The Land Is Our History

The Land Is Our History

The Land Is Our History

Indigeneity, Law, and the Settler State

MIRANDA JOHNSON

OXFORD
UNIVERSITY PRESS

Oxford University Press is a department of the University of Oxford. It furthers the University's objective of excellence in research, scholarship, and education by publishing worldwide. Oxford is a registered trade mark of Oxford University Press in the UK and certain other countries.

Published in the United States of America by Oxford University Press
198 Madison Avenue, New York, NY 10016, United States of America.

Library of Congress Cataloging-in-Publication Data
Names: Johnson, Miranda C. L., author.
Title: The land is our history : indigeneity, law, and the settler state /
Miranda Johnson.
Description: New York, NY : Oxford University Press, [2016] | Includes
bibliographical references and index.
Identifiers: LCCN 2016010046 | ISBN 9780190600020 (hardcover : acid-free paper) |
ISBN 9780190600068 (paperback : acid-free paper) | ISBN 9780190600037 (updf) |
ISBN 9780190600044 (epub)
Subjects: LCSH: Aboriginal Australians—Legal status, laws, etc. | Indians of
North America—Legal status, laws, etc.—Canada. | Maori (New Zealand
people)—Legal status, laws, etc.
Classification: LCC KIA1.A9 J64 2016 | DDC 342.08/72—dc23 LC record available at
https://lccn.loc.gov/2016010046

Front cover image: Gunybi Ganambarr, "Mungurru" (2013). Gunybi works in North East Arnhem Land, Australia. This image represents Gunybi's mother clan, the Dhalwangu. The parallel wavy lines take the flow of water to the open ocean, Mungurru, where waters from other Yirritja clans merge and mingle. The hunter's harpoon floats incessantly between the coastal saltwater estates of these clans. It is also here that the feminine thunderclouds take up life-giving water to rain back over the hinterlands. The transformation of saltwater into fresh and back into salt mirrors the soul as it changes its outward form from corporeal to ethereal and so on. Image and description courtesy of Buku-Larrngay Mulka Art Centre, Yirrkala.

9 8 7 6 5 4 3 2 1

Paperback printed by Webcom, Inc., Canada
Hardback printed by Bridgeport National Bindery, Inc., United States of America

Contents

Acknowledgments

THIS BOOK HAS been a long time in the making. I have racked up many debts to many individuals and institutions. The project began as a dissertation at the University of Chicago, which itself would never have come to completion without the dedicated supervision of Dipesh Chakrabarty, Bain Attwood, Jessica Cattelino, and Bill Novak. To Dipesh and Bain I owe a very special thanks for inspiring in me the idea that I could apply for a PhD program in the United States and helping me get there. My graduate education at Chicago was a mind-altering experience. I am profoundly grateful to Jessica for her support and advice throughout the dissertation-writing phase and beyond.

I could not have entered an expensive American PhD program without financial support. I thank the New Zealand Tertiary Education Commission for what was then a very generous scholarship for overseas study, the Top Achiever's/Bright Futures scheme, now sadly no longer offered. I am grateful for the funding that the University of Chicago provided me in my last two years of study. A Committee for Institutional Cooperation American Indian Studies Graduate Fellowship at the Newberry Library in Chicago and an award from the American Philosophical Society Phillips Grant Fund for Native American Research supported initial research into legal cases in Canada.

The research for the dissertation and later the book has taken me from Regina to Nhulunbuy, the Whanganui and Mackenzie rivers, and all sorts of archives in between. I would like to thank the many people I encountered on these travels who helped me along the way. Specific thanks are due to archivists at Library and Archives Canada in Ottawa, the National Archives of Australia, and Archives New Zealand for their assistance at the desk and behind the scenes. In Calgary, Alberta, I read through files at the University of Calgary Special Collections, and the Glenbow Archives relating to Justice William Morrow and the Dene caveat case I discuss in Chapter 3. Many

thanks to the Legal Archives Society of Alberta for the permission to repro-
duce photos from their holdings of Morrow's materials. I made use of Ted
Woodward's collection at the University of Melbourne Archives and other
files relating to the Gove land rights case held by the Australian Institute for
Aboriginal and Torres Strait Islander Studies in Canberra. In all these places,
archivists and librarians were immensely helpful and granted me access to
more than I had hoped for. Thanks also to the Northern Territory Library
for permission to use an image from their collections. In Wellington, friends
and former colleagues at the Waitangi Tribunal and the Alexander Turnbull
Library went out of their way to find me the documents I needed and continued to help with last-minute requests. The Turnbull Library granted permission for the last image in the book. Paul Hamer at the tribunal kindly
granted me permission to use his photo from a Whanganui river inquiry hearing and helped with other details. Their commitments to public service and
scholarship make New Zealand a better place. Faron Levesque, James Dunk,
and Aden Knaap, all fine scholars themselves, provided me excellent research
assistance at different times. I am deeply grateful to Will Stubbs and Gunybi
Ganambarr for the use of the cover image and to Tim Stallman for drawing
the maps.

   In the course of researching this book, I met deeply committed scholars,
lawyers, community leaders, judges, and many others involved in fighting
for justice for indigenous peoples. They helped me to focus my research in
crucial ways. In Canada, I thank in particular the late Lloyd Barber, Marian
Dinwoodie, Walter Hildebrandt, John Leslie, Val Napoleon, Stewart Raby,
and Arthur Ray, all of whom gave me considerable time and assistance in
learning about law, rights, and activism in a country I knew very little about.
In Australia, Bain Attwood, Ann Curthoys, Penny Edmonds, Nicholas
Peterson, and Deborah Bird Rose made useful suggestions and offered critical insights as the project developed. The late Alan Ward introduced me to
native title issues in Australia and helped me think about comparisons with
law and justice in New Zealand. Monica Morgan and Wayne Atkinson discussed with me the Yorta Yorta people's long struggle in the courts. In New
Zealand, staff at the Waitangi Tribunal went out of their way to help me understand the complexity of treaty claims. I thank in particular Paul Hamer,
James Mitchell, and Barry Rigby. Maarire Goodall met with me for a series
of long conversations about the setting up of the tribunal, the Lands Case
I discuss in Chapter 5, and issues of biculturalism. Jenny McLeod and David
Young helped me understand much better the long history of the Whanganui
River. Sir Edward Durie, then Law Commissioner, made time in a hectic

schedule to discuss with me his role and work at the Waitangi Tribunal. Tony Ballantyne, Barbara Brookes, Aroha Harris, Charlotte Macdonald, and Mike Stevens talked through various aspects of this research with me in the broader contexts of New Zealand and Māori history. Thank you all.

As well as research funding, the availability of sources, and help from participants, the other key ingredient for writing this book has been time. I have been immensely fortunate to hold two postdoctoral fellowships. These provided me space, salary, collegiality, and the time to write. In 2008, I joined the Society of Fellows, University of Michigan, under the directorship of Donald Lopez. There, I was surrounded by brilliant colleagues in the Society and the Department of History who challenged my thinking and expanded my vision. In particular, I thank Sepideh Bajracharya, Deirdre de la Cruz, Philip J. Deloria, Kriszti Fehervary, Zeynep Gürsel, George Hoffmann, Nancy Rose Hunt, Lara Kusnetzky, Farina Mir, Christian de Pee, and Damon Salesa, for their friendship, insights, and critical feedback.

In 2012 I was appointed to a postdoctoral fellowship at Race and Ethnicity in the Global South, a center sponsored by Professor Warwick Anderson's Australian Research Council Laureate Fellowship at the University of Sydney. I am grateful to Warwick for his support and for organizing a manuscript workshop for my book. I thank Ann Curthoys, Lisa Ford, Ricardo Roque, Tim Rowse, and Christine Winter for their excellent comments. Particular thanks to Sally Merry who provided wonderful suggestions for improvement.

Colleagues at the University of Wisconsin-Madison in the Department of History and the American Indian Studies program were inspiring collaborators for the two short years I worked there. In the midst of political chaos and destructive attacks on this beautiful institution, they offered friendship, beer, and intellectual stimulation for which I will always be grateful. Many thanks to Sana Aiyar, Ned Blackhawk, A. Finn Enke, Nan Enstad, Pernille Ipsen, Steve Kantrowitz, Neil Kodesh, Florencia Mallon, David McDonald, Leah Mirakhor, Nancy Mithlo, Mitra Sharafi, Karl Shoemaker, and Jim Sweet.

In the Department of History at the University of Sydney I am surrounded by colleagues who have welcomed me and my family into the fold of another culture and country. Grateful thanks to Andrew Fitzmaurice, John Gagné, Chris Hilliard, Peter Hobbins, Chin Jou, Michael McDonnell, Kirsten McKenzie, Penny Russell, Hélène Sirantoine, and Sarah Walsh for ongoing support and camaraderie. Frances Flanagan, Tamson Pietsch, and Sophie Loy-Wilson are close readers and dear friends. I also thank my students who open up new worlds to me.

Susan Ferber at Oxford University Press made incisive and acute comments on my writing just when I most needed it. I thank her and the production team at OUP for all their wonderful work in turning the manuscript into this book.

Friends far and wide have nurtured me and held me tight when I needed it most. Anita Chari and Rosa Williams have been at my side since graduate school. Even though we're now separated by oceans and continents, the love holds fast. Rochona Majumdar, Ana Levy-Lyons, Vasaré Rastonis, and Larisa Reznik, all warmed me up in the cold Midwest and continue to encourage me on. Zeynep Gürsel, Lara Kusnetzky, and Nancy Hunt made Ann Arbor a home away from home and are lifelong friends. Bain Attwood and Claudia Haake are generous beyond words. Old friends from New Zealand nourish me still. In particular, Sandy Callister, Jocelyn Chalmers, Aroha Harris, and Kirsty Willis remind me where I belong. Josie Karavasil read the whole manuscript and cheered me on to the finish line. New (old) friends in Australia, Shona and Jack Thomson, always go beyond the call of duty, as do our Bondi community of Tina, Oliver, Sue, and Sally. Tamson Pietsch and Ruth Higgins now feel like kin. Kirsty Gover is a brilliant interlocutor and dear heart. She has read and re-read countless drafts of this book and made incisive criticisms that vastly improved it.

The formidable intelligence and deep political commitments of my mother, Cecilia, are behind the words in this book. She raised me and my brother Lucien to care about what matters most and she shows us how it is possible to keep going in the face of pain and loss. We are both so fortunate. My father Louis, who died when I was ten, lives on in our family humor, and his poetry binds us together. My brother's tenderness and astonishing creativity sustain me and many others.

When I was in the process of leaving the United States, I met Michael Goodman. Not only did he follow me halfway around the globe so that we could build a life together—leaving family, friends, job, and community—but he then also had to put up with the never-ending demands that this book continued to make on us as we both began anew in Australia. His brilliant and critical mind pushed me to think harder and write better. His love carried me through the hardest years of this project and made it possible, finally, to bring it to an end. He is extraordinary. Our beloved son Louis is now taking us on a new journey. They are the lights of my life.

A Note on Terms

THIS BOOK USES the identifying terms of the period in naming indigenous groups. So, for instance, when discussing activism in the early 1970s in Canada, it uses the term "Indian" because this was the term in contemporary use, by "Indians" and others. Although the terms "Aboriginal people" or "First Nations" are now generally, if not unilaterally, preferred, these terms are not used until later in the book since they emerged from the legal discussions of aboriginal title and treaty rights that earlier chapters discuss. Likewise, early chapters in this book refer to "Aborigines" rather than the now officially recognized term "Indigenous Australians." Maori words are not given macrons in Chapter 5 whereas in Chapter 6 they are, thus Maori becomes Māori. In 1987, Māori was recognized as an official language in New Zealand. This recognition was intended to encourage the speaking of the language more widely and the use of correct pronunciation, which the macron indicates. When referring to particular linguistic and tribal groups, the book refers to the names they took for themselves in making their claims to the state—Dene, Yolngu, Whanganui, and so on. The term "indigenous peoples" indicates a general and more abstract grouping of people across the three countries who were pursuing their rights, differentiating themselves and being differentiated from "settlers," and at times claiming alliance with other colonized groups.

The Land Is Our History

The Land Is Our History

Introduction

If our rights are meaningless, if it is inconceivable that our society have treaties with the white society even though those treaties were signed by honourable men on both sides, in good faith, long before the present government decided to tear them up as worthless scraps of paper, then we as a people are meaningless.
—HAROLD CARDINAL, *The Unjust Society (1969)*

THE LATE 1960S was a watershed moment for politics from below. Students protested immoral wars, civil rights activists urged the end of racial segregation, and anti-colonial revolutionaries called for the overthrow of imperial rule. New social and political movements forced their demands onto national and international agendas. Inspired by those movements, minority indigenous peoples in Australia, Canada, and New Zealand made distinct and unexpectedly powerful claims about their rights and the justice owed to them. Going beyond demands for civil rights, indigenous activists issued radical challenges to the settler states that surrounded them by pointing out that they were the prior occupiers and first peoples of the land. They insisted on their sovereignty and demanded recognition of their land and historical treaty rights. By pressuring governments and wider publics to respond to their claims, which were ultimately concerned with the ongoing survival of their communities, indigenous peoples changed both their own status and the founding story of the settler state.

These three Commonwealth countries were the product of nineteenth-century colonization when white settlers, mainly from the British Isles, flooded into the Americas, southern Africa, and the Pacific. Intending to create new, more egalitarian, societies on what they saw as vacant or under-utilized lands,[1] they dispossessed the original inhabitants through wars and sporadic frontier violence and by the use of specially designed legal instruments for the seizure of land. Decimated by introduced diseases and other consequences of dispossession, surviving indigenous peoples were pushed to the edges of colonial territories. By the end of the century, settler states, "uniquely destructive of indigenous rights,"[2] had usurped the original inhabitants on lands they now called theirs. In Australia, Canada, and New Zealand, settler societies began to define their own sense of nationhood as they achieved self-government and political independence from Britain.[3] At the same time, these three "Neo-Europes" in particular retained strong cultural, economic, and legal ties to Britain well into the twentieth century.[4] Notably, these settler states, politically independent from the metropole but culturally and economically dependent on Britain, were constructed in terms that excluded the recognition of surviving indigenous nations.

Despite dispossession, marginalization, and neglect, indigenous populations in fact began to increase again in the twentieth century. National governments considered new ways of incorporating these young and growing populations into the domestic workforce. Following World War II, governments in Australia, Canada, and New Zealand outlined what they saw as progressive policies of assimilation by which they envisaged indigenous peoples becoming full citizens who aspired to the same things that other settlers did.[5] In this rendering, there was only one nation in the settler state, and it was, in cultural terms, a white settler nation. In the late 1960s, indigenous activists rejected progressive policies of assimilation as yet another example of colonization. They argued that their people had maintained their own collective identities as distinct nations within the settler state, and these nations were now under threat from assimilation. Thus, they broke apart the assumption of white policymakers that the nation-state was a single unity, arguing instead that the settler state was comprised of many nations.

In a dire context of new threats to indigenous lands as mining and development projects expanded to the remote regions of the three countries in the late 1960s, indigenous leaders urgently demanded that the settler state recognize their peoples' land rights. These, they believed, would help them protect their collective identities. Faced with the intransigence of settler governments to recognize these rights, in the 1970s, young activists and older leaders brought claims for land and treaty rights to the courts and commissions of inquiry of the settler state. These were institutions that had been hostile to such claims in the past. For the first time, the histories and traditions relating to the lands and identities of indigenous peoples were taken into account by legal institutions.[6]

The Land Is Our History explores how established leaders and young activists engaged legal strategies and what the larger outcomes of claims were for them and particularly for the settler states to which they appealed. Excavating connections between legal cases on new mining and development frontiers of Australia, Canada, and New Zealand from the early 1970s through to the mid-1990s, this book shows how activists—in concert with white judges, lawyers, and others—fashioned a new definition of indigeneity in the context of legal struggles. This emphasized that indigenous peoples' identities were inextricably bound to the land. Importantly, this definition of indigeneity could be translated into a set of distinct rights at the level of the state.[7] It also offered local communities new ways of imagining themselves as culturally unique and as having a kind of sovereignty within their own territories, and sharing certain predicaments with other indigenous peoples in other locales. Indigeneity thus allowed for multiple kinds of engagement including with other indigenous peoples across vast terrains and markedly different cultures, and also with settler states forced to reckon with indigenous demands. Eventually, the transnational circulation of indigeneity gained traction at the level of international law.[8]

Fracturing national myths and making new stories of origin necessary, indigenous peoples' claims challenged authorities to acknowledge the origins of the settler state in devastating dispossession and even attempted genocide. In a global moment in which national governments in the three countries were decrying apartheid and racial oppression in other parts of the world, indigenous claims had a particular purchase. Speaking to more local traditions of fairness and equality, although also complicating them, activists urged the settler states to recognize their distinct rights.[9] By doing so, settler states would be redeemed and indigenous peoples' vulnerable identities would be preserved.

The redemption of the settler state was necessary so that a new story could be told about the co-founding of Australia, Canada, and New Zealand by indigenous peoples and settlers.[10] This was the import of the charges laid by the young Canadian Cree activist, Harold Cardinal, in 1969. He proposed that the honor of the settler nation was at stake in the recognition of treaties made with his community. The only way to ensure the settler nation's esteem and moral righteousness, he argued, was through the acknowledgment of indigenous peoples as "coeval" treaty partners with distinct rights to the land.[11]

Activists timed their demands impeccably. In a moment of acute public uncertainty as the three Commonwealth countries finally dissolved economic and cultural ties to Britain and sought out new postcolonial identities in the Asia-Pacific region, indigenous peoples changed the status quo. Making the most of this moment of national insecurity, activists pressed governments to acknowledge that, like other colonized peoples around the world, they too had been unjustly treated. Nonetheless, they insisted that they had maintained a distinct connection to the land, an identity that needed to be protected from the threats that new mining development on remote frontiers and assimilation policy across settler states posed. Influenced by global anti-racist and anti-colonial discourses, the complex and distinctive claims that indigenous peoples made arose from their particular historical experience of settler colonialism and its phenomenally intrusive but not totally fatal impact on indigenous communities.[12]

The basis of indigenous peoples' claims in the 1970s was that the lands and waters of their ancestors were their history. Without rights to these domains, they argued, they would no longer be indigenous. This claim, which yoked together place, history, and identity, was also made by groups that had been dispossessed of much of their territory and wanted to reestablish connections to places of significance to them in order to restore a sense of who they were in the wake of dispossession. Claims for indigeneity were, therefore, different from human rights discourses that privilege the individual in establishing the grounds for non-discrimination. Indigenous claims were collective ones for "peoplehood" based in distinctive histories and relationships with each other and to their territories.[13] At the same time, indigenous peoples demanded something different from anti-colonial revolutionaries who fought for autonomous, sovereign nation-statehood.[14] In keeping with their traditions and uses of specific regions, activists argued for something like local territorial rights based on the central importance of place to indigenous identity.[15]

Although indigenous peoples demanded something seemingly more limited than did anti-colonial revolutionaries and different from human rights advocates, in another sense they wanted something even more transformative. As the American Indian legal scholar Vine Deloria explained, the assertion of a profound and inextricable relationship with the land went beyond a political claim. In a foreword to a key text in the globalizing indigenous rights movement in 1974, Deloria argued that the authors' conception of a "fourth world" of indigenous peoples offered a "vision of human existence beyond that of expediency and the balancing of powers and speaks to the identity crisis that has gripped every land and its peoples."[16] The notion that indigenous identity as it came to be defined transnationally in the 1970s spoke to something existential helps to explain why such claims were so provocative and why they had the widespread effects that they did. Indigeneity appealed widely to many who were disenchanted with postindustrial modernity.

Taking account of the broad appeal of claims for indigeneity as well as the specific context in which such claims were constructed, this book argues that they were astonishingly successful in the last three decades of the twentieth century in the three Commonwealth states. This success was astonishing because, prior to this period, indigenous peoples had little influence on state policymaking. In the 1970s, the success of claims for indigeneity was in large part due to the fact that these claims provided a way forward for the specific identity crisis facing Australia, Canada, and New Zealand. Throwing off their imperial ties, these countries needed new stories of foundation that would help to cohere them as they faced intensifying internal and external pressures and locate them more convincingly in their own regions.[17] The stories that indigenous peoples told of their attachment to and use of the land in order to win recognition of their rights in courts of law and commissions of inquiry served this need extraordinarily well. Focusing on how indigenous claims helped to reframe the national identities of these three countries in particular, this book does not survey the development of indigenous activism in the United States. In that country, the rise of "Red Power" and the American Indian Movement in the 1970s did not bring American identity into question in the ways that indigenous rights movements in the other countries did, although American Indian activism was profoundly influential on activists in the countries examined here.[18]

In fact, indigenous peoples' claims, although challenging, were not entirely novel. The construction of indigeneity in the late twentieth century recalled an older, pre-nationalist, European belief in the "interdependence of tribe and place." Historian Anthony Pagden explains that local, "indigenous" Europeans used the argument of "an inalienable right, grounded in nature rather than in the political or civil order, to be ruled only by a member of their own tribe or clan" to contest empire within Europe.[19] This idea traveled with Europeans as they colonized new lands. In the late nineteenth century, settlers in Australia, Canada, and New Zealand described themselves as the natives, asserting a sense of belonging to new lands that tied their identity to these places.[20] Following World War II, as new waves of immigrants arrived from southern Europe, settlers sometimes referred to themselves as the "first people" of the land.[21] These claims to native-ness and first-ness permitted settlers to construct an autonomous relationship to the British empire that emphasized their belonging to and rights in the settler dominions. Later, it enabled settlers to differentiate themselves from the non-white immigrants arriving on their shores. Such claims neatly erased the rights of and wrongs committed against indigenous peoples in colonized territories. By reclaiming indigeneity in the last decades of the twentieth century, those people—the survivors of colonization—made a provocative assertion of their *prior* and *continuing* occupation of and belonging to the land that challenged white settlers' self-conception of rightful belonging.[22]

Based on extensive archival research into legal case files, government policy debates, discussions in the press, and interviews with key participants in the three Commonwealth countries, this book demonstrates how indigenous activists established claims for indigeneity by carving open institutional spaces previously closed to them. Phrasing their claims in the moral terms of colonial injustice and offering a way to redeem national honor through the recognition of their rights, activists opened up a new space of law in which their demands could be examined and adjudicated. This was particularly surprising since in the past they had not often received a fair hearing. For most of the history of the settler state, colonial authorities had represented indigenous peoples as uncivilized and as unreliable witnesses in court, initially because as non-Christians, they could not take oaths. Their evidence was dismissed.[23]

One of the key and enduring changes that this book examines is how indigenous claimants accessed and opened up legal institutions in new ways in the 1970s. They persuaded judges that their own histories needed to be taken account of in evaluating their rights claims. For this to happen, judges expanded legal evidentiary practice, finding old common law precedents for the admission of indigenous oral traditions and other evidence usually regarded as inadmissible hearsay. Responding to indigenous claimants' demands for fair treatment, judges tried to accommodate rather than dismiss or exclude the different ways in which they gave expression to their histories. In the remote areas about which many claims were made, claimants also pressured judges to shift hearings from formal courtrooms to their own settlements and sites of significance to them. This meant that at least for the duration of the hearing, legal personnel were subject to the protocols and expectations of indigenous peoples in places they asserted were theirs.

The reforms to evidentiary practices and the shift in the location of hearings that indigenous peoples instigated opened up access to powerful institutions. Courts are usually considered spaces of asymmetrical power in which legal claimants are poorly positioned to change their status. Indigenous claimants in the 1970s turned these sites into places of more creative dialogue.[24] Especially when they were able to do so on their own lands, indigenous peoples taught judges, commissioners, lawyers, and others new things about their own histories and laws, and they demonstrated in compelling ways why those places were of such significance to them. These stories humanized their struggles and made a deep impression on legal actors. In several key legal cases in the 1970s, the affective impact of indigenous testimony prompted judges to respond positively, within the constraints of the common law, to indigenous peoples' demands for rights and justice.[25] In some instances, the stories that indigenous peoples told in the space of law even served to enlist non-indigenous legal actors in their activism, taking legal claims from judges' "heads to their hearts" as one lawyer for Maori claimants in New Zealand put it.[26] Moved by such stories, in numerous cases judges used their decisions to compel governments to recognize a wider set of indigenous rights. This book relates the biographies of some of these actors to show how their own preconceptions and experiences, as well as their philosophies of law and ideas about justice and national history, drove them to support, and reframe, indigenous struggles for justice.[27]

The admission of their testimony redefined the legal and political status of indigenous peoples as bearers of distinct rights. Their histories were translated into forms of legal proof demonstrating their unique and historical attachment to place and the descent-based nature of their communities. In the space of law, claimants gave evidence of their ancient and continuous relationship to and use of the land since time immemorial, to use the common law phrase as they often did. Those groups who had made historical treaties with settler states, such as Cardinal's community among others in Canada, and Maori tribes in New Zealand, argued that they understood those agreements as acts of international diplomacy since they recognized the political status of each party.[28] They brought elderly witnesses to the stand to present their memories and oral traditions of such agreements. Leading judges in the highest courts of the land concurred with some of these arguments, thereby giving such narratives a newfound power within institutions of the state.

The fact that the three settler countries shared an Anglo common law tradition was key to the circulation of indigenous rights discourses around Australia, Canada, and New Zealand. In all three countries, indigenous claimants translated their broad claims into core common law idioms of property and contract in order to win rights and redress. However, the kinds of property rights and contractual obligations that indigenous peoples made claims about were quite different from the ways those doctrines were usually understood. Indigenous claims sparked a revitalization and reinterpretation of colonial doctrines including "aboriginal (or native) title" and treaty-making. In terms of legal discourse, both aboriginal title (first developed in the United States in the early nineteenth century), and treaty-making (a practice begun with tribes in North America in the seventeenth century) had, with a few exceptions, been ignored or relegated to legal insignificance by lawyers in the settler states for most of the twentieth century.[29]

Indigenous claims brought aboriginal title back into circulation. This is a form of collective property right that recognizes the historic and ongoing attachment of indigenous peoples to their lands.[30] It was useful to indigenous peoples because it gave them stronger rights than those of use and access that had been awarded to them on an ad hoc basis prior to the 1970s. Further, because it foregrounded their ongoing presence on and attachment to the land, it conveyed great symbolic as well as economic value. The recognition of aboriginal title promised to give tangible legal form to the expression of indigenous peoples' historical claims as "first peoples" who were the prior occupiers of the land. It overturned popular historical representations of vast areas of unoccupied land, purportedly "free" of prior owners and available for the taking.[31] Unlike other property rights, claimants to aboriginal title in the 1970s and 1980s did not have to show that they exercised exclusive ownership of the lands under claim; although neither could they sell lands so recognized on an open market.[32] Implicitly, the revitalization of aboriginal title recognized a kind of inherent sovereignty held by indigenous peoples as autonomous groups with their own laws and forms of government prior to the arrival of white settlers, who had maintained a degree of autonomy despite colonization.[33]

The other kind of claim that indigenous peoples brought to law in Canada and New Zealand concerned the fulfillment of historical treaty promises. This avenue was not available to Aboriginal activists in Australia, since no treaty had been made or upheld with Aborigines by the colonial state in that country.[34] Even in Canada and New Zealand, not all indigenous peoples were members of tribes that had negotiated treaties in the past or saw themselves as beholden to treaty obligations in the late twentieth century. Those who did make treaty claims used the idea of a contract to hold settler states to account, specifically referring to what they had lost and the redress and restitution they demanded in the present. More broadly, treaty claims levered open a moral space in the state. Claimants argued that treaties were actually of fundamental importance to the settler states in a postcolonial age—they represented broader social contracts according to which settler states had grounded their authority. Most radically, activists used treaties to emphasize their peoplehood in international terms. Insisting that treaties were agreements between nations, indigenous claimants pushed courts and commissions of inquiry to interpret treaty provisions in ways that gave more weight to their understandings. Responding to these assertions, in the 1980s, lawyers and judges imported principles of treaty interpretation from international law in order to legitimate the oral traditions and the communal interpretations of historical agreements made by indigenous peoples.[35]

Settler governments were initially more prepared to address treaty claims than those for aboriginal title. They thought that breaches to treaty promises could be easily remedied, but they worried that recognition of aboriginal title would legitimate indigenous claims for autonomy. Doing so would break apart the unitary notion of "perfect" sovereignty premised in one rule of law. According to this idea, the power of the settler state was based in unity and homogeneity and the state could not therefore recognize plural legal orders as existing in its own territory.[36] However, once actors in the space of law began to debate the extent and significance of aboriginal title rights, it became clear that governments had to formulate policies that would lay out how such rights could be recognized and what the implications of doing so were for acknowledging pluralism in the settler state.

Furthermore, aboriginal title promised something of use to the settler state: a connection to an ancient indigenous past that could situate those countries in their own geographies in comprehensive terms. In the 1980s and 1990s, aboriginal title was reworked as a doctrine fundamental to the common law tradition of each of the settler states. In the case of Australia, it was recognized in that nation's common law for the first time in the groundbreaking 1992 legal decision, *Mabo v. Queensland (no. 2)*.[37] As Australian Prime Minister Paul Keating put it in his powerful "Redfern speech" soon after the *Mabo* decision, "We cannot imagine that the descendants of people whose genius and resilience maintained a culture here through fifty thousand years or more . . . and who then survived two centuries of dispossession and abuse, will be denied their place in the modern Australian nation."[38] Admitting to injustices by redressing treaty breaches and recognizing aboriginal title simultaneously attempted to redeem the state and establish it in new terms.

Beyond political rhetoric, the cases that indigenous peoples brought to law contributed to the construction of a new archive. This archive was filled with testimonies of indigenous peoples about their connection to place, their traditions regarding the use of specific lands and waters, and their memories of treaty negotiations. Claimants tried to control access to these stories, given in support of rights claims, and their use in the public domain. This was hard to achieve, since the legal archive became a critical source from which the modern settler state could reclaim an authoritative, ancient, and even sacred past.[39] The incorporation of indigenous history into the state was similar to processes in other postcolonial states in the twentieth century. Indian nationalism, for instance, was imagined through claims to ancient Hindu traditions in an attempt to purify it of European influence.[40] In Australia, Canada, and New Zealand, new national stories were created around the legal doctrine of aboriginal title. The recognition of these rights as continuous over time enabled the state to affirm its own continuity. Aboriginal title constituted a "bridge" between pre-colonial indigenous occupation and the imposition of sovereignty by the settler state.[41] In other words, the histories of indigenous peoples' inextricable attachment to the land became a *pre*-history for the settler state, situating it in relation to an indigenous past.

Emphasizing the settler state's connection to an ancient, indigenous past was part of the project of dissolving ties with Britain. Liberal settler states no longer had to be imagined as deriving from a blurrily European location. They had their own "ancient constitution."[42] However, there was a twist. Whereas in other postcolonial states, the formerly colonized achieved self-government and sovereign independence, the recognition of native title in settler states took consideration of minority indigenous peoples' full sovereignty off the table.

Within and beyond the space of law, indigenous leaders claimed a new constitutional status as "first peoples" and even co-founders of the nation. They reimagined treaties as founding contracts in which two parties, first peoples and settlers, came to terms about how they could live together. Further, the new legitimacy for their histories that claimants demanded from the law increased the value of indigeneity among a broader public. Recognition of their rights even seemed to promise a distinct form of local self-determination achieved by returning to the lands of their ancestors. In the course of bringing legal claims, activists cultivated a new historical consciousness among their communities about their relationships to the past.

Yet the focus on traditions about treaty promises and evidence of connection to land in court often privileged the experiences and stories of men over those of women and old people over younger generations.[43] Legal claims created new grounds for exclusion as well as opportunities. Those who saw themselves as indigenous but were unable to prove a place-based identity or whose claims were left unresolved were excluded from the political status of "first peoples" and the benefits that such could bestow. As they won greater recognition of their indigeneity in the public sphere, in the space of law indigenous peoples became increasingly subject to sharp legal determinations of who they were and were not. Urban-based indigenous communities fared poorly in trying to win determinations of their land rights. These distinctions sowed the seeds of new conflicts between indigenous communities located in different places.

Even those claimants who were successful in translating their histories into legal proof and who won their rights could find that their aspirations were diminished and their identities sometimes distorted in the process.[44] This occurred notably in terms of a conceptual relationship between indigeneity and ideas about history. Activists insisted on their distinct histories that nonetheless made them coeval with settlers. Those in the most densely settled parts of settler states emphasized indigenous agency in holding on to key traditions despite intensive colonization. Those on remote mining frontiers demonstrated the survival of their cultures to settler officials in the face of new threats. Indigenous peoples on remote frontiers and in urban areas saw themselves as being in history and having historical agency. However, in court, they had to prove the "cardinal" principle of continuity of attachment.[45] The idea of continuous attachment to land was frequently interpreted by judges, and the settler public, not as a measure of historical survival and agency but as a demonstration of ahistorical indigenous authenticity. This was a judgment based on phenotype, language retention, and stereotypical ideas of what constituted traditional practices. For many white legal professionals, indigenous peoples were considered to be the more authentic the less they had been touched by the historical forces of colonization, or in fact any historical forces at all.[46] In demonstrating to non-indigenous audiences their collective survival, indigenous peoples thus inadvertently invited the fixing of their identities to an unchanging and primordial past often based on persistent images of noble (or sometimes brutish) savagery. They found that the coeval-ness they asserted in bringing their claims into the courtroom could be denied by legal evidentiary processes that were supposed to accommodate them.

Foregrounding the aspirations of those who played a critical role in these decades of change, from the late 1960s to the late 1990s, as well as the frustrations and disillusionment of activists and legal actors, reveals the complex and mixed results of indigenous claims-making. Rather than a zero-sum game in which indigenous peoples either lost everything or were completely victorious, a fragile truce was established in the 1970s and 1980s. This temporary compromise was held together by concessions on each side. The state agreed to accommodate certain aspects of indigenous claims, including creating regimes for the recognition of treaty and land rights. In return, indigenous peoples had to forgo violence and assertions of full sovereignty and submit their claims to settler law.

THIS BOOK FOLLOWS a broadly chronological organization in connecting legal claims in Australia and Canada in the 1970s to those in New Zealand in the 1980s and 1990s. Within each chapter the narrative tacks back and forth in time to explicate the historical conditions of claims-making and highlight local moments of success, failure, and change. The chronology charts the emergence and development of a legal strategy as well as the effects of indigenous engagements with law. Using this chronology highlights a significant shift in settler states. When indigenous claims emerged in the 1970s, they engaged with a largely social democratic form of governance beginning to grapple with some implications of the broader politics of decolonization. By the 1990s, all three countries, and New Zealand in particular, had embraced policies of neoliberalism and globalization. At the same time, an international discussion of indigenous rights to self-determination had become more significant. However, these same rights were being hotly debated within the settler states as some refuted the idea that indigenous peoples deserved special justice in a context of increasing wealth discrepancies and radical cuts to state services. As marginalized indigenous peoples pushed their issues from the local to the global, some of their arguments for distinct rights began to lose traction within the settler state itself.

Chapter 1 argues that the historical timing of indigenous claims in the late 1960s was crucial to opening up a new space for dialogue in the state. It examines in detail how indigenous activists in Australia and Canada on new frontiers and in urban centers constructed a very particular rights history in part out of older state practices that supported contemporary claims. Emphasizing a distinctive history of connection to the land, activists effectively refuted the value of policies of assimilation and forced governments to consider land-based self-determination. However, activists also discovered that settler governments would not negotiate with them about specific rights to land. In order to force governments to do so, indigenous peoples had to go to court, which became a strategy of first resort in the 1970s.

Chapters 2 and 3 focus on two of the earliest legal cases in pursuit of indigenous land rights in Australia (Chapter 2) and Canada (Chapter 3) in the 1970s. In the "Gove land rights case" that Yolngu people brought to court in 1970 and the "caveat case" that Dene people in the Mackenzie Valley mounted in 1973, indigenous witnesses had their histories admitted into court for the first time. Although the immediate outcomes of these cases were not entirely successful ones for the claimants, the stories about indigenous identities and forms of belonging they told in court, and some aspects of the decisions issued by judges, sparked political change. Both cases pushed federal governments to reconsider previously firm stances against recognizing distinct indigenous rights. Realizing that public will and understanding of indigenous claims was shifting, national political leaders created commissions of inquiry to investigate more broadly how indigenous claims might be addressed given the novelty and complexity of the issues they raised. Chapter 4 examines the workings of and connections between three commissions of inquiry in Canada and Australia: the Indian Claims Commission (Canada); the Woodward Commission (Australia); and the Berger Inquiry (Canada). Indigenous peoples used these commissions to advance their own historical research agendas and expand on ideas about their place-based identity. In the process, they began to show that a hegemonic story about the making of white men's countries was insufficient since they were now asserting their indigeneity as "first peoples" of the land. They splintered national stories that were the basis of an old social contract in which indigenous peoples' rights were forgotten, and invited new ones that recognized indigenous peoples as co-founders.

The history of Maori activism is quite different from indigenous activism in Canada and Australia. While taking account of the global shifts that similarly affected New Zealand, Chapter 5 explains how activists contested the symbolic value of the Treaty of Waitangi, made by the British Crown with some Maori chiefs in 1840. In the late 1960s, the treaty was officially celebrated as creating "one people," founding a national myth of racial harmony. Activists refuted this interpretation, arguing instead that the treaty was a "fraud" and needed to be renegotiated in the present. They pushed for the creation of the Waitangi Tribunal in 1975 to examine Maori grievances arising from the treaty. In that institution, and in a key legal case in 1987 known as the "Lands case," Maori leaders took their demands to the national stage. Judges in the Lands case awarded Maori a new role as partners with the Crown who should be consulted with about wide-reaching economic reforms directly affecting them. Even more radically, one of the judges suggested that Maori were "guardians" of the national estate who would protect it from the sale of state assets that the incumbent Labour government was undertaking in the late 1980s.

Although not adopted universally, the idea that Maori people had a unique and important role in nation-building as partners with the Crown and guardians of the national estate was compelling. It implied that a notion of the social contract was being renegotiated in New Zealand. However, in taking on this role, Maori were also asked to bear the burden of "indigenizing" the settler state. This is examined in Chapter 6 in relation to a specific claim in the Waitangi Tribunal concerning rights to the Whanganui River. The burden of indigenizing was not shared by other groups and it served to bind Maori identity more tightly to the construction of a postcolonial "Aotearoa/ New Zealand."[47]

Indigenous legal claims of the 1970s through to the 1990s had dramatic effects. Activists rejected assimilation and asserted that they were different from but also coeval with settlers. They demanded recognition of their distinct rights and sparked innovations in statutory, common, and constitutional law. Going beyond the law, activists helped to create new public traditions about the origins of the settler state as a product not only of white endeavor but also of indigenous sacrifice and survival. They showed how indigenous peoples could, and should, be considered central actors in a story of postcolonial change. The costs, however, were significant and unanticipated by leaders in the early 1970s. The compromise they reached with the settler state was fraught and vulnerable to shifts in larger political ideologies from social democracy to neoliberal reform. This book examines the profound yet also wavering changes that indigenous claims wrought in Commonwealth settler states at a critical historical juncture.

1

Citizens Plus

NEW INDIGENOUS ACTIVISM
IN AUSTRALIA AND CANADA

ON 14 AUGUST 1963, the Commonwealth (federal) parliament received a petition from a remote Aboriginal community in Australia's far north demanding an inquiry into their land that, the petitioners asserted, was "sacred" to them and "vital to their livelihood."[1] This was not the first such petition sent to the parliament, but it was the first presented in two languages (English and a Yolngu dialect) and employing Aboriginal designs. Mounted on stringy bark panels and framed by stylized images of native flora and fauna painted by local artists, the typewritten, bilingual petitions were formally and politically experimental. The hybrid form that the petitions took startled parliamentarians, who had recently signed off on a land ordinance that would excise areas of the Aboriginal reserve in question for the purpose of leasing it to a bauxite mining company.[2]

The Yolngu-speaking leaders from northeast Arnhem Land who made the petitions were outraged that they had not been consulted over the use of their land. They turned that outrage into an original artistic and political expression. The "bark petitions," as they have become known, presented an argument for the coeval and yet distinct status and rights of this indigenous people and are now prominently on display in the National Archives of Australia as one of the country's "founding documents."[3] However, premised in an assertion about Yolngu people's deep and inextricable belonging to the land, the claim that the petition made was barely legible to settler society at the time. Confused and condescending press reports referred to the petitions as a "novel plea" and incorrectly identified the "tribal group" making it.[4] Nonetheless, ten years later, claims like those made by Yolngu people on this remote development frontier were being made by indigenous peoples across Anglo settler states.

In the 1960s, indigenous peoples' lands in the remote north of both Australia and Canada came under threat from an emergent mining boom. On these new frontiers, which had not been extensively settled by white farmers, indigenous peoples had largely held on to their lands—at least in practice if not according to settler law. However, as large-scale mining ventures hunted for resources to feed growing markets in Asia and the United States, federal governments began to open up these rich northern areas by improving access to them. Governments believed that improvements in infrastructure in remote areas would help to modernize small northern populations of indigenous peoples.[5] Rarely consulted about development projects, indigenous leaders in remote regions protested incursions on their lands and sought a nationwide audience for their demands.

The beginning of the mining boom on new frontiers coincided with sharpening indigenous discontent about government policies of assimilation in the densely settled souths of Australia and Canada. In the 1950s, influenced by global struggles for decolonization and responding to demands of indigenous soldiers returned from fighting in World War II, federal governments created policies of assimiliation that would transform indigenous peoples from wards of the state into equal and productive citizens. In countries that prized homogeneity over difference, however, the idea of assimilation assumed that being an equal citizen meant becoming the same as the majority population of white settlers. According to critics of the policy, assimilation seemed like a new instrument for destroying indigenous peoples' distinctive collective identities.

Indigenous leaders in both countries responded to the double threat of the mining boom and assimilation by connecting struggles in remote areas with those in urban centers. They demanded equal wages in the pastoral industry as well as in the factory, full enfranchisement for all indigenous peoples irrespective of their administrative status which had previously excluded them from voting, and access to state housing and public health services in the inner city and on far-flung reserves. These were protests that called to mind those of civil rights and anti-Apartheid activists elsewhere. Indigenous activists also made demands that arose from the specific form of colonization that their communities had experienced. They argued that indigenous people were entitled to the same benefits as other citizens *and* to additional rights that would protect their collective identities as distinct nations. These included rights to the preservation of language and culture, to hunting and fishing as promised in historical treaties, and access to sacred sites. Since these aspects of identity concerned relationships to and use of land, activists argued that what they needed most was land rights. The emergence of a land rights struggle in Canada and Australia at the same time was not simply serendipitous but a common strategic response to similar historical forces.

In Canada, activists arguing for their rights as citizens and as distinct cultural and historical communities used the concept "citizens plus" to indicate the specificity and uniqueness of their demands.[6] It was an innovative and effective idea for widening participation in a shared struggle and gaining nationwide attention. As "citizens plus," indigenous peoples in the majority settler states asserted their rights as coeval citizens in the context of the settler state, and they insisted that they were distinct nations with their own territories and even a right to local self-government.

The concept of indigenous peoples as citizens plus expanded the notion of citizenship in settler states without threatening political dissolution. Rather than arguing for revolution, indigenous leaders drew on and reinterpreted aspects of the history of indigenous-state relations. They pointed out that settler authorities had acknowledged the importance of their ways of life on the land in the past—for instance, in Canada in treaties made with them or, in the case of the Yolngu, by reserving lands for their ongoing use and occupation. Using these precedents, activists demanded the fulfillment of treaty promises and stronger recognition of their land rights. By recognizing their rights as citizens plus, they hoped governments would have to consult with indigenous communities about mining developments and also forgo policies of assimiliation.

THE AUSTRALIAN GOVERNMENT'S proposal to lease the land in northeast Arnhem Land that the "bark petitioners" claimed was theirs did not entirely ignore the needs of local people. The conflict between the government and Yolngu leaders concerned how different authorities perceived what those needs were. Yolngu people wanted to ensure rights over their land and its use since it was and would continue to be critical to the preservation of culture and identity in the wake of the massive transformations that a mine would bring. National politicians believed that the mine would bring benefits to this remote community and would help Aborigines' transition to modernity. Blending an argument about mining opportunities with the policy of assimilation, Minister for the Territories (which included the Northern Territory) Paul Hasluck claimed in April 1963, before the bark petitions were sent to Canberra, that the mine would help to "advance" the Aborigines who lived on reserve land in the area. Hasluck promised that royalties would be paid into a special trust fund held for local people. Compensation would be made, "probably in the form of a series of cottages to be built for them." Sacred places, or what Hasluck referred to as "totemic sites or spirit centres," would be preserved, at least for the "older generation, for whom the ancient traditions are strongest." Like other policymakers, Hasluck assumed that as younger people were incorporated into the national and global economy they would let go of their ancestral heritage. Although he did admit that they would need land in order to "meet the future needs," he did not think they needed distinct land rights.[7] Hasluck's argument assumed that white men always knew what was right for Aboriginal people, as Yolngu leaders pointed out: "The white men think that they are too good for Aboriginal people and therefore he says to himself that he could go ahead and do what he likes, by moving into someone else's land and do all the damage as he could."[8]

Hasluck was a firm supporter of assimilation. In 1951, he announced that welfare measures in Australia shared the objective that "all persons of aboriginal blood or mixed blood would live like white Australians."[9] For Hasluck, assimilation supplanted older policies of segregation and protection that had allowed groups like the Yolngu to live separately from white Australians, paid them rations rather than wages, and discouraged their engagement with mainstream education. The reserve lands that Yolngu people saw as theirs, for instance, had been established in 1931 for the temporary benefit of "nomadic tribes" in order to "preserve the Aboriginal race" until it died out or remnants moved into white communities.[10]

Postwar assimilation policy in Australia, as in Canada, intended to integrate burgeoning indigenous populations more fully into white society. The policies debated by white authorities in this period sometimes emphasized racial assimilation, especially in Australia (there is more than a hint of that in Hasluck's 1951 statement), and even, at its most extreme, the biological absorption of "half-caste" Aborigines.[11] More usually, these policies referred to social and economic integration pursued through housing, education, and health reforms.[12] Often well-intentioned and with a desire to close the gap between the growing indigenous and majority non-indigenous population, assimilationists sought to do away with the distinctive status—official and unofficial—applied to indigenous peoples that they believed had stigmatized them as inferior or backward. Rejecting older colonial discourses in the era of decolonization and civil rights, policymakers gave greater emphasis to the idea that indigenous peoples, who had formerly been treated as wards, should now be offered the entitlements, and take up the responsibilities, of full citizens.[13]

Extending the federal franchise to indigenous peoples was one important legal development in making them citizens. In 1960, Canadian Indians living on reserves were awarded the unconditional right to vote in federal elections; in Australia, Aborigines were enfranchised at the federal level in 1962.[14] Prior to those reforms, enfranchisement had often depended on the degree of civilization indigenous peoples were regarded by the state as having attained and their location on or off reserve lands. New policies encouraged communities to move off reserve lands. In some instance governments forcibly relocated groups they saw as vulnerable. In Canada, policymakers contemplated the dissolution of "treaty status" by which Indians whose ancestors had made treaties with colonial authorities were distinguished administratively from those without treaties, or who had accepted land "scrip" or freehold title to small plots of land. According to some state officials, the Indian Act (1876) which regulated how status could be maintained or lost and placed those with status under the administration of the Indian Affairs, was based on outdated ideas of wardship. It was significantly reformed in 1951, removing some coercive measures.[15]

Nonetheless, critics pointed out at the time and subsequently that postwar assimilation policies bore similarities to earlier interventions into indigenous communities. Moreover, reforms still "assumed that the purpose of Indian policy was the end of Indians."[16] Indigenous communities imagined different futures from those applied to them in assimilation policy. While they, too, demanded equal rights with other Australians and Canadians, spurning ideas of wardship and the "civilizing mission" on which it was based, they wanted to retain key aspects of their identity. Certain aspects of their status, in part identified and administered by the state, recognized that indigenous peoples' identity was premised in a distinct use of and relationship to the land. They now sought to turn that recognition into a set of rights, ones that would protect their identities and their lands. On mining frontiers in particular, they needed stronger rights to land than simply use and access, or other ad hoc grants made to them that were not firmly based in common or statutory law. As Hasluck's comment attested, allowances made by governments for the practice of traditions and rituals assumed that such practices would be discontinued once younger generations had moved away from remote areas or were employed in development projects.

A key strategy of indigenous activists in the late 1960s was the new interpretation of their status as "citizens plus" that they forced on policymakers and wider publics. While white policymakers assumed that the historical status of indigenous peoples as wards of the state was degrading and exclusionary, indigenous peoples began to emphasize how treaty status in Canada, for instance, or lands reserved for "nomadic" Aborigines in Australia, recognized their distinct historical status, and this was necessary for them to maintain their identities. Thus, they reinterpreted key colonial doctrines and events such as treaty-making to show how earlier incarnations of the state had acknowledged their land rights. They argued that these rights should be given full recognition now. This was a subtle argument, prone to being misconstrued, but it became remarkably effective in opening up a new political space for indigenous claims in the 1970s.

AN ARGUMENT FOR Aborigines as citizens plus did not gain traction in Australia until their equal rights were more firmly secured. For most of the 1960s, activists focused on struggles against discrimination and changing the Australian constitution. Those struggles, often carried out in the cities and country towns of southeastern Australia, established Aborigines as coeval citizens. In the late 1960s, new arguments for "land rights" emerged, mainly in remote areas, shifting the focus away from equal rights to the distinct rights of Aborigines.

Protests about the racial discrimination against Aborigines grew in intensity in the mid-1960s, influenced by events in the United States. In 1965, Charles Perkins, one of a very small number of Aboriginal students at the University of Sydney, helped to organize a busload of white students to take a "freedom ride" into the hinterland of New South Wales to protest segregation in country towns and other forms of racism that Aborigines experienced in their day-to-day lives. As Perkins later discussed, he had experienced considerable discrimination as a young boy in central Australia, before moving to Sydney.[17] Like the American freedom riders, the Australians were met with hostility and often heckled and blamed for causing social disruption by locals in the towns they visited. At one point their bus was even driven off the road, but no one was killed. They attracted wide national and international press coverage, and Perkins appeared in national dailies swimming with Aboriginal children in a swimming pool from which they had previously been excluded.[18]

· Activists were concerned with the formal as well as informal obstacles and discrimination that Aborigines faced. Perhaps the signal nationwide movement was for a referendum that proposed repealing provisions in the 1901 Constitution which prohibited the Commonwealth from making special laws in respect of Aborigines and excluded them from census-taking. The 1967 referendum is popularly although erroneously remembered by Aboriginal and non-Aboriginal people as when "Aborigines got the vote" and it received over 90 percent support by the Australian electorate in 1967.[19] What the referendum actually did was sanction the Commonwealth parliament to make

laws in respect of Aborigines by including them in what is known as the constitution's "race power," although it did not require the parliament to do so. In
contrast to Canada (and New Zealand), the Commonwealth government in
Australia did not take direct responsibility for Aborigines' welfare. Until the
1967 referendum, Aboriginal welfare had been overseen by missionaries and
humanitarians in the nineteenth century and later by individual state governments. The referendum also required officials to count the Aboriginal population as distinct in national censuses.

The referendum, which promoted a sense of "inclusion, acceptance, goodwill, and the future," [20] opened the door for the creation of special assistance
programs for Aborigines. It even created a space that activists could push
wider open as momentum grew for land rights legislation at the national level
in the 1970s. This idea was entirely novel in the Australian context where
native title had never been recognized, in the courts or by the legislature, and
no treaties had been officially entered into with indigenous groups by colonial
authorities. The history of non-recognition in Australia was quite distinct
from what had occurred in Canada and New Zealand, where some treaties
were negotiated and the idea of indigenous land rights had been discussed in
the past. In large part, this had to do with the unique form of colonization
on the continent. The first Australian colony of New South Wales was, from
the beginning, one of settlement, initially for the punishment and reform of
convicts. None of the later Australian colonies were significant trading posts.
Few informal economic alliances between Europeans and indigenous peoples
were established as they were in North America, and no diplomatic or military alliances were formed between particular European groups engaged in
inter-imperial rivalry and Aboriginal people. In other settler countries, the
historical agreements forged between indigenous peoples and the Crown
continued to be recognized in a special "trust" relationship between individual groups and the settler state. This trust relationship with, or fiduciary
duty to, Aboriginal people was not observed by the Commonwealth government in Australia.[21]

The struggle for constitutional change in 1967 did not foreground the
issue of land rights per se. Members of the primary organization pushing for
the "yes" vote, the Federal Council for the Advancement of Aborigines and
Torres Strait Islanders (FCAATSI) established in 1958 to remove discrimina-
tory legislation in Australia and press for equal rights for Aborigines, did raise
the issue of land rights at times in their discussions and meetings, demanding
compensation and even the right to develop "tribal lands" that were identified
as Aboriginal reserves, but it was not a central concern.[22]

Some Aboriginal leaders in settled areas had protested the dispossesion of their people historically. In the 1870s, for instance, Kulin people on the Coranderrk mission station in Victoria had demanded rights, as one leader William Barak put it, to "my father's country."[23] Sixty years later, the Australian Aborigines' League based in Melbourne, which included former residents of Corranderrk, petitioned King George V as well as the Commonwealth government for redress for what Aborigines had lost, particularly in terms of land expropriation. William Cooper, secretary of the league, thought that having dedicated Aboriginal representation in parliament—akin to the Maori seats in the New Zealand parliament—would help to alleviate the problems that Aborigines faced, including landlessness, and improve their condition as a race of people.[24] In Sydney, the Aboriginal activist Fred Maynard created the Australian Aboriginal Progressives Association in 1924, based on the model of the Universal Negro Improvement Association in the United States. The association battled against the New South Wales Aborigines Protection Board which had oversight of Aboriginal people and ruled their lives in radically intrusive ways including removing children from their parents. One of Maynard's ongoing campaigns concerned bringing the relocation of Aborigines from traditional lands that had been taken over by white farmers to national attention.[25]

For these leaders and activists, notions of "land" or "country" were associated with a range of experiences and entitlements. Those included ancestral connection, moral outrage at dispossession, a shared sense of racial difference, and the desire for economic security. However, their protests largely fell on deaf ears as there was little sympathy on the part of the settler public or Commonwealth government for the recognition of distinct land rights for Aborigines. Even in the late 1960s the recognition of Aborigines' land rights seemed unlikely despite awareness on the part of some policymakers of the recognition of native or customary land tenure in other places including within Australia's own colonial protectorate of Papua. Since there was no precedent for such recognition in Australia, many activists were circumspect about the possibility of Aboriginal people winning recognition of their land rights any time soon.[26]

Yet, in the early 1970s, the idea that Aborigines had distinct land rights, based on a distinct and historical relationship to the land, became a matter of widespread debate and a key issue in the 1972 Commonwealth election. It would become the central issue of Aboriginal affairs in the following three decades. What made this issue imaginable and debatable—if not yet fully recognizable at law—was a notable shift in the emphasis of activist discourse, from equal rights to land rights, and a change in the ideology of government policy in respect of Aborigines, from assimilation to self-determination.[27] Scholars also began to play an important role in exposing the "destruction of the Aborigines" and critiquing a notion that colonization in Australia was justified because it was empty.[28] By the early 1970s, demands for "land rights," government debates about "self-determination," and the survival of Aboriginal identity despite colonization, became discourses that were inextricable from one another.

The "birthplace" for modern land rights is often considered to be the walk-off in 1966 at the Wave Hill station in central Australia by Gurindji stockmen who complained of inequality in wages as well as racial discrimination in working conditions and the poor treatment of Aboriginal women on cattle stations.[29] Most pastoral workers in the Northern Territory at this time were Aboriginal, and they earned on average only about one-quarter of the wage that non-Aboriginal men did for the same job.[30] The Conciliation and Arbitration Commission granted Aboriginal stockworkers equal wages but this would not take effect until the end of 1968. In 1966, the Gurindji stockmen argued that the land occupied by the station, which at the time was leased to a British company Vestey's that owned a number of cattle stations in the Northern Territory, was their traditional land and contained important sacred sites. At the end of the year, twenty-six men and women turned the "walk-off" into an occupation, establishing a camp at Wattie Creek on the station, close to a sacred dreaming site.

A protest that began as a claim about equal rights and the delay in implementing the Commission's grant soon became key in the emerging struggle for land rights. It was significant that such demands were made by those in the remote "outback" who could make a persuasive argument that imminent threats to their lands endangered their ways of being Aboriginal because they looked and sounded like traditional Aborigines.[31] Moreover, at Wave Hill, Aboriginal union representatives, southern white activists, and local Aboriginal leaders drew a crucial connection between land rights and self-determination for Aboriginal people.

Two of the Aboriginal union leaders who became central figures at the Wave Hill strike had recently visited Kenya at the invitation of a government minister. They were impressed with cooperative farming schemes there. If even "primitive Massai tribesmen just out of the bush" could run such farms then they could too, they were reported as saying.[32] The white writer and communist Frank Hardy, who became another central figure in the protest, connected an issue of "inalienable" tribal land rights at Wave Hill to the

Communist Party's recent endorsement of the right of Aborigines to "control their own affairs" and to "preserve and develop their own culture including language."[33]

Like other activists before them, Gurundji people at Wave Hill petitioned the federal government for the opportunity to buy the lease over the station. Even the Northern Territory government suggested that the Commonwealth transfer to them a "home area" although not the entire area of the pastoral lease. "It was urged that Government should recognise the emerging spirit of independence and initiative of the Gurindji," explained Nugget Coombs, the chairman of the recently formed Council of Aboriginal Affairs, to relevant government ministers in 1971, "and work with them in an attempt to assess the practicability of their plans."[34] The petition and the proposition it led to, however, were rejected by the Commonwealth for fear that it would lead to a spate of land claims. Many of the Gurindji protestors remained in the camp they had established at Wattie Creek without having their land rights formally recognized.[35]

The Commonwealth government was not yet prepared to recognize Aborigines' land rights, but the idea of creating land "trusts" for Aborigines was broached by the state government of South Australia around the time of the Gurundji strike. In 1966, the South Australian parliament passed the Aboriginal Lands Trust Act which enabled some lands reserved for Aboriginal groups to be vested in a statewide trust. Like some of the activists involved in the Wave Hill protest, promoters of the law in South Australia viewed the recognition of land rights as a key facet of the self-determination campaign.[36] Politicians who supported the new legislation referenced international law relating to indigenous peoples. For example, they cited the International Labor Organization's (ILO) protection of indigenous peoples' tribal lands in convention 107 (1957) as evidence for the need to recognize indigenous rights in Australia.[37]

Debates during the passage of the Aboriginal Lands Trust Act showed that the notion that Aborigines were in a period of transition was still paramount. The vesting of land was seen by those promoting the legislation as recognizing Aborigines' past connection to their lands in preparation for moving into a modern future, in much the same way that Hasluck described the "older" Yolngu people's attachment to land. Critics of the bill asked what such notions had to do with political emancipation. As one academic at the time put it, "I think they [Aborigines] have to undergo much more education before they can become sufficiently detached to deal with the problems that will come before the Trust."[38] Even supporters argued that the vestment of land was important "even if in years to come [such lands] are only somewhere to go at weekends to see where their forebears lived."[39]

White politicians and experts did not think about Aboriginal land rights as a long-term prospect nor one that was necessary for Aborigines in achieving a degree of independence. The idea that indigenous peoples were entitled to self-determination and that this could be realized through recognizing land rights as core to their collective identity was still some way from becoming a salient political demand.

At the national 1968 Aboriginal Advancement Conference, a year after the constitutional referendum, however, a new national campaign was launched by activists. Organizations from across the country resolved that together they should urge

> the granting of Aboriginal land rights, and in particular the granting of full title and rights to compensation with respect to all existing Aboriginal Reserve land throughout Australian and the provision of land for all Aboriginal groups seeking to live on, use, and develop land in their traditionally occupied areas.[40]

As these activists anticipated, land rights would become the critical issue for Aborigines in remote and even in densely settled parts of the continent in coming years. Furthermore, the recognition of Aborigines' land rights would come to be associated with an idea of "self-determination" and the turn away from the policy of assimilation, which was no longer sustainable as the civil rights of minorities became an international issue and, at the same time, new social movements demanded rights to identity. Indigenous peoples, like other colonized and racially marked groups, demanded the right to define themselves and frame their own futures, according to their deep and abiding attachment to the land.[41] This meant going beyond demands for civil rights and making the case for distinct rights.

However, the idea that indigenous peoples had a right to self-determination based on their connection to the land faced significant challenges in the Australian context. The distinct rights of Aborigines raised particularly complex issues in a country where there was no prior recognition of land rights and no history of treaty-making. Governments in the late 1960s and early 1970s were reluctant to inquire into these problems, in large part because the substance of those rights were unknown and the ways they might be evidenced was not yet clear.

IN CANADA, TOO, indigenous peoples had long protested being dispossessed of their lands. Earlier generations had laid claims to land and maintained particular customary practices such as hunting and fishing even in the face of laws that restricted such activities. They had petitioned parliament, the British monarch and Privy Council, and even the League of Nations for acknowledgment of their peoplehood and recognition of what they had lost.[42] In contrast to Australia, some groups in Canada had taken their claims to the courts in the late nineteenth and early twentieth centuries. Those claims were based on treaty promises that leaders argued had been breached or concerned lands taken by settlers without any treaty negotiations taking place.

In some parts of Canada, Indian leaders had negotiated agreements with imperial and colonial authorities beginning in the eighteenth century and continuing into the early twentieth century. Pre-Confederation treaties made in what are now the eastern provinces of Canada and those made following Confederation in 1867 across the west—although not in much of northern Canada and what became British Columbia—varied considerably in their contents and execution. Earlier treaties were primarily concerned with facilitating trade and affirming political alliances; the later "numbered" treaties made in the western provinces demanded extensive land cessions from Indians in return for small payments in kind and money. Those treaties also created reserve lands.[43]

Although the contents of these treaties appear to be straightforward, their negotiation at the time and the interpretations made of them later demonstrate that they were complex events, understood differently by the parties involved and setting very different expectations for each side that changed considerably over time. In the mid-nineteenth century, for instance, Colonial Office officials in Britain advocated the making of treaties with indigenous peoples as a humane practice, protecting them from predatory settlers, although they also worried about the possibilities that colonists would evade the terms.[44] As colonial governments achieved more political independence in the late nineteenth century, settler policymakers and judges generally interpreted treaties as deeds of surrender; this was the case in the leading judicial decision on Indian land rights, *St Catherine's Milling and Lumber Co. v. The Queen* (1888) in which the majority of the Canadian Supreme Court justices found that Indians had rights of occupancy but not of ongoing ownership.[45] However, Indian groups remembered treaties as recognizing their status as political entities and offering protection and care from the British monarch.[46] Whatever they hoped the treaties promised them, most Indian groups experienced extensive dispossession, as well as the curtailment of hunting and fishing rights following treaty signings.[47]

In the early twentieth century, Indian leaders in the east and west of Canada brought their claims to court. This included the Nisga'a in British Columbia who claimed their lands had been stolen from them since no treaties had been made with them. Although they were allocated communally owned reserves in the late nineteenth century, the provincial government began whittling away the extent of these reserves as the settler population in the province grew.[48] Attempting to stifle a wave of legal activism, the government prohibited the use of band funds administered by the Department of Indian Affairs to pay lawyers to prosecute legal cases. The prohibition, an amendment to the Indian Act, was made in 1927 and not repealed until 1951.[49] Even after this date, plaintiffs who wanted to sue the Crown may have had to seek permission to do so from the provincial government in the province where they were bringing their case.

In the early 1960s, and with greater intensity in the early 1970s, Indian leaders and organizations returned to the courts and began to win more attention for their claims than their predecessors earlier in the century, including the Nisga'a. As was the case in Australia, the timing of Indian activism with pressures on the settler state in the context of global decolonization was key to their success in drawing out a new and effective narrative about their claims.

Many of the same conditions existed in the early twentieth-century campaign by Nisga'a leaders for the recognition of their aboriginal title rights as in the 1960s and 1970s. These included an economic boom that led to the further expropriation of native lands; the residential schooling and legal education of Indian leaders including Peter Kelly and Andrew Paull (who were, however, not admitted to the bar since, as enrolled status Indians, they could not vote); and the support that the Nisga'a leaders received from a small coterie of white lawyers.[50] However, that earlier campaign failed primarily because of a lack of political sympathy in settler society and the representation of Indians as wards of the state. As Peter Kelly later lamented, Indians continued to be regarded as "simply a dependent people."[51] What made the difference in the later period, therefore, was a changing appreciation of Indians as equal citizens rather than as wards, and an emergent public discourse about indigenous peoples' rights in the context of global decolonization.

Following World War II, Indian leaders and settler politicans had proposed remedying breaches in treaties. For the first time, the federal government actually sought out the opinions and ideas of Indian leaders themselves. Leaders used the opportunity to demand their right to local self-government, although these demands were not given much attention by government ministers.[52] One important proposal that was discussed at length was for the creation of a nationwide "Indian Claims Commission," inspired by the example of the United States Indian Claims Commission that operated from 1946 to 1978. The idea gathered signficant political support in Canada, and in 1965, a bill that proposed the creation of such a commission came before parliament. One member of parliament argued that the public relations work that such a commission might achieve was critical to raising the esteem of Canada in the eyes of other Commonwealth countries in the era of decolonization:

> We have only to think of the discussions that have been going on in London between the Prime Ministers of the various Commonwealth nations to understand how significant it is that if we in Canada are to be a self respecting member of the Commonwealth we have got to take action within our own borders. . . . The job that has to be done by this legislation, in effect, is parallel to the job which has been done by Britain in granting India her freedom and independence.[53]

The commission was not created but, in any case, Indian activists did not wait to be given the political rights they sought. In 1969, policy proposals by the new Liberal government galvanized Indian protest across the country. The government issued a "white paper" that proposed dissolving Indians' treaty status which placed them under the administration of Indian Affairs.[54] Prime Minister Pierre Trudeau and his advisors regarded the treaty status of some Indian bands as retarding them. The practice of a special administration of Indian affairs was, Trudeau believed, incommensurate with the platform of an equal and "Just Society" on which his party had been elected. By treating individual Indians as "wards" of the state, such a form of administration only further exacerbated the "Indian problem." Instead, Trudeau argued that Indians should be encouraged to claim the rights and perform the duties of Canadian citizens so that they could "demand what they consider just."[55] The new policy, Trudeau explained, would encourage "our Indian and Inuit population . . . to assume the full rights of citizenship through policies which will give them both greater responsibility for their own future and more meaningful equality of opportunity."[56] Trudeau's preference for an unmarked citizenship was itself in part a response to the widespread claims to equality that had become politically salient in the era of decolonization.[57]

With this position, the Liberal government created a moral opening that activists made good use of, although to different ends. According to Trudeau and other liberals, Indians had to throw off their distinct status in order to become full citizens of modern settler states.[58] Indian leaders, however, were adamant that they must retain their historical rights to maintain their distinct identities. Accordingly, they saw the White Paper as a further attempt to assimilate them into an individualized form of citizenship that would destroy their collective lives and identities as Indians. The proposals, they argued, were another example of colonization by settler states, not decolonization. The White Paper proposals denied the history of recognition that had already been awarded to Indian people, primarily in the form of treaty-making. As the young Cree activist Harold Cardinal put it in leading the political charge against the government, Indians had to reject the Liberal government's emphasis on equality at the expense of difference. "If our rights are meaningless, if it is inconceivable that our society have treaties with the white society even although those treaties were signed by honourable men on both sides, in good faith, long before the present government decided to tear them up as worthless scraps of paper, then we as a people are meaningless."[59]

As well as claiming rights as equal citizens, Indian activists employed a term already in circulation to describe their distinct political status. They claimed they were "citizens plus," a term that had been coined to express the idea that Indians had additional rights to their equal entitlements with other Canadian citizens—in particular, that they had the right to maintain their own culture and choose their own future. The term was used in a 1964 report that examined Indian bands' social conditions; it was issued by the Canadian federal government's Department of Citizenship and Immigration and commonly referred to as the "Hawthorn Report" after its main author, New Zealand-born anthropologist Harry Hawthorn.[60] The Hawthorn report, which was mainly concerned with Indians' transition to modernity, argued that Indians were "citizens plus" because "in addition to the normal rights and duties of citizenship, Indians possess certain additional rights as charter members of the Canadian community."[61] The report specified that the "additional rights" of indigenous peoples included the right to choose their own future rather than have one foisted upon them. Advocating an "ordinary respect for what values and institutions, languages, religions and modes of thought, persist in their own small societies," the Hawthorn report asserted that indigenous peoples should be allowed to choose whether they continued to live according to the norms of their own societies. "Almost certainly some Indians will choose not to accept what we regard as the benefits of our society, and will choose instead what they regard as the benefits of theirs."[62]

Indian activists took up the term "citizens plus" to oppose the proposals in the White Paper and offer instead a new concept that would protect their distinct identities. In another polemic to which Cardinal contributed entitled "Citizens Plus," also known as the "Red Paper," the Indian Association of Alberta called for the "preservation" of Indian history and Indian rights. "The only way to maintain our culture," asserted the Association, "is for us to remain as Indians. To preserve our culture it is necessary to preserve our status, rights, lands and traditions. Our treaties are the basis of our rights."[63] In asserting the historical nature of their rights, Cardinal and other activists recovered an image of treaty-making as an honorable best practice. Whereas many in settler society likely viewed treaties as simply expedient instruments of empire, and Indians as dupes, Cardinal offered an image of Indians at odds with that of the White Paper. He insisted that they were and long had been political actors, with their own histories of political action and organization. Their inherent nationhood had been recognized by colonial officials in negotiating treaties, even thought the promises made in those treaties had not always been upheld and treaty bands had been vulnerable to the whims of state policymakers. Indians, in other words, were coeval with settlers, and they maintained their political distinctiveness on their ancestral lands.[64]

Trudeau's government ministers were surprised by the depth of the antipathy to the White Paper and put the proposals on hold. Instead, they turned to the problem of addressing treaty grievances by finally establishing an Indian Claims Commission. The idea of appointing a commissioner to discharge remaining government obligations deriving from the treaties had, in fact, been proposed in the White Paper. In that proposal, however, the commission was represented as the penultimate work of Indian administration, after which treaty obligations would have no further political meaning or effect. The Canadian Indian Claims Commission (CICC) that was established in 1969, following extensive protests of Indian leaders, took on a very different orientation. It became a central institution in the explication of a new history of treaty-making: that such treaties recognized the rights of, in a notable change of terminology, *Aboriginal* peoples to their peoplehood as distinct and enduring. By establishing those rights in the historical authority of treaties, CICC reports and the wide-ranging scholarship it spawned demonstrated that Indians had collective rights as political entities, not only rights as individual citizens. The CICC instituted a research program in regional areas that encouraged the collection of local histories, oral traditions, and other forms of ethnographic evidence that supported Indians' version of treaty negotiations and gave more weight to the notion of Indians as "citizens plus."[65]

At the same time as status Indian leaders were demanding their treaty rights, leaders of communities with whom colonial authorities had never made treaties were demanding recognition of "aboriginal title" to lands they said their people had never ceded. This included Inuit people in the Arctic, Métis communities, and Indians in British Columbia and parts of the north. The federal government initially dismissed their claims, and the CICC was not given the jurisdiction to hear or make recommendations on aboriginal title. However, the government was eventually forced to change its position following the renewed legal activism of Nisga'a leaders who brought the first contemporary aboriginal title case to court. Led by Frank Calder, in 1969 the Nisga'a began the action against the province of British Columbia, claiming that their nation's title to land had never been extinguished.

After two rulings against the Nisga'a plaintiffs in the lower courts, the Supreme Court of Canada found for the first time in Canadian legal history that aboriginal title did exist according to the British Proclamation of 1763. This proclamation had limited legal settlement in the thirteen colonies east of the Appalachian mountains and recognized "Indian territory" west of the proclamation line. However, the justices in *Calder et al. v. Attorney-General of British Columbia* (1973) split (3–3) on the issue of whether such title had been extinguished. A seventh judge found against the Nisga'a claimants on a matter of jurisdiction on the grounds that they had not obtained permission from the province of British Columbia to sue the Crown. His decision pushed the matter of aboriginal title back into the political realm.[66]

The Nisga'a claimants failed on a technicality, but *Calder v. Attorney-General* marked a legal turning point in the recognition of Indians' land rights in historical terms as well as launching the careers of some of those involved. A few years later, the Nisga'a's lawyer, Thomas Berger, chaired the Mackenzie Valley Pipeline Inquiry that investigated the claims of Dene people in the Northwest Territories to their land rights in the context of a proposed oil and gas pipeline that would connect Arctic reserves with the United States market. The inquiry was a turning point in the appreciation of the injustices being inflicted on remote northern peoples and brought their claims to nationwide attention.[67]

According to one of the justices in the Calder case, the ethnohistorical evidence that had been prepared in support of the case made a new approach to aboriginal rights necessary. Mr. Justice Hall argued that such rights had to be ascertained "in the light of present-day research and knowledge disregarding ancient concepts formulated when understanding of the customs and culture of our original people was rudimentary and incomplete and when they were thought to be wholly without cohesion, laws or culture, in effect a subhuman species."[68] Notably, however, neither expert historical testimony nor histories provided by Nisga'a claimants were central to the decision which for the majority of the justices turned on the question of extinguishment of title rather than on proof of attachment given by Indians.[69]

Leading Indian organizations saw the case as a breakthrough. George Manuel, chief of the National Indian Brotherhood, issued a statement affirming that the Brotherhood "do not regard this decision either legally or morally as a defeat. . . . This judgment indicates . . . that the court has not as yet ruled definitively on the existence of aboriginal rights. . . . [W]e believe that it is now the duty of this government to rule on the question."[70] The publicity surrounding the case had immediate political effect: Trudeau reversed his opinion that aboriginal title rights could not be recognized in Canada. On 8 August 1973, the government issued a "Comprehensive Claims" policy that distinguished the claims of groups without treaties from treaty or "specific" claims and paved the way for the resolution of aboriginal title claims.[71] The federal government would negotiate modern treaties that guaranteed certain rights to groups in exchange for the cession of their aboriginal title rights. As new mining and infrastructural developments in Canada's north were proposed, remote communities began to pursue recognition of their aboriginal title rights, insisting that their identities were at risk.

The influence of external factors, particularly anti-colonial and anti-racist ideas, was extremely important in changing perceptions of indigenous rights, as demonstrated by the reversals of policy by the Liberal government. Mr. Justice Hall's comments in the Calder case that Indians should no longer be regarded as a "subhuman species" surely hit a nerve in the anti-racist present of the 1970s. However, decolonizing discourses were not adopted into the language and strategy of Indians in Canada wholesale. The importance of the local concept of "citizens plus" was crucial for distinguishing the claims of indigenous peoples from those of other racially marked or minority groups seeking civil rights but not distinct rights. Indigenous activists significantly adapted the language of decolonization as they made their demands to settler states. In so doing, they found that local concepts could be remarkably effective in bringing their demands to public notice.

THE IDEA PURSUED by governments following World War II that indigenous peoples should bear equal rights to those of other citizens in settler states opened a door that activists pushed wider in fighting for the survival of their identities as indigenous nations. Given the long-standing representations of indigenous peoples as racially inferior in Australia and Canada, the achievement of a status as modern, equal citizens should not be underestimated. But it was not enough. Being an equal citizen in the settler state did not guarantee that indigenous communities on the new mining frontiers would have the power to say how their lands could be used. It did not enable those in settled areas who had already been dispossessed of their lands to reconnect with their ancestral places and protect vulnerable identities. Indeed, if equality was to be achieved through assimilation, it actually threatened indigenous peoples' identities.

In Australia and Canada, the argument that indigenous peoples were coeval and had distinct additional rights to their lands as citizens plus brought communities together in a shared struggle. Younger activists such as Charles Perkins and Harold Cardinal saw demands for equal and distinct rights as linked to those of more remote communities such as Yolngu and Nisga'a. Even if tactics between younger and older generations differed, a shared sense of what it meant to be indigenous was beginning to emerge. This identity was one framed around the expression of deep historical connection to the land. Soon, indigenous leaders would begin to forge links with those in other countries too, creating new organizations such as the World Council of Indigenous Peoples and developing a global argument about rights to indigeneity that they would take all the way to the United Nations.[72]

The nationwide connections that leaders built between urban and remote communities was critical not only for indigenous peoples' sense of who they were but also for generating momentum and forcing national governments to acknowledge their demands. FCAATSI and the National Indian Brotherhood did vital work in bringing activists together to share tactics and information. They mounted nationwide campaigns, for instance, pushing forward a "yes" vote on the constitutional referendum in Australia, and opposing the White Paper in Canada. The success of both these campaigns showed that indigenous peoples might be minorities in their own homelands, but they could win wider sympathy for their causes and exert strong moral pressure on governments to change their policies about indigenous rights.

Despite indigenous success in these campaigns, the settler state remained intransigent about giving full recognition of indigenous land rights or aboriginal title. In experimenting with notions of local self-determination, governments might broach the question of limited land grants and consider breaches of particular treaty promises, but they were reluctant to consider claims for "territorial rights." They dismissed indigenous communities' capacity for substantive political autonomy and their insistence on their own distinct nationhood. Moreover, governments were focused on spurring national economic growth by opening up new lands for the resource boom particularly as Australia and Canada cut economic ties with Britain. In the face of this intractability, indigenous leaders shifted strategy. They had to make recognition of their land rights a priority. Rather than using violence to achieve their ends, established and new leaders on the new frontiers of both countries joined forces in turning to the courts.

2

Australia's First "First People"

If we were without the land, there might be none of us.
—AFFIDAVIT OF DADYNGA MARIKA (1969)

IN MAY 1970, Yolngu leaders traveled the 700-plus kilometers from their home on the Gove Peninsula, east Arnhem Land, to Darwin, the capital of Australia's Northern Territory. It was the beginning of the Dharratharramirri or "knock 'em down" season when gusting winds from the southeast flatten the tall grasses, and the dirt roads become passable again; it was also seven years after the Yolngu had sent their "bark petitions" to Canberra. They were heading to the Northern Territory's supreme court to appear as key witnesses in the country's first-ever native title hearing. The leaders, who were most of the named plaintiffs in the case, were suing Nabalco, a Swiss bauxite mining company and the Commonwealth (federal government) of Australia. They claimed the company had unlawfully invaded their land on the Gove Peninsula since the government had not consulted with them prior to issuing the mineral lease.

The legal case that Yolngu leaders mounted was a new strategy for them and for Aboriginal people across the continent. *Milirrpum v. Nabalco Pty. Ltd. and the Commonwealth of Australia* (1971), commonly known as the "Gove land rights case," raised a host of legal and moral issues.[1] By going to court, indigenous peoples forced the question of whether they even had standing in the law, particularly if they wanted to present testimony of their attachment to land based in oral traditions and usually considered hearsay. The judge, Mr. Justice Richard Blackburn, did establish a precedent for the admission of Aborigines' distinct evidence of their attachment to land which was crucial for later claims, although he decided he could not find a precedent for the recognition of Aborigines' distinct land rights.

Beyond the law, the case brought to the fore of political debate questions about the recognition of Aborigines' rights and their distinct status in the settler state. In his 1967 Boyer lectures broadcast nationally on ABC radio, the anthropologist

W. E. H. Stanner, who appeared as an expert witness in the Gove case, had referred to a "Great Australian Silence" in the treatment of Aborigines. As he put it, the "forgetting" of the Aborigines was not simply absent-mindedness, but "a cult . . . practiced on a national scale."[2] The Gove land rights case broke the silence. Using terms such as "invasion" and contesting the Commonwealth's presumption that it owned the peninsula, Yolngu people made it clear to the judge, lawyers, and the media covering the case that theirs was a morally righteous cause and that they deserved justice as Australia's "first people."

UNTIL THE PROPOSAL for developing a bauxite mine was made, the Gove peninsula was a virtually "unheard of spot" in the rest of Australia. By the end of the 1960s, land on this remote frontier, including the world's "most valuable airstrip" as one news report claimed, was at the center of an ownership battle

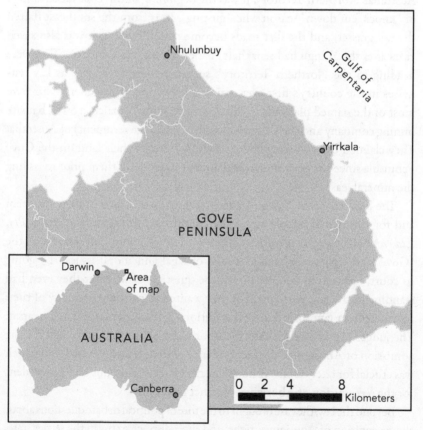

FIGURE 2.1 Map of the Gove Peninsula, Northern Territory, Australia. Map by Tim Stallmann.

that was gaining nationwide attention.[3] At least a day's drive from Darwin, depending on the season, the peninsula is part of what is known as Arnhem Land, named by a seventeenth-century Dutch explorer. Until World War II, when it served as a defense post for Australian and American troops, the Gove peninsula was rarely visited by Europeans.[4] However, despite the assumptions of Australian journalists in the early 1970s who tended to depict them as naïve and previously untouched, the people who had inhabited the area for tens of thousands of years had been trading with outsiders along the coast long before Europeans arrived. In the early eighteenth century, decades before Captain Cook charted the southeast coastline of Australia, groups in Arnhem land began to deal in trepang (sea cucumber) with Macassan traders and allowed some Macassans to establish temporary settlements in the area. The trepang trade was prohibited in 1907 by the recently created Commonwealth government, which had direct responsibility for the Northern Territory, as it began to tighten customs restrictions around Australia's coastlines, and alcohol became a trade item in the far north.[5]

Cross-cultural economic interaction in the area was not cut off by these prohibitions. In the inter-war years, Japanese pearlers visited the Gulf of Carpentaria, into which the peninsula protrudes. Yolngu people worked with Japanese fishermen, but in the early 1930s relations between some of the groups soured. In 1932, Yolngu people at Caledon Bay killed five Japanese fishermen following an escalation of tensions; then a white policeman sent to investigate the deaths was himself killed. A 1931 ordinance that had established an Aboriginal reserve as a "sanctuary" in order to protect the locals and encourage a missionary presence in the area did not appear to have been effective.[6] Authorities in Darwin promised a punitive expedition, a common response to frontier conflict in the Australian outback. Mission organizations and an anthropologist, Donald Thomson, intervened, advocating a peace mission instead. Thomson visited Yolngu people to find out their concerns and following his recommendations, the Commonwealth government approved the Methodist Overseas Mission to establish a station at Yirrkala. Yolngu oral histories tell of welcoming the mission in to the area and inviting Wilbur Chaseling of the Methodist organization to live among them to help establish peace in the midst of increasing clan warfare and the conflict with outsiders.[7]

Permanent residences were built on the banks of the Yirrkala creek in 1935, which by 1970 were home to a mobile population of about 600 people. The third such mission in Arnhem Land, Yirrkala began humbly when missionaries erected a shed in which to preach to Gumatj and Rirratjingu clans, who camped on the creek for several months of the year. The first resident missionary couple, Chaseling and his wife, encouraged Yolngu people to stay at the station throughout the year, and members of other clans, including the Djapu, settled in the village as mission residents grew plantations of bananas, cassava, and other tropical crops, some of which were sold to merchants who would visit the mission by boat from Darwin. The Chaselings ran a tight enterprise, following a principle of "no work, no pay" at the station.[8] Wages were paid to mission residents at first in the form of flour and tobacco. Missionaries based their religious teachings on the "dignity of labour." Chaseling also preached religious tolerance and sought to find analogies between Christian and Yolngu beliefs and religious practices.[9]

In addition to granting permission for mission stations, the land ordinance of 1931 had provided for the excision of certain areas if gold or other mineral deposits were found. Mining ventures would have to pay the government royalties, part of which would be used to provide for the welfare of the local Aboriginal inhabitants. In 1953, following the discovery of considerable bauxite reserves, the government passed a Minerals Ordinance vesting the minerals in the Crown. A number of companies made unsuccessful applications for minerals leases. Finally, in 1963, the Commonwealth government excised 140 square miles (more than 300 square kilometers) from the reserve in preparation for granting a mining lease. Neither Yolngu inhabitants at Yirrkala nor the resident missionary, Edgar Wells, was consulted.

Angered at this lack of consultation, Wells assisted leaders at Yirrkala in preparing and sending the "bark petitions" to parliament in August 1963. The unexpected success of the petitions in gaining nationwide attention prompted the parliament to establish a select committee inquiry into the "grievances of the Yirrkala Aborigines."[10] The inquiry recommended that compensation be paid to the people at Yirrkala and their sacred places respected, but it did not recognize Aboriginal people on the peninsula as owners of the lands they inhabited nor did it suggest they had political authority over their territory. The reserved land was Crown domain and Yolngu people were not considered to bear inherent sovereignty with distinct rights to their lands, as Native Americans on reservations were in the United States; therefore the government was not required by law to recognize their claims. This precarious legal situation was not fully appreciated by Yolgnu people when they first heard of the bauxite mining proposals.[11] In 1968, after a number of applications failed to eventuate in substative proposals, the government made an agreement with Nabalco Pty. Ltd. and issued a mining lease which came into effect at the end of that year.

Yolngu leaders were not totally opposed to the Nabalco mining venture. They did, however, want the title to the land that the company was mining legally recognized as theirs so that they could have a say in the extent of the mining operations and negotiate royalties with the company themselves. At an impasse with the Commonwealth government, which refused to recognize their claims, Yolngu leaders and their supporters turned to the courts. It was the first time any Aboriginal community had tried to prosecute native title rights. Mounting a novel legal claim entailed more risk and more work than any of those involved in the case—the Yolngu leaders, the Methodist mission, the lawyers hired to prosecute the case, or the anthropologists brought in to provide expert testimony—could have anticipated at the time. Yolngu people were supported by the Methodist Commission for Aboriginal Affairs, first convened in 1962, which had affiliated with the Federal Council for the Advancement of Aborigines and Torres Strait Islanders (FCAATSI). The commission had recently expressed its backing for Aboriginal self-determination and land rights and, given the fact that many Yolngu were Methodists, the case was clearly within its area of duty and concern.[12] The commission therefore approached a Melbourne legal firm to produce a legal opinion on the possibility of mounting a land rights claim. No legal firms had expertise in this area, so one of the partners at the firm, Frank Purcell, hired a young white activist and lawyer, John Little, to write a memo. Little had spent some time in northern Aborignal communities and had already undertaken research into the recognition of native title rights in other Anglophone settler jurisdictions. Purcell also invited a Melbourne Queen's Counsel, Edward (Ted) Woodward, to give his opinion.

Woodward later recalled his bemusement at the invitation since he had never had professional dealings in Aboriginal affairs prior to the case, nor any personal interactions with Yolngu people and their culture.[13] Nonetheless, the more he read about the issues, especially the history of reserve in east Arnhem Land, the stronger his moral commitment to the land rights case became. As he recounted in his memoirs, his motivation was clear: to "protect Aboriginal rights. . . . I simply felt that the whole process was so obviously unjust that there should be a legal answer to it."[14] His involvement in the case would make him an important player in Aboriginal land rights when they became a national issue in the early 1970s following the Gove land rights case.

Little, on the other hand, was more radical politically, and this soon led him to become frustrated with the compromises for which Purcell and Woodward argued. In late 1969 when Purcell tried to negotiate a compensation deal with Nabalco and the government on behalf of his Yolngu clients, Little accused him and other lawyers of "patronising" the Aborigines and "giving up" on the land rights case. He argued that the lawyers should be about fighting for Yolngu people's territorial control of the whole peninsula.[15] After Mr. Justice Richard Blackburn's decision against the Yolngu plaintiffs, Little turned away from Australian law altogether. In a letter to a Yolngu leader in January 1972, Little accused Purcell, Woodward, and others of betraying the Yolgnu people. He advocated a different strategy: that the Yirrkala leaders mount a campaign of armed resistance against the inherently racist state.[16] Little's position did not receive much of a hearing at Yirrkala, although some other activists around Australia also advocated violence against the state.

Woodward and Purcell were certainly invested in due process and in securing a good deal for Yolngu people by legal means. They were also intellectually excited by the case, and Woodward searched widely for comparative legal examples in preparing the suit. The broader issue at stake was not just how specific Yolngu rights to their land might be recognized, the lawyers realized, but in much larger terms how Australian law might incorporate the doctrine of native title, as other Anglophone, common law colonies had done.[17] The anthropologist Diane Barwick later suggested that it was an anthropological network stretching from Australia to Canada that helped to provide comparative legal materials useful to the lawyers in making their arguments. According to Barwick, the anthropologist W. E. H. Stanner, who was an expert witness in the case, was given extensive material on native title rights by Thomas Berger, lawyer for the Nisga'a people in British Columbia who were concurrently pursuing their aboriginal title claim.[18] Closer to home, in Australia's own protectorate of Papua, the native title rights of indigenous people had been recognized by the Australian High Court as early as 1941.[19] Why had native title never been recognized on the mainland? Could the country be brought in line with its peers and even its own dependencies?

Following the trail of native title jurisprudence in other Anglophone colonies, the lawyers focused on the question of finding a legal precedent for the recognition of Aboriginal land rights in Australia. They also collected evidence of long occupation of east Arnhem Land by Yolngu clans, which they realized would be necessary proof of title.[20] If they could show that there were precedents for the recognition of Aborigines' land rights in earlier acts or ordinances passed by the Australian parliament or in colonial instructions, and if they could prove that Yolngu people had exercised long-standing rights of use and occupation, they believed they would be able to make a strong case for the recognition of native title in the common law.

In the memo that Woodward and Little prepared in June 1968, they argued for taking the land rights case to court. "There is at least a good argument that the aboriginal clans of East Arnhem Land have a title to their traditional lands recognized by our law, the exact strength or extent of which remains to be seen, but which probably is as good as fee simple without the customary reservations of minerals, etc.," they argued. The lawyers did not think that a collective claim to the land would cause a legal problem; indeed, they encouraged the Yolngu clans to sue "in a representative capacity" and they further exhorted them to "act as though their land is really theirs and not as though they are there on sufferance."[21] The memo was translated into Yolngu dialects and presented to the recently formed Yirrkala Village Council for discussion and action.

It was persuasive. President of the Yirrkala Village Council, Dadynga (Roy) Marika, agreed that going to the "white man's law" in order to gain recognition of Yolngu land rights was a necessary step. If successful, the community might be able to control the activities of the mining men on the peninsula, he argued. Roy Marika, born in 1931, was a younger brother of the first named plaintiff in the case, Milirrpum Marika.[22] Leaders of the Rirratjingu clan, the Marikas' eldest brother, was Mawalan, whose paintings had adorned the bark petitions of 1963. They claimed direct descent from three creation spirits, an ancestry bestowing a special status on them within their clan and among Yolngu people generally.

In an affidavit signed on 18 March 1969, Marika recounted how Yolngu people were promised that the mining companies would consult with them about where they would build and that they would respect their sacred places. But the mining men were now working near Yirrkala: "at Birridjimi, Wallaby Beach as it is sometimes called by white people, the jungle has been bull-dozed [*sic*] and buildings and a bore put there without my permission [referring to his role as representative of the Village Council] or consultation with me." Even more distressingly, the company had begun to bulldoze a road up the sacred hill of Nhulunbuy ("Mt Saunders" as it was "sometimes called by the white people") in order to put a water tank on the top of it.[23]

Roy Marika had appeared before the select committee inquiry that visited Yirrkala in 1963 following the presentation of the bark petitions and he had spoken extensively with the politicians. In the late 1960s, he became a good friend of Dr. H. C. ("Nugget") Coombs, an eminent public servant appointed chairman of a new federal government advisory body in 1967, the Council for Aboriginal Affairs. Yet all this political talk over land use had failed to win Yolngu people any security. As Marika put it, "In the old days and under our aboriginal law [*sic*] if a stranger came to the country of a clan without the permission of that clan, the clan pushed the stranger off immediately." The clans living at Yirrkala had not been able to push the new mining company strangers off, although some locals had pulled out survey pegs that had been laid out in advance of building a new town to service the mine.[24]

The stakes were high. As he warned his Yolngu kin, without their land rights they might in fact cease to exist as a people. He was possibly thinking of the fate of other dispossessed Aborigines in the Northern Territory, like the Larrakia in Darwin who served for Yolngu spokespeople as a powerful negative example of the destructive effects of European settlement.[25] "Perhaps we do not understand how we could be without the land," admitted Marika. "But if we were without it we might be without our dances, songs, stories, sacred places, names and the madayin. Perhaps if we were without the land there might be none of us."[26] "Madayin" refers to the effects of a non-human force upon humans as

FIGURE 2.2 Outside the courtroom, Canberra, during the Gove land rights case, 1971. L-R: Galarrwuy Yunupingu, Frank Purcell, Ted Woodward, Roy Marika, Milirrpum Marika. Photographer unknown. Photo credit: National Archives of Australia, A1200, L88859.

well as naming a ritual object.[27] Thus, Marika connected the loss of land with loss of meaning in the stories and rituals that made Yolngu people who they were. The risk was too severe. It was time for another approach.

MILIRRPUM V. NABALCO PTY LTD was heard in the Northern Territory's Supreme Court in Darwin in May 1970. Recognizing the far-reaching nature of the case, which raised questions of "high moral principle," the *Canberra Times* provided regular coverage.[28] Media reports covered many of the issues at stake, including the shame that white Australians did (or should) feel in respect of the dispossession of Aboriginal people and the problems of law that were debated in court. Reports also considered the complexity of the attachment of the Yolngu to their land.[29]

Lawyers for the Yolngu plaintiffs argued that the claim for native title rights raised a matter of utmost importance for the nation: how British sovereignty over Australia had been acquired and whether it had been done legally. The native title rights of the continent's Aboriginal inhabitants had been given neither positive recognition nor had they been explicitly extinguished, the lawyers pointed out. "Where is the difficulty in saying that if the Crown did not accept its obligation willingingly, the courts would remind it of them?" they asked rhetorically.[30]

Led by the Commonwealth's legal team, the lawyers for the defendants denied from the outset that the Yolngu clans held a property interest in the Gove peninsula. In fact, they questioned whether the plaintiffs even had the right to sue the mining company and the government. Despite the fact that the government was providing some legal aid to the Yolngu's lawyers, its own lawyers claimed that the case was frivolous. Absolute title to land in Australia was vested in the Crown, they emphasized, reiterating the commonly told story about Australia that justified settler colonization: "At the time at which the Crown acquired sovereignty," the defendants' lawyers asserted, "the said territory was without settled or civilised inhabitants or settled law." Furthermore, it was Crown policy

> that the said territory be, and in fact it was, settled and administered in a manner inconsistent with the existence or continuation or any interests in any land within the said territory in the aboriginal native inhabitants thereof other than such rights as might be expressly conferred by or under the authority of the Crown.[31]

According to this argument, even if some Aboriginal inhabitants did have an interest in land at the time of colonization, the fact that this interest was

not explicitly recognized by the Crown at that point in time meant that neither "native title" nor anything resembling it existed in the present moment.
Whereas the Yolngu's lawyers sought to establish that the burden for extinguishment lay on the Crown, since native title rights existed a priori, Crown
lawyers took the opposite approach. They argued that if native title rights were
to be recognized now, the burden was on the plaintiffs to show that such had
been recognized in the past. They doubted that the plaintiffs could do this.

Agreeing with the lawyers for the plaintiffs, Justice Blackburn acknowledged that the case concerned matters of national significance. As he explained
in his 150-page decision, the case brought to the fore "great and difficult moral
issues" for the court and the country. However, restating a racial theory by
which some peoples were considered more civilized than others, Blackburn
also revealed that he thought colonization in Australia had been carried
out "by a more advanced people of a country inhabited by a less advanced
people,"[32] thus lending some credence to the argument of the Commonwealth
lawyers. His reiteration of civilizational difference had legal implications for
it suggested that he thought indigenous peoples did not bear inherent rights;
they could only be granted them by the sovereign state.[33] A product of empire,
Blackburn was born in 1918 and fought with the Australian Imperial Force
during World War II in the Middle East and New Guinea, after which he
took up a Rhodes scholarship at Oxford. He held posts as a legal academic in
Australia for seven years before going into practice and he made quick progress into the judiciary. Although he had no previous experience in matters of
Aboriginal rights, while living in the Northern Territory he was president of
the Aboriginal Theatre Foundation.[34]

Blackburn believed that the case deserved a full and fair hearing.
Commonwealth lawyers then put other procedural obstacles in the plaintiffs'
way. They argued that Yolngu testimony should not be admitted because it
was simply "hearsay," hoping to make it impossible for the plaintiffs' lawyers to
make a compelling case about use and occupation of the peninsula. It became
clear from this objection that the major battle in the case would be fought
over the admission of Aboriginal and expert anthropological testimony into
court, even before the substantial legal matter of native title rights was argued.
Commonwealth lawyers objected to the admission of hearsay statements such
as this one: "My father (who is now dead) said to me, 'this [referring to a particular piece of land] is land of the Rirratjingu.' "[35] They argued that normal
evidentiary rules could not be overridden, "either because of the novelty of
the matters in issue, or because of the difficulty of communicating with the
aboriginal [sic] witnesses and understanding their evidence."[36]

It was true that admitting the testimony of Yolngu witnesses, as well as that of expert anthropologists, was new in the Australian common law.[37] The admission of both types of evidence was rare in other settler countries also. As the plaintiffs' lawyers discovered, the only other case they could find where expert anthropological evidence had been admitted into a common law court was a 1968 treaty rights case from British Columbia concerning the hunting rights of Squamish Indians.[38] In terms of admitting indigenous testimony into court, the Yolngu's lawyers drew on New Zealand examples. Ted Woodward became aware of the use of Maori "folklore" in land cases there following the visit of a Maori Member of Parliament, Matiu Rata, in June 1970.[39]

Making their argument for why both Yolngu testimony and expert evidence should be admitted into court, the plaintiffs' lawyers argued that it was critical to examining the substantive legal issue of whether Yolngu people had a recognizable land title. The Aboriginal testimony that would be presented, they argued, demonstrated a "well-established social system based upon membership of a clan," patrilineality and exogamy, and territorial rights given by "spirit ancestors" that imposed particular responsibilities on different individuals and clans.[40] The lawyers emphasized the "intense spiritual connection between aboriginals and their land," and argued that "their relationship with their land is therefore timeless and inextinguishable."[41] They also claimed that the Yolngu and anthropological testimony was complementary. "It is convenient to record the aboriginal evidence under the same general propositions which were used in relation to the evidence of anthropologists," they submitted to the judge.[42]

Blackburn dismissed the Commonwealth's argument, insisting that rules of evidence had to be applied "rationally" rather than "mechanically." Neither the "novelty" of the case nor the "unusual difficulties associated with the proof of matters of aboriginal law and custom" were reasons for excluding Aboriginal testimony.[43] Despite what he called the "'notorious fact' that Australian aboriginals have no writing" and the problem that Yolngu testimonies could not be compared with written records, Blackburn searched the rules of evidence for a way he could admit them. In his view, applying the rules of evidence rationally meant finding an argument within the common law for the admission of oral testimony of a second- or thirdhand nature.[44]

He turned to an exception to the hearsay rule known as the reputation principle. This refers to the production of local and usually oral knowledge about customary rights, in particular those concerning land boundaries. By using the reputation principle, Blackburn refuted the Crown lawyers' arguments that the hearsay evidence of Yolngu witnesses was simply individual or private knowledge, untestable outside of the conditions of its production.[45] Instead, Blackburn used this exception to the normal rules of evidence to legitimate the collective, founding myths that bound the community together in a "system of laws." Crown lawyers had disputed even the existence of Yolngu law on the Gove peninsula. Blackburn instead argued that while Yolngu people may not demonstrate law as sovereign command, they certainly demonstrated respect for their own law and they transmitted legal norms to younger generations. Members of the community, Blackburn averred, clearly felt obliged to follow rules of conduct established in their legal system.[46] Thus, the evidentiary principle that Blackburn used to admit Yolngu testimony itself served as a recognition of their distinctiveness.

Blackburn pointed out that what made rights public in nature was the process by which such rights came to be, not how externally verifiable they were. "Rights affecting a large number of people are those which are likely to be truly stated, because large numbers of people are likely to know the truth and error is thus 'sifted,'" Blackburn explained, quoting common law evidentiary expert John Wigmore.[47] For his own purposes, then, what mattered was that a number of different Yolngu testimonies supported each other in terms of the kinds of rights to which they referred.

He paid particular attention to the evidence that Yolngu leaders presented about the origins of their spiritual attachment to the land. Giving their evidence over two weeks in the Darwin courtroom in May 1970, they saw their role as teaching the court about their ownership of the land. It was a role for which they expressed faith in themselves, which was perhaps hardly surprising given their long history of interactions with outsiders. Yet it may have signaled a quite radical change in Yolngu politics since leaders were now prepared to reveal information they had been previously keeping away from the prying eyes of outsiders.[48] Time was now of the essence, however. As the Yirrkala Village Council had put it a year earlier, "If only he [the judge] studied about the Aboriginal people and their law and customs, then he will know that he is damaging their precious belongings. This has been done because he doesn't really know our law and customs and also he doesn't recognize that every bit of land is precious and owned by different tribes of people of the two moiety."[49]

Some of the most persuasive evidence they presented recounted founding myths. Roy Marika explained to the court how the creation spirits gave the land to particular people:

Q. If you were to take the Judge there [to the Gove peninsula], could you show him all the Rirratjingu land?

A. [Interpreted] I would take him to all of this country and say: "This country is Yiritja—this country is Dua."

They made that place, and again he set down all of the things. For all the Dua people he gave that land. The story, the ceremony, the songs.

Djangkawu [the creation spirit] gave everything to and for the Dua people. Your country here. Your song; and your law. To another group this is yours. Again he gave this sacred law; he gave this law for the old people, not for the young people and not for the women.[50]

Yolngu male leaders not only told the judge about their founding stories. They also presented ritual objects, including *rangga* or walking sticks, which, according to the lawyer Ted Woodward, were like "title deeds." One newspaper report described these objects somewhat pejoratively as "stones, sticks, and other sacred tribal artefacts,"[51] and the Commonwealth lawyers initially dismissed their evidentiary weight, doubting they had "any value from [a] legal point of view."[52] They were no doubt surprised, then, that Blackburn not only admitted the evidence of the plaintiffs but was also, according to Woodward, quite captivated by the objects presented to him in chambers,

in the absence of any females and with appropriate use of the singing sticks and invocations, I suppose you would say, of the spirits of the early ancestors. In a way it was a little incongruous to do that in a judge's chambers, producing the sacred objects from their brown paper wrappings and so on. It would have been much more impressive had it been able to be carried out on the land in question, but there were practical difficulties about that.[53]

Other witnesses explained their use of land and tried to explain matters of permission to the judge. Milirrpum Marika, describing how Djangkawu had given the land and the law to Rirratjingu moieties, was asked to explain how different people gained permission to hunt on other people's land. He explained: "Your word permission . . . that's through your way, the way you say it. Our permission name that Djangkawu gave, he said it through this way: to live, to walk to travel for singing ritual, for hunting, for learning and understanding, those things are one, not a lot. Those things are strangers for us to understand, to go to that country, to the aboriginal country."[54]

The issue of permission, and the complexity of the negotiations around rights of permission, were not clearly explained to the court, nor were they drawn out by the plaintiffs' lawyers or the anthropologists.[55] According to the anthropologist Nancy Williams, who did behind-the-scenes translation and transcription for the Yolngu people in the lead-up to the case and attended all the hearings in Darwin but did not provide expert testimony, the evidence presented in court by Yolngu witnesses was badly distorted by inadequate translation. Williams criticized the Yolngu's lawyers for not grasping key concepts, particularly to do with the issue of permission. Most damning was her criticism of the expert anthropologists, Stanner and R. M. Berndt, who were hired to place the Yolngu arguments in a wider anthropological framework and presented their evidence to the court on 8 and 9 September 1970 when it reconvened in Canberra. Particularly concerned about whether the judge would recognize rights of Aborigines to their land in economic terms, she charged both men with a "consistent failure" in understanding basic Yolngu concepts.[56] Indeed, Blackburn was particularly unpersuaded by the anthropologists' and lawyers' arguments that Yolngu clans had both spiritual and economic attachments to distinct territories.

Stanner had seemed an obvious choice because of his national standing and his clear sympathy for Aborigines and their rights. A professor of anthropology at the Australian National University in Canberra and a member of the Council for Aboriginal Affairs along with Nugget Coombs, Stanner was a leading figure in the study of Aboriginal Australia. Although he was not an expert in Yolngu culture nor could he speak any Yolngu dialects, he was keen to accept the job of expert witness since he saw the potential for the case to become a matter of wide interest. In particular, he thought the case offered an opportunity to push an idea of Aboriginal sovereignty onto the national agenda in the distinct terms of Aborigines' ancient and sacred attachment to land. This sovereignty, he argued, was of an "indissoluble" kind and was not premised on the occupation of land or territory. Rather, Aboriginal sovereignty was manifested by the strength of the spiritual link between the individual and the ancestor (mythological or human) from whom succession to particular areas derived. As he explained in his testimony to the court, in the Aboriginal worldview, land-use was "beyond the capacity of mankind to do anything about. . . . It is part of the endowment of the very universe."[57]

The spritual attachment of Aborigines to their land was not exclusive of a notion of property, he believed, and Yolngu clans certainly recognized themselves as landowners. Aborigines' ancestral link to place might be translatable into a European notion of rights. In an unpublished paper in 1969 given to the lawyers preparing the case, he argued that there was an idea that Aborigines belonged to the land rather than the other way around. The idea was true enough but "apt to seem vague and mystical to people in the European tradition."[58] Stanner recognized the importance of specifying the attachments of Aborigines to their land, yet he did not have the extensive knowledge of Yolngu practices that would show how individual clans owned particular territories that could be mapped and delineated.

Echoing the desire of Yolngu leaders to teach outsiders about their law, Stanner was an ardent advocate of the idea that contemporary white Australians now needed to learn about the ancient worldview of Australia's indigenous peoples. This was particularly necessary in a moment in which the country was searching for a new national identity and sense of place in the world as it moved away from its relationship with Britain. As he had explained in the 1967 Boyer Lectures, "there is stuff in aboriginal life, culture and society that will stretch the sinews of any mind which tries to understand it . . . after, not two centuries, but three hundred centuries of human affairs in this country."[59]

The other anthropologist who was hired to present evidence on behalf of the plaintiffs, R. M. Berndt, took what he saw as a more pragmatic approach. An anthropology professor at the University of Western Australia he had already published several books on Aboriginal culture in Arnhem Land by the time the Gove land rights case came to court, a number with his wife and fellow anthropologist Catherine Berndt. The Berndts first visited Yirrkala in the late 1940s and developed a lifelong interest in Yolngu people.[60] In northern Australia and in New Guinea, the Berndts encountered the hard edge of colonial dealings with indigenous people. They worked in the Northern Territory in 1944 as welfare officers investigating the notoriously bad working conditions of Aboriginal laborers in the cattle industry and they wrote a highly critical report for the federal government.[61]

For Berndt, like Stanner, the contemporary welfare of Aboriginal people was a pressing concern that framed his scholarly interests, but he pursued an academic career rather than one in public affairs. Berndt was more circumspect than Stanner about what the outcome of the legal claim would be for the Aboriginal claimants themselves. He also became increasingly concerned about the status of anthropological knowledge in the court as it became clearer during the case preparation that the specialized knowledge of the anthropologists could not be easily consumed by the lawyers. In a letter dated 25 February 1970, before the hearings began, he reiterated his concerns to Frank Purcell that an adversarial setting was not the best place for such complex and novel legal issues to be addressed, especially when it was in the interests of the lawyers representing the mining company to "bend" the facts of the case. Like Williams, he had observed how much difficulty the lawyers were having in understanding the anthropological concepts and so he advised them to stick to simple evidence. He also expected that expert anthropological o-pinion should be accepted for what it was: expert opinion. Berndt proposed that he was "an intermediary between the Aborigines and the legal practi-tioner. Aborigines say this or that (stage one); anthropologists interpret this, placing what is said in a wider perspective and in relation to the issue being debated (stage two); the legal practitioner accepts what the anthropologist says and casts it in a meaningful legal context (stage three)."[62]

Berndt did not argue for a reframing of the national story out of the Gove land rights case. In fact, he thought the best thing that the Yolngu people could hope for would be limited land rights, respect of sacred sites, and a good compensation package. He had made a similar argument in 1964 just after the government had decided to allow mining leases on part of the land. Knowing from his other experiences in the Northern Territory that the indig-enous peoples in the area might simply be pushed to one side, Berndt argued at that time that they must be provided their own capacity to develop and exploit natural resources.[63]

Whereas Stanner argued for the spiritual significance of Aborigines' at-tachment to their land and their distinctive role in a rewriting of the na-tional story, Berndt argued for specific socioeconomic solutions for the Yolngu people. He emphasized the importance of understanding social facts rather than coming to grips with larger spiritual narratives. Even so, the bigger moral and political issues that the Gove land rights case raised could not be entirely suppressed. As Berndt admitted in a scholarly article on the case, the land was considered by the Yolngu people as the "natural heritage of man" rather than as property that could be bought and sold.[64] This question of how Aborigines understood their relationship to the land and why it mattered that such a relationship be recognized by Australian common law could not be contained as an issue of specific anthropological fact. As Berndt's aside revealed, the questions that the Gove land rights case provoked were conceptually complex.

Blackburn accepted the evidence provided by the two anthropologists, but he regarded it as a collection of facts rather than interpretations. It was the judge who retained control of how much authority would be given to the evidence presented. In this regard, he said that he attached more weight to Berndt's evidence than to Stanner's since Berndt had spent long peri-ods studying Yolngu social organization whereas Stanner had, by his own admission, only spent a few days with Yolngu people assessing how their practices accorded with his research elsewhere in Aboriginal Australia.

Nonetheless, Blackburn doubted many of the specialist terms that both of the anthropologists and the Yolngu's lawyers introduced into the court, arguing that the Yolngu witnesses' own testimony did not often match what the anthropologists said. In a critical finding for future legal cases and for the broader recognition of Aborigines' rights in Australia, Blackburn had made a clear argument for admitting Aboriginal testimony into court. By recognizing that Yolngu people obeyed their own legal system, Blackburn introduced an idea of plurality into Australian common law. There was not only not one law in Australia nor was the common law the first legal system. Yolngu people, as Blackburn saw it, had deep, abiding, and ancient spiritual connections to the lands they inhabited, recognized in their legal system.

However, Blackburn would not recognize a spiritual connection in the common law framework of property rights, at least not without guidance from legislators. As Williams had feared, the judge was so persuaded by evidence of the Yolngu people's spiritual attachment to the land that he could not see their relationship as one commensurable with English ideas of property. He concluded that the "clan is not shown to have a significant economic relationship with the land," and had a "more cogent feeling of obligation to the land than of ownership of it." Putting it another way, he defined Yolngu people's relationship to land in terms opposite to that of property owning. "[I]t seems easier, on the evidence, to say that the clan belongs to the land [rather] than that the land belongs to the clan," he stated, which became a frequently quoted phrase after the case.[65]

An Australian court was unable to recognize that Yolngu people had property rights when they expressed their attachment to the land in ontological statements such as "if we were without the land there might be none of us." In order to win such rights, they would need to show more exploitative and exclusionary use of the land they claimed. Or the Australian government would have to create a specific category of property right that could recognize such a distinctive form of ownership. In effect, Blackburn sent the Yolngu native title claim back to the Commonwealth parliament to deal with.

BITTERLY DISAPPOINTING FOR those awaiting it at the Yirrkala mission station, Blackburn's decision received wide publicity in the Australian press. "Gove: A Dubious Legal Decision" argued one headline. "Yirrkala Men Say Law Is Immoral," proclaimed another.[66] The media coverage throughout the case, and particularly following the decision against the Yolngu plaintiffs, showed that the idea that some Aborigines may hold distinctive rights in respect of their lands was gaining public acceptance.

In response to public pressure following the case and the subtle judicial directive that Blackburn gave, the incumbent conservative government issued a new policy for granting long-term leases to some remote Aboriginal communities. The policy would provide "them with an effective base for their economic future,"[67] continuing to take the assimilationist view that "traditional" Aborigines should be assisted in modernization as they became more like other citizens of Australia.[68]

Others, however, argued that Aborigines' traditional association to particular areas should be recognized as a distinctive kind of land tenure. This would provide them with the capacity to make their own decisions and imagine their own futures, as the Australian Council of Churches argued in a submission to a parliamentary committee on Aboriginal affairs. Indeed, without their land rights, the Council of Churches argued, "Aborigines will be without the right and power of decision-making in the determination of their own future development."[69] This notion of self-determination was based on the idea that their attachment to the land was of a spiritual rather than political or economic nature, as Stanner and indeed Blackburn had argued in the Gove case. Peter Cullen, a spokesperson for the Council of Churches, wrote to Melbourne's *Age* newspaper, explaining that "an Aborigine regards his land with its visible manifestations of their creation in a profoundly spiritual or religious way."[70]

The focus on spirituality by critics of government policy implied a cultural, rather than political and economic, basis for self-determination, as if these elements were separable. Although Yolngu claimants emphasized spiritual needs and cultural identity, they clearly did so in order to assert their political authority over and economic use of their lands. In the petition they submitted to the prime minister shortly after Blackburn's decision came down in which they expressed their shock at the decision, they repeated in condensed form some of what they had told the court. Now, however, they gave more emphasis to rights of permission that only they should have the capacity to grant:

> The land and law, the sacred places, songs, dances and language were given to our ancestors by spirits Djangkawu and Barama. We are worried that without the land future generations could not maintain our culture. We have the right to say to anybody not to come to our country. We gave permission for one mining company but we did not give away the land. The Australian law has said that the land is not ours. This is not so. It might be right legally but morally it's wrong. The law

must be changed. The place does not belong to white man. They only want it for the money they can make. They will destroy plants, animal life and the culture of the people.[71]

Yolngu leaders had, perhaps, learned what an Australian government needed to hear. In this petition, they demonstrated how representations of sacred law could be invested with a powerful moral and political charge.

Even more significantly, they had also realized that in order to win local territorial rights they actually needed to establish why the maintenance of their collective peoplehood mattered for the Australian nation. They did so by starting to call themselves "first" people. In a press conference Yolngu leaders held in Canberra after presenting the petition to the government, Roy Marika explained to the gathered reporters, "I am the first Australian and you and your culture are the second Australians."[72] As he had written privately to Frank Purcell a year earlier, "We want the area that every group has been owning—by singing, story, painting—as well as all the other things that Aborigines have in their minds; or the life of the people will be destroyed. That's why they say 'No' not to put any more prospecting camps or townships. We are the owners and we are the first Australians."[73]

By calling themselves "first Australians," Yolngu leaders achieved something that the legal decision had failed to do for them. They undid assumptions about their backwardness, or their place in a narrative of transition. As first people, they were not "behind" other Australians. Rather, they were narratively prior to them. Perhaps because it became so ubiquitous so fast, this often overlooked claim was, in fact, a revolutionary moment in Australian public life. It effectively changed the terms of the discourse about Aborigines needing to catch up and instead began to establish their singular importance for the nation. As "first people," Yolngu and other Aborigines provided the nation with an ancient past that it was looking for in a moment of global, post-imperial uncertainty. They also charged the nation with a unique responsibility for ensuring that its first peoples were able to maintain their ancient connection to the land.

The shift to a rhetoric of "firstness" by Yolngu leaders, and their role in opening up legal and political consideration of Aboriginal rights in Australia, changed their status in the country. As a consequence of the land rights case, Yolngu leaders became spokespeople for Aboriginal people in national terms. Yolngu people were, henceforward, often referred to both as the most authentic Aborigines in the country and as the leaders of political change for indigenous Australians. They were at the forefront of pushing for constitutional reforms that would recognize Aboriginal rights through the 1980s and 1990s, including a proposition to make a nationwide treaty.

Despite the fact that the first-ever native title case failed, therefore, Yolngu people succeeded in that their story of the land, their relationship to it, and even their inherent rights over it, changed the political environment in Australia regarding Aborigines' land rights. The story of inevitable colonization which the Commonwealth lawyers had told in the legal case gradually lost its power as justification for colonization. In its place, the idea that Aborigines had distinct rights because of their long and vital association with the land gained ground. As Galarrwuy Yunupingu, who worked as an interpreter in the legal case and became prominent in Aboriginal politics in Australia through the 1970s, put it after the case, "the land is our history." He continued,

> Land most important in Aborigines mind. . . . Land is footstool, foundation of everything that we talk, do, individual Aboriginal person. Quality of life, way we speak, act, way we live, food for person all relates back to land.[74]

By 1977, when Yunupingu addressed the National Press Club as a national leader in the struggle for Aboriginal rights, he told a story of the Yolngu land rights as the beginning of far-reaching changes in Australia. "My father, Mungarrwuy, and I lodged a land claim on behalf of our Gumatj clan and our mother clan, the Rirratjingu, whose leader was Milirrpum. It was a petition, written on bark."[75] Yunupingu began the address speaking the language of the Gumatj clan or, "in one of the languages of Australia. I spoke it like this for my own people, at Yirrkala, who will be listening. I spoke it like this for all Aboriginal Australians, everywhere, our brothers and sisters. Now let me speak it again in the English language . . . for our European Australian brothers and sisters, who have given us back so much of our land, at last."[76]

By speaking first in Gumatj, Yunupingu was also reminding the audience seated in front of him that the Anglophone settler state could be reconceived as having been founded in Aboriginal languages, languages that existed prior to the arrival of the "Europeans." Yunupingu spoke emphatically as a "First Australian" whose heritage was now endowing the nation with a new, ancient past.

YOLNGU LEADERS GRASPED something that few of the white professionals involved in the Gove land rights case, except Stanner, fully appreciated. To win greater security over their lands, livelihoods, and futures they would have to change how they were represented in Australian public life. In particular, they needed to explain why their historical attachment to the land mattered for the nation itself. Calling themselves the "First Australians" was an inspired act of rhetoric that pushed back against the narrative of inevitable and justifiable dispossession, challenged white settlers to reconsider their own identity, and asserted another origin for the settler state. In that sense, the discussions about the case initiated a revolution in the historical consciousness of both indigenous peoples and the Australian nation.

These outcomes depended on the willingness of Yolngu leaders to risk a great deal in preparing for the case and seeking out justice for themselves and other Aboriginal people. Some of those risks paid off, particularly in the sense that Yolngu people carved open a new space in law in which they voiced their demands, taught their own law, and expected to be heard. Their actions pushed Justice Blackburn to begin a reform in evidentiary practices by admitting indigenous peoples' traditions into court that endures in Australian law today and went on to influence lawyers in other countries too. However, Yolngu leaders did not stop the mine from being built nor could they mitigate all the social effects that the construction of the new town of Nhulunbuy had on the Yirrkala mission. Furthermore, Blackburn's focus on the Yolngu people's spiritual attachment to land downplayed their coeval status as modern political actors with economic and social rights, although some of their land rights were eventually recognized following a statutory change in 1976. The focus on spirituality at the expense of other realms of life would also have long-lasting consequences for indigenous rights claims in Australia.

3

Frontier Justice and Self-Determination in Canada's North

We are no longer the enemy. When the government decides that they will develop a dialogue and deal with us on just terms then we can move out of the courts and to the more civilized bargaining table.

—INDIAN BROTHERHOOD OF THE NORTHWEST TERRITORIES (1973)

IN APRIL 1973, two years after Justice Blackburn delivered the decision against the Yolngu plaintiffs in northern Australia, Indian leaders in Canada's Northwest Territories (NWT) brought to court the first-ever collective land claim in the region. Like the Yolngu leaders, the Dene leadership initiated legal action following a government proposal allowing new resource development on their homelands about which they had not been consulted. In this instance it was the Mackenzie Valley oil and gas pipeline project that would connect reserves in the Arctic Sea with pipelines already feeding southern Canada and the United States. The process of going to court focused Dene leaders on a new story about their peoplehood. In particular, they crafted a story about their collective attachment to the land that would be recognizable as land rights. The idea that land rights would serve to protect the Dene identity was novel and it entailed a careful selection of traditions and practices from community members to sustain it.

The court also became a site for the creation of another story, this one for the Canadian nation about the importance of the "last true frontier" to national identity.[1] The story was told by the judge, Justice William Morrow, and it was a new version of an old myth. In Morrow's telling, the frontier was a place in which Canadian nationhood was formed through the collaboration of natives and newcomers. These co-founders both privileged self-sufficiency on the land and shared in its spoils. Morrow's story of the frontier differed from older versions in that indigenous peoples were given a central and ongoing role, rather than being represented as a vanishing race that was inevitably overpowered by the might of the British empire. Indeed, according to Morrow, Indians embodied the core values of the tradition and therefore needed to be protected from large-scale developments for the nation's good.

The stories of Dene peoplehood and of a revised frontier tradition converged in the courtroom as indigenous leaders and the judge pushed forward the idea of aboriginal title. There were significant consequences for everyone involved. Morrow, radically at the time, gave full recognition to Dene people's aboriginal title rights, thus helping to inject their rights activism with a new power. From being largely a "forgotten people who were in great need of many kinds of help and who were receiving almost none" in the 1950s, as one anthropologist put it, by the mid-1970s Dene claims were being discussed in the Canadian parliament.[2] At the same time, the judge offered redemption for the Canadian nation and a new vision of the past that enabled Canadians to more firmly express their desire for sovereign independence. This was critical at a moment in which Canada's external sovereignty was under threat from American and Soviet competition for Arctic oil resources and, at the same time, the country's ties to Britain were loosening. Internally, the integrity of the nation was imperiled as Québec nationalists demanded the separation of that province from the confederation and even engaged in violence to further their aims.

For indigenous claimants, representing themselves as engaged in a dialogue with the state rather than using violence to achieve their ends was morally powerful. But having to go to court to win a place at the more "civilized bargaining table" had unexpected costs.[3] In the process of having their land rights recognized by Canadian lawyers, they found their identities as indigenous peoples being fixed in space and time and even their coevalness being denied. For in order to show themselves as continuously attached to the land, indigenous witnesses were asked to produce static images of themselves as nomadic hunters who prized life on the land over all else. There was little room in the court, or in the new public space they had won for themselves, for them to grapple with the far-reaching changes to their social worlds and political desires that rapid economic development had already brought about.

WHEN DENE LEADERS in the NWT launched a land rights campaign in the early 1970s, their social, political, and economic world was in great flux. "I am not an old man," explained Phillip Blake, a social worker, in 1975, "but I have seen many changes in my life. Fifteen years ago, most of what you see as Fort McPherson did not exist."[4] The growth of new and existing settlements was one manifestation of the transformation of Canada's northernmost region and largest territory.[5] Over a thirty-year period, from 1941 to 1970, the

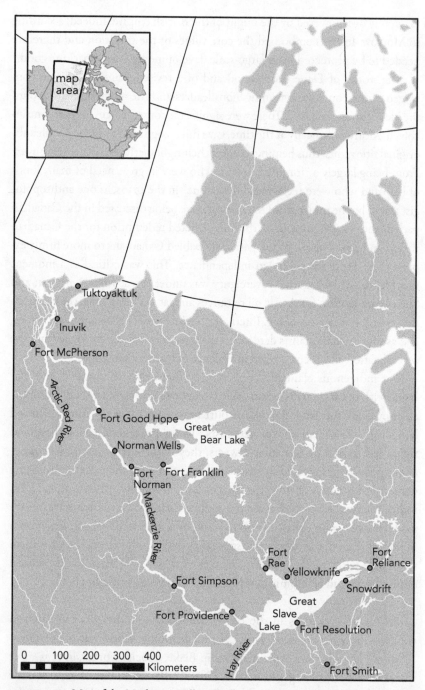

FIGURE 3.1 Map of the Mackenzie Valley, Northwest Territories, Canada. Map by Tim Stallmann.

population of many settlements in the Mackenzie region increased more than 50 percent. Indigenous northerners had begun to take up year-round residences following World War II, as the terminal decline of the fur trade meant that indigenous peoples lost one of their major forms of employment, and disease outbreaks, especially of tuberculosis, threatened small communities.[6] Encouraged by federally subsidized housing programs, many families moved into the larger settlements like Fort McPherson where they had better access to health care and education as well as oil-heated homes.[7]

The NWT population as a whole grew exponentially in the postwar period jumping from 12,028 in 1941 to 42,610 by 1976. In 1971, the "treaty" or "status" Indian population was 7,108, an absolute increase of more than 60 percent from thirty years earlier. As elsewhere in Canada, the native birthrate boomed as access to health care improved.[8] Staggeringly, the non-native population in the NWT increased more than 600 percent (from 2,290 in 1941 to 16,225 in 1971).[9] Newcomers in a steady stream were moving into the territories as mining and other industries expanded and federal government offices enlarged their operations. By the 1970s, according to one observer, a "numerical swamping of the native population by southern-derived whites" was under way.[10] Nonetheless, when Inuit, non-status Indians, and Métis were included in the ethnic breakdown, indigenous peoples still outnumbered the non-indigenous in the territory. This was a very different from most of the rest of Canada, where indigenous peoples constituted a tiny minority of many provincial populations and only made up about 2.5 percent of the national population.[11]

The new northern frontier had been formally opened by Progressive Conservative Prime Minister John Diefenbaker in March 1958. Drawing on myths central to Canada's agrarian frontier past, Diefenbaker announced a new destiny for the Canadian nation, yoking the potential for the nation's mid-century growth to the "opening of Canada's northland."[12] Distinctively, the new frontier proclaimed by Diefenbaker was not based in pioneering on the land but, rather, extracting resources from underneath it, which the federal government oversaw since the NWT's natural resources were in its domain. This required vast investment in new infrastructure, projects that were dependent on foreign, particularly American, capital.[13] The rhetoric about the new northern frontier of the postwar period revealed continuities as well as differences from that about the nineteenth-century agricultural frontier in Canada. In the previous century, the "Britain of the North" saw itself closely aligned with "home."[14] Extensive transportation and communication networks strengthened ties to the metropole, to the extent that some claimed the railways connecting western primary produce with east coast ports provided Canada with a "British nationality."[15] In a new moment of nationhood in the 1950s, Diefenbaker proposed a more independent Canada, referring to widespread concerns that Canadians would be economically overpowered by their southern neighbor. But he had to acknowledge that the country's economy was becoming ever more tied to that of the United States, trying to reassure the Canadian electorate that the government would encourage foreign investors to "partner" with the Canadian people and would "deny the present plan of certain American companies that do not give to the Canadian plants their fair share of the export business."[16]

Americans, along with the Soviets, were also competing with Canada for access to the rich oil resources in the Arctic sea. One of the Canadian government's major aims in modernizing the north was to assert its sovereignty over this remote frontier in order to bring international competition to an end. At the same time, needing to maintain good relations with the United States, the Canadian government did not make militaristic claims. Rather it engaged in a process of "gradual acquisition," hoping that the United States would give implicit recognition to Canada's northern domain. Tensions with the United States came to a head in 1968 when oil was discovered in Prudhoe Bay in Alaska. The following year, in search of the most efficient route to ship the oil south, an American supertanker transported the Alaskan oil across the Northwest Passage without asking permission from the Canadian government. The event provoked an uproar among the Canadian public both for political and environmental reasons, and Canadians exerted pressure on their government to make the nation's sovereignty over Arctic waters explicit. However, the newly elected Liberal government was unwilling to make a strong claim about Canadian sovereignty and jeopardize its relationship with the United States.[17]

The issue was resolved not by diplomatic means but economic priorities: the shipping of oil through the Northwest Passage was more expensive and riskier than building a pipeline that could connect northern oil reserves to those in the south. American corporations and the Canadian government turned their attention to that problem. In 1970, the Canadian government issued the first guidelines for the construction and operation of a northern oil and gas pipeline. Soon the federal government would have a new battle on its hands, this time with Dene people in the NWT who argued that the lands the pipeline would cross were theirs and that the government had to recognize their territory before it could lease it to a pipeline company.

As well as these larger geopolitical tensions, the legal battle that Dene leaders took to court in 1973 had its antecedents in simmering discontent about political representation and control over local resources within the NWT. Once status Indians won the federal vote in 1960, and increasing numbers of newcomers arrived to work in the mining industries and supporting businesses, the electorate expanded radically. Yet there was only one representative for most of the area in the federal parliament. Indigenous and non-indigenous residents of the NWT began to demand the devolution of political power and autonomous provincial status so that they could have more say in how resources were exploited. Demands for self-government in the NWT pushed the government to create a commission of inquiry in 1965, known as the Carrothers Commission. It recommended increased self-representation, and so the federal government devolved more responsibilities to the Territorial Council.[18] Although the Carrothers Commission made no mention of what role Indian people might or indeed should play in a more representative Territorial Council and prospectively a province, the Council began to take more responsibility for Indian affairs.[19] In the late 1960s and into the 1970s, the management of Indian affairs became a key area over which the federal government and the Territorial Council competed for control. Sometimes this worked to the detriment of Dene people, yet it also opened up new political opportunities and a space in which to push for their own claims for increased independence.

In this context, Dene people began to mount a considerable critique of government institutions. They argued that their people were increasingly dependent on government welfare and frequently compared their loss of autonomy in the present with the control they used to have in the past. Government publications advocated rapid economic development and modernization as the solution for the "human problems of the north." Locals disagreed.[20] The vision for the north that they conjured, with some nostalgia, was one premised on a subsistence way of life in a pre-welfare period of independence. As Ted Bugghins put it, comparing life now to that prior to World War II, "They never used to have Welfare in them days. If you were going to take your family to the bush, you used to go to Hudson's Bay Store and that's where you'd get all your supplies from. . . . White man made the people more poor than what they used to be in the olden days."[21] In a similar vein, Mary Rose Drybone, a social worker from Inuvik, criticized government programs in her community in which "we the Dene people have no say." Drybone recalled her life in the bush as a young girl: "When you are in the bush like a family everybody takes part in doing everyday chores. My dad would go to visit the traplines by dog team . . . and then my mother would be busy tanning hides and us children would cut wood or haul some clean snow for cooking and drinking water."[22] Some leaders sought solutions to the problems of delinquency and dependency that they saw around them from within their own traditions and histories, advocating land-based self-determination. Alexis Arrowmaker, a Dogrib chief from Fort Rae, led a return-to-the-land movement in the early 1970s, establishing a camp at Snare Lake where he would teach young people bush-craft and hunting and trapping skills.

Dene leaders also pursued political change. Spurred by the nationwide protest about the White Paper which had proposed dissolving the Department of Indian Affairs and doing away with Indian "treaty status", sixteen chiefs from across the north created a new organization in 1969 to represent their interests, the Indian Brotherhood of the Northwest Territories. The Brotherhood, like other provincial indigenous organizations formed at this time, was formally recognized by the Department of Indian Affairs and Northern Development (DIAND) and represented issues of local concern to the federal government. However, the organization saw itself as accountable primarily to Indian communities, as well as having a wider political and educative role in the NWT. According to its charter, ratified in 1970, the Brotherhood was committed to "uphold[ing] the rights and interests of the Indian people of the NWT" and to giving "voice to the opinions of the People of the NWT." The Brotherhood insisted on the reinstatement of the DIAND office at Yellowknife which had recently been closed. They also emphasized the importance of the yearly treaty payments as symbolic of the "special relationship" between the Crown, now represented by the federal government, and Indian people. Finally, the Brotherhood hired a lawyer, Gerry Sutton, to carry out a research project into the legal implications of treaty grievances.[23]

In 1971, a new young leader, James Wah-Shee, was elected president of the Indian Brotherhood. He would lead the organization through its first legal case about treaty and aboriginal rights. Wah-Shee had studied business administration in Madison, Wisconsin, and was a member of the Company of Young Canadians working the Northwest Territories, a government-sponsored project that harnessed the energy of political youth movements around the country for social development, along the lines of the American Peace Corps. He hailed from Alexis Arrowmaker's community and, like the older leader, he too looked back to a time when Dene identity was inextricable from the land. Against Prime Minister Diefenbaker's vision of the north, which promised a future of development in terms of resource extraction, Wah-Shee wrote of "yesterday's vision" as a founding story of connection to the land. In a poem later published in a history of what would become known as the Dene Nation, he wrote:

> *North dream of mine*
> *My father's too*
> *You are us*
> *And we are you.*[24]

Wah-Shee's and the Indian Brotherhood's first major campaign was to secure land rights as the Canadian government pursued the idea of the gas and oil pipeline. In June 1972, the Minister of Indian Affairs and Northern Development, Jean Chrétien, had tabled what he saw as extensive "social guidelines" to accompany the construction of the pipeline, which would be an engineering feat because of the extreme environment. According to these, applicants would have to "set up special orientation and consultation machinery to familiarize its staff and employees with the culture and aspirations of native people and of territorial residents generally."[25] Although the guidelines gave some attention to the needs of northerners they did not recognize the land rights of Dene, Métis, and Inuit peoples whose lands were involved in the pipeline proposals. The government had not directly consulted the chiefs or the Indian Brotherhood of the Northwest Territories about the proposals.

On 3 April 1973, a young chief and member of the Indian Brotherhood, François Paulette, along with fifteen others, applied to lodge a caveat under the Land Titles Act in order to protect their communities' interests to 400,000 square miles of land that the pipeline would cross. The caveat they sought from the Northwest Territories Supreme Court would not recognize the Dene people's land rights in the first instance but it would demonstrate their interest in the land prior to their title to it being investigated. In supporting their claim over the unpatented Crown land, the applicants argued that they had used and occupied the area since time immemorial. Yet much of the unpatented land was covered by Treaty 8 and Treaty 11 in which those who signed the treaties had purportedly ceded much of the area now claimed.

Historical treaties were initiated by the federal government in the wake of earlier mining projects. The negotiation of Treaty 8 in 1899, which covered a vast area in northern Alberta and the Lesser Slave Lake of about 840,000 square kilometers, was triggered by discovery of gold in Klondike and the expectation that thousands of gold diggers would be traversing Indian people's territory. An order in council that established the Treaty 8 commission claimed that Indians in the area were "inclined to be turbulent and were liable to give trouble to isolated parties of miners or traders who might be regarded by the Indians as interfering with what they considered their vested rights."[26] From the government's perspective, the treaty was intended to pacify indigenous peoples and make way for the miners.

Treaty 11, the last of the "numbered" treaties made in western Canada,[27] was negotiated in 1921 following an oil strike in the Mackenzie district.[28] Some Indian leaders and missionaries in the area had been pressing the government to make a treaty with local communities in order to afford them protection and economic assistance, but the government had refused until the prospect of widespread oil drilling pushed the government to assert its sovereignty and bring Indians under its authority. Although one local missionary involved in the treaty-making process hoped that the agreement reached would benefit both sides and ensure an ongoing relationship of good faith, the actual negotiations throughout the Mackenzie Valley were tense and resulted in considerable misunderstandings of what had been promised by the government.[29] Like other numbered treaties, Treaty 11 extinguished Indians' title to the lands they inhabited and hunted over and in return colonial authorities gave communities implements, including guns and ammunition for hunting, and also promised to establish land reserves.

By the 1930s, some Dene people were boycotting "Treaty days" when annuities promised in the treaties were paid because they thought their hunting and trapping rights, which the Treaty Commissioner Duncan Scott had assured them would not be taken away, were being seriously curtailed.[30] Mostly focused on those rights, Dene people's lands were not affected by widespread white settlement since the northern climate was not conducive to farming. Promised reserve lands, which elsewhere were created to transition Indians to an agricultural way of life, were never established in the NWT. If the federal government had extinguished aboriginal title rights in the north de jure it had not done so de facto. Like the Yolngu leaders, Dene people believed the land was theirs.

Dene leaders, like others across Canada at the time, argued for another interpretation of treaty-making. These agreements, they contended, established an ongoing relationship of goodwill between the Canadian government and Indian polities. Treaties were diplomatic alliances of peace and friendship rather than instruments of land cession, as some leaders had argued in earlier unsuccessful hunting rights cases.[31] The annual treaty payments, which the Indian Brotherhood had demanded be reinstated in 1969, were one important sign of that ongoing relationship. In 1970, the chiefs objected to the abnegation of the diplomatic relationship on the part of the Canadian government in issuing the pipeline guidelines and creating a national park without consulting them.

The application for the caveat was a strategy intended to force a political negotiation with the Canadian government, as the Indian Brotherhood itself pointed out. By using such a strategy, the Brotherhood hoped to create a platform for demanding justice in moral terms as well as winning legal rights. In its recently created newspaper, *Tapwe*, which connected remote Indian communities of the Territories and informed non-Indian people about local issues, the Brotherhood criticized the "sham game of consultation" that the government had thus far engaged in. "We are no longer the enemy," asserted the Brotherhood. "When the government decides that they will develop a dialogue and deal with us on just terms then we can move out of the courts and to the more civilized bargaining table."[32]

The Brotherhood's moral charge—to establish "just terms"—presumed coevalness between treaty partners. However, other commentators portrayed the Dene leaders as incapable of making a trenchant legal claim. In case notes for the *Alberta Law Review*, Ronald Pearson described the caveators and their communities as "the least politically and socially developed of all the native groups in Canada." He doubted whether the Dene could establish a claim to land title based on their "primitive use" of the land as hunters and gatherers.[33] According to Pearson, since the Dene used the land "primitively" they could not be coeval with white civilization and would not have standing in a Canadian court of law. The contradictory representation of Dene people as modern political actors, on the one hand, and confined to a primordial past, on the other, became more pronounced in the course of the legal hearings.

The Brotherhood's application for a caveat over land whose aboriginal title had not been extinguished was urgent and timely. They had been waiting to pursue their legal claim for the outcome of the Calder case, decided on 31 January 1973, in order to gauge its political effect, which was positive even though the case itself failed on a legal technicality.[34] The leaders were also aware of the Alaska Native Claims Settlement Act that had been passed by the United States Congress in 1971. Under that act, Native Alaskans had ceded extensive land and sovereign rights in exchange for becoming shareholders of resource developments managed by village corporations.

Due to the unusual nature of the caveat—that it was based in a claim to aboriginal title—the Registrar of Titles forwarded it to the Northwest Territories Supreme Court. The court had been in operation for less than twenty years (it was created in 1955) and it was mostly concerned with criminal cases in Indian settlements. This was the first time the court had been asked to broach explicitly the question of aboriginal title and the land rights of northern people.[35] Justice William George Morrow, who was generally considered to be sympathetic to Indian issues and who had petitioned for Dene land rights to the Canadian Exchequer Court in 1965 when he was working as a lawyer in the region,[36] immediately saw the broader significance of the application. Before he would hear the case he imposed a "land freeze" over the entire region in which the chiefs claimed an interest. This meant that no one could assert their rights to the land in question without first having made an agreement with the caveators. The "land freeze" sparked controversy in the local and national press, as well as innumerable puns in headlines and cartoons.[37]

The first day of the hearings, held in Yellowknife, was covered by a number of journalists from the Northwest Territories and beyond. "Feeling each other out as cautiously as boxers in the first-round, six lawyers representing the federal government and 7.000 [sic] treaty Indians began their legal battle Tuesday over who owns the western Arctic," wrote Steve Hume, a journalist for the *Edmonton Journal*. In "the northern capital's stuffy little courtroom above the post office before a packed public gallery that left spectators standing four deep in the doorway" were territorial councilors, Dene leaders, government officials, executives of the Indian Brotherhood of the Northwest Territories, and other lawyers.[38]

The presence of the Crown lawyers was particularly unusual. Morrow's actions in issuing the "land freeze" and hearing the case had attracted a high degree of interest from the federal government. The Crown lawyers claimed that the court had no jurisdiction over the application other than to file it and leave a hearing to the Federal Court. Morrow thought otherwise, implicating the Crown lawyers in the colonial attitude of the "south" toward the "north," and at the same establishing his sympathies as a man of the north. "According to some people we are still a colony," he quipped. "It may be that in retaining its colonial hold over the N.W.T. it (the Crown) has picked its court." He countered their argument that he had no jurisdiction to hear the case, suggesting that if the Crown had never obtained title to the lands in question perhaps jurisdiction for the case lay not with the federal court but at an international level.[39] The Crown lawyers almost precipitated a constitutional crisis but the appeal court judge found that Morrow did have the jurisdiction to hear the case. Morrow began the case in the summer of 1973. Crown lawyers refused to attend.

Legal commentators at the time saw the caveat case as a turning point in federal Indian policy. Would Morrow's court "characterize dealings with the

Indians as being benevolence on the part of the Crown," or would the case
"elevat[e] a unique system of tenure to inclusion as a property right under the
common law of real property?"[40] In other words, would the court interpret
the claims of the chiefs in purely moral terms, in which case they should be
resolved by the paternal state in respect of its obligations due to its wards, or
would the court recognize the indigenous claimants as bearing inherent rights
to their lands?

Morrow, like Justice Blackburn in the Gove land rights case, was motivated by moral concerns. Nonetheless, he framed the issue before him
in terms of legal rights, and he was more optimistic about finding a form
of property title that would cover the unique claims of Indian groups.
Following the arguments of some of the judges in the Calder case that
aboriginal title was something that Canadian courts could recognize,
Morrow believed that Dene people did have a legal claim to aboriginal title
rights in the Mackenzie Valley and so their case deserved to be heard. The
Brotherhood's decision to wait in bringing the caveat until after the Calder
decision seemed to have paid off.

In order to substantiate the claim, the Brotherhood's lawyers argued that
the court must examine local Indian people and find out what exactly was the
evidence for their title in terms of usage and length of occupation. The court
would also need to learn about how Dene people interpreted the treaties their
leaders had signed. Adding to these concerns, the Brotherhood worried that
key elders would die before they could record their testimony. Their argument
for examining Indian witnesses had a deeper political purpose. Like other provincial organizations around the country, the Brotherhood was beginning to
undertake historical research in support of a claim to Dene peoplehood. As
well as substantiating their claims to law and to the Canadian government,
Indian organizations saw their research programs as furthering the development of a new consciousness among Indian people about their own political
histories.

In the lead-up to the caveat case, the Brotherhood applied to the recently created Indian Claims Commission for funding for historical research.
Arguing that what it called "action-research" must "remain within our community in order for it to contribute to our short-term objective of informed
negotiations and our long-term objective of independence within Canadian
society," the Brotherhood proposed building a "core" of "native field workers."
They would ascertain what lands were used by local communities and their
"views" of the land, as well as convene a number of experts who would help
the organization think about broader economic and social development and

an administrative structure in the eventuality of a land and compensation settlement. Armed with thorough field research, the Brotherhood hoped that
it would be better prepared for negotiation with the government and that
the research process itself would be a "very valuable self-study and learning
process for our people.... The eventual settlement agreed upon by us with
the Minister will provide nothing less than the resource base for our future as
independent Canadians."[41]

Pushing their way to the negotiating table with the Canadian government via a legal claim was a process that brought the goals of achieving land
rights and self-determination goals together. However, it was riddled with
contradictions. The Brotherhood needed to be able to demonstrate the historical nature of their rights to the Canadian government—and indeed the
wider Canadian public—in the strongest evidentiary and legal terms possible. This meant that some of the legal arguments their lawyer made potentially contradicted the very memories the Brotherhood was trying to legitimate. For instance, a central argument was that because the treaty promises
had not been kept, notably to establish reserves of one square mile per family
of five, the Dene people's aboriginal title rights had not been extinguished.[42]
Accordingly, if the treaty promise to establish reserves had been kept, their
land rights would have been extinguished. Not all treaty promises were, therefore, to be considered sacrosanct. In evidencing their rights, Dene people confronted another set of contradictions. Wanting to define their own historical
understanding of the rights in the service of self-determination became risky
inside this court. As they discovered in the hearings, if Dene individuals asserted an identity that was too stridently political, they would not be recognized as authentically Indian.

When Morrow took his court around Indian settlements in the caveat
area in the summer of 1973, he aimed to record the testimony of elderly residents who had been present at some of the treaty signings, the most recent
of which had occurred in 1921. In his decision on the case, which cited the
precedent of *Milirrpum v. Nabalco* for the admission of hearsay evidence according to the reputation principle,[43] Morrow wrote, "It is fortunate indeed
that their stories are now preserved."[44] He meant that it was fortunate that
such stories had been "preserved" in his court as evidence, taken under oath
and subject to cross-examination. Thus, Morrow intimated a further purpose
in recording Indian testimony in court: that the state's legal archive could be
expanded and changed by incorporating this indigenous people's perspective
on their history.

FIGURE 3.2 L-R: James Wah-Shee, Julian Yendo, William Morrow, during the caveat hearings, 1973. Photographer unknown. Photo credit: Legal Archives Society of Alberta, Morrow fonds, 106-G-3.

ON THE FIRST DAY of the hearings, Morrow announced his intention to take the court "to the people." He advised the caveators' lawyers to prioritize the testimony of those who "may not live long enough" should there be further legal action. The lawyer appointed by the Crown to attend the hearings immediately withdrew from the case, adopting a new tactic in order to undermine the hearings. If the testimony were not subject to cross-examination in the usual adversarial manner, its validity could be called into question. Thrust into the role of inquisitorial judge and concerned that his objectivity might be seen to be at issue, Morrow appointed another lawyer as amicus curiae (friend of the court) to cross-examine witnesses.[45]

He then got down to the nitty gritty of organizing the "circuit court." He decided how many communities could be visited by flying the court party around the Mackenzie Valley on his DC-3 plane, for how long, and where the court party would be housed while visiting the settlements. Would there be enough sandwiches on board the plane to feed the accompanying journalists as well as the lawyers, scribes, and others? Asked about whether the judge and lawyers should wear their robes while out on the circuit, he concluded that they should. "I think that robing does distinguish us from the Government," he explained to the court, "and it also reminds the lawyers and the judge as they put their stiff collars on that for hundreds of years they have been maintaining a tradition of fairness and honesty. . . . If we let the little things go the first thing you know we will let the big things go."[46]

By the time the caveat case came to court Morrow had been working on and off in the Northwest Territories for fourteen years. First he had been employed as a defence lawyer and then as a judge, a position for which he and his wife had moved from their home in Edmonton, Alberta, to Yellowknife. He was very familiar with taking court parties on a circuit, a practice begun by his predecessor Justice John Sissons who believed that justice should be taken to "everyman's door."[47] Sissons and Morrow made regular visits to remote communities usually in the summer months and they both argued for stretching the law to fit to local custom so that it would, in Morrow's words, "coincide with what is 'just.'"[48] By hearing cases in the places where local people lived, Morrow involved a wider range of witnesses than might be the case if they were required to come to a larger town, and he gained an appreciation for what issues really mattered to people in various locations and why.

As adaptable as the common law was, Sissons and Morrow were, quite self-consciously as the comments on robing attest, importing foreign procedures and imposing symbols of Canadian sovereignty over the north. Morrow would regularly unfurl a Canadian flag in the courtrooms and other locations where he held a court session. So, while he may have wanted to distinguish his court from southern federal politics he certainly put the signs of Canadian power on display. Federal officials saw the practice of a circuit court as helping to establish effective occupation. The Minister of Indian Affairs who initially approved Sissons' idea for a circuit court in late 1950s was quite clear about what such a show of justice could achieve: "there would be a very real advantage in having this demonstration of Canadian sovereignty and administration on a high judicial level throughout these regions where administration is tenuous and where United States activities are bulking so large at the present time," he wrote to the Minister of Justice.[49]

Morrow, the "hiking judge," was notorious for his dedication to the job and for his efficiency.[50] Keeping to a rigorous hearing schedule sometimes meant that, when time was short, he heard cases on board the plane. And if there was no dedicated court room, which was the case in most of the outlying settlements, he would set up in a schoolroom or local hall. In one instance during the caveat case the court convened beside a lake at card tables borrowed from a local woman and in another instance at the bedside of an elderly and ill Indian man.[51]

FIGURE 3.3 Hearing evidence at Colville Lake, during the caveat case, 1973. Photographer unknown. Photo credit: Legal Archives Society of Alberta, Morrow fonds, 106-G-1.

Morrow loved the outdoors and admired those who "lived close to the land"; he often combined a court circuit with hunting and fishing expeditions.[52] As he wrote in his memoir:

People living close to the land have a special quality about them. They are unselfishly concerned about their families and their way of life and that has a beautiful simplicity that cannot be improved upon. Whether that person is a fisherman from Newfoundland, a farmer from Saskatchewan, or a hunter from Arctic Bay, the concerns are the same and the attitudes are identical. These people are the "salt of the earth" and no country can be strong without them.[53]

An avid photographer, he captured proud images of his hunting trophies and time spent with friends out on the snow or in the river valleys of the north. It was not simply the thrill of the chase that motivated Morrow; he also saw himself as participating in the social ethic of frontier life, framed by the "unselfishness" of northern people. He distributed his kill among family and friends and often carried a case of rye with him to share with the Mounties and others on whose hospitality the court party might depend when out traveling the circuit. This "hunter ethic" was discussed at length during the hearings by the expert anthropologist June Helm and referred to by Dene witnesses as well.

According to accounts in various press reports, the Brotherhood and many local leaders saw Morrow as *their* judge, someone who was "aware of all the traditional and cultural implications of the land at stake."[54] Morrow had earned this trust from his adjudication of earlier cases and, in particular, by presiding over the Hay River Commission in 1968 that had investigated claims that the Justice of the Peace and the Royal Canadian Mounted Police at the settlement were taking too much of the law into their own hands.

Fashioning himself as a man of the north demonstrated to the national audience following the case and to the federal government in particular why he was uniquely placed to listen to and authorize Indians' knowledge. His familiarity with communities along the Mackenzie and his understanding of some of their social and economic relations meant that he was often able to make witnesses feel comfortable in a formal legal setting. This role as "insider" led Morrow to claim a position beyond that of judging the case at hand and applying the law. Morrow claimed to be an arbiter of what constituted authentic "Indian history." In so doing, he imposed limits on indigenous identity that would have significant consequences for Dene people.

MORROW HAD TO find a way to admit into court the Indian history that he and the Indian Brotherhood deemed so important to the case. Aware of the precedent that had been established by Justice Blackburn in *Milirrpum v. Nabalco*, Morrow used the reputation principle in order to admit the Dene people's public traditions as well as personal memories of treaties and land use. The transcript shows how the testimony of Indian witnesses was molded in court to fit the evidentiary expectations that the reputation principle set. For instance, Baptiste Cazon, a chief of the Fort Simpson Slavey band of about twenty years' standing, discussed traditions of the long-standing attachment of Fort Simpson residents to lands that "had always been considered to be theirs." Following clarification from the lawyer as to a difference between "knowing" and having "heard," Cazon explained, "The history away back—the history don't say where the people came from, but once upon a time it was covered with water, and there was a time a history—before the white people—so at one time there was an ice age, and at one time the country was all flooded, but we come from this country, and as far as we know we did not come across from overseas. We did not have that kind of history at all." The transcript continues:

Q: I am not saying you have to know. I am just asking you what you have
   heard, what your legends might say or even what your religion says. Is
   it true from what you have said that from your knowledge about your
   history, and so on, you did not come from overseas?
A: No, I did not say that.
Q: You did not come from overseas?
A: We did not come from overseas. At one time the water covered the whole
   dry land in this part of the country, and at one time there was a winter for
   a long time. That is what I said. It is one thing we do not know, and we do
   not have to know.
A: What you are saying is that as far as you know you have always been there?
Q: Yes, as far as I know.[55]

Cazon spoke for his people—"We did not have that kind of history at all"—and he was addressed by the lawyer in a representative capacity—"You [as a people] did not come from overseas?" he asked, further emphasizing that this evidence was of a collective nature, a tradition that was well known and publicly accepted within the speaker's community.

Others provided eye-witness accounts of treaty negotiations. Michael Landry, an eighty-seven-year-old of Fort Providence who had attended a meeting about Treaty 11 in 1921 in his community, told the court that he remembered that local people were given nets, shells, and flour when the treaty "money" was first paid, and that there was a policeman who gave out the goods. The judge wanted more information, through the sworn interpreter, about Landry's personal circumstances and his way of life.

THE COURT: Is he not married?
THE INTERPRETER: He is married and still lives like the old days. He is nomadic. He goes to his old trapping grounds and now gets a pension.

The lawyer acting as amicus curiae, Dietrich Brand, continued the examination, referring more particularly to what Landry remembered about the treaty "signing":

Q: Before the Treaty was signed, did you consider yourself to be a Canadian?
A: Yes, he said before the white men came, he figured it was his own land.
THE COURT: When they made their "X"'s, can he remember if each man made his "X" like that, or did somebody else take the pen and push their hand?
THE INTERPRETER: Yes, he says it is pretty hard for him to tell. Nobody knew how to write in those days.[56]

Landry not only provided a personal memory of the treaty event but also practiced what Morrow recognized as a traditional hunting way of life, which may have added weight to the credibility of his evidence in the judge's eyes. As Morrow was careful to establish, in order to prove distinct land rights the Dene claimants needed to show that they still "earn[ed] their living from the land in the time-honoured way."[57] This was clearly not the case for the majority of Dene people in the early 1970s. Yet the evidence of elders such as "nomadic" Landry was attributed more weight by Morrow, and even became a standard by which other witnesses' evidence was assessed. This evaluation was based not simply on factual accuracy but also according to a moral scale of measurement. The fact that some people did still engage in a traditional subsistence way of life signified to Morrow that such was still possible and even desirable.

As the hearings progressed, it became clear that Morrow's court preferred oral traditions and collective memory to the documentary archive, particularly when the latter was mentioned by Indian witnesses themselves. For instance, when Brand asked the first named applicant François Paulette, then a chief of the Chipewyan Fort Smith settlement, whether the Chipewyans had ever surrendered or sold their lands to the government, Paulette began to relate the findings of his own archival research. Morrow intervened,

Chief Paulette, you may have done some research and you may have reached a conclusion. That is not what the question is asking for. The question is, from the legends or the stories or the talk that has come down over the generations, I think you are entitled to answer from that, what you picked up from your forebears but not what you have read.[58]

Morrow made it clear that Indian witnesses could not act outside evidentiary terms that demonstrated a long-standing and traditional attachment to land. Paulette was the same generation as Harold Cardinal and James Wah-Shee. Even though these younger leaders energized the demands and legal claims of Indian communities and had more formal schooling than many in their parents' generation, they could not show that they knew too much in terms of literate knowledge. As Morrow began to establish in these hearings, the authentic "native expert" was preferably a male elder who transmitted oral traditions but did not engage in archival research or express concerns about social problems in the settlement. When Alexis Arrowmaker raised issues of alcoholism and housing in the settlements, Morrow explained that while he had sympathy for the chief about these concerns, such were beyond the scope of aboriginal title hearings. "I can't help you today with these other problems," he said.[59]

Very few women provided testimony in the hearings. Morrow favored men's evidence of hunting and trapping over that of women, reflecting his understanding of a traditional economy based on a particular use of the land. Some of those women who did present their testimony, often about what they remembered their kinsmen having done, found the demands of producing the right kind of evidence nerve-wracking. Elise Murphy, a sixty-four-year-old resident of Fort Rae, recalled how her father was reluctantly made chief during the treaty discussions in 1921. Her father accepted the treaty payments, she said, because an agreement was reached that as "long as the sun is rising in the east and setting in the west and the river flows and as long as they never changed, there won't be any laws about the game, and also he mentioned about the map, how big the land he is going to use for his people. This is how the Treaty was paid." Sutton, the lawyer for the Indian Brotherhood, pressed her on this point. Was a particular piece of land mentioned in the treaty? Murphy changed the story: no land was mentioned at the treaty signing. "They hadn't mentioned anything about land, they didn't say they were getting money for the land." Indeed, Murphy further admitted that she could not "see" a map nor could she read or write. "I don't know how to write," she stated. "I can't tell you a lie, I must tell you the truth. Do you feel I am not telling you the truth because you keep asking me these questions?"[60]

Murphy's anxiety about her own credibility revealed the paradoxical position that indigenous witnesses found themselves in when asked to provide reputation evidence. On the one hand, witnesses such as Murphy had to transmit to the court the oral understandings of their ancestors. In so doing, they showed that the transmission of knowledge in their communities still operated in the ways that it might have done in the past and therefore met the conditions of the reputation principle. On the other hand, in providing "declarations of the dead" they were not represented as being coeval with other actors in the court, specifically the lawyers and judge. Indeed, their coevalness was denied as they were expected to present evidence of continuity in tradition in which they fully participated. Thus, Murphy's illiteracy was perhaps embarrassing to her because it made her seem less modern and less credible, yet it was also a sign that she was authentically indigenous in the terms being established by Morrow.

Murphy's tentativeness on whether the cession of land was explained at the treaty signings revealed the effects of political shifts on historical memory for community members. As Indian leaders emphasized new issues, particularly land rights, which they hoped would in turn lead to self-government, local people found themselves being asked to recall things in terms they did not usually use. Murphy may well have been responding uncertainly to new expectations that the Indian Brotherhood as well as the court was in the process of establishing. Did her memory accord with a contemporary idea of land rights? Indian witnesses were asked to provide evidence that would prove land rights in terms of long-standing traditions, even though the concept itself was novel and did not necessarily resonate with their own memories of what they had been promised.

The fact that land rights was a new idea was attested to by the American anthropologist June Helm. She had worked with Dene communities since 1955 and presented expert testimony to Morrow's court. She said that nobody really thought the treaties were about land in the decades following their signing. However, about 1967, when Department of Indian Affairs officials had begun to raise the prospect once again of establishing small reserves for Dene people, she began to hear comments like, "We did not know, nobody told us we were giving away our land." As she elaborated, at the time of the treaty signings, Indian people did not even understand the concept of land ownership or sale. "How could anybody put in the Athapaskan language through a Métis interpreter to mono-lingual Athapaskan speakers the concept of relinquishing ownership of land?" she asked the court rhetorically.[61]

Helm's argument is supported by evidence from an earlier set of hearings about the treaties, when Dene people revealed a very different understanding of land from that being employed by settler authorities. In 1959, a commission of inquiry traveled to the Northwest Territories charged with recommending remedies for the unfulfilled treaty provisions of Treaties 8 and 11, in particular the failure of the government to set aside reserves. The commission appointed two local leaders, Baptiste Cazon and James Koe, and heard from a number of community members. Observing a widespread suspicion of the government, the report they wrote expressed their difficulties in explaining to "the Indians" that "it is possible to separate mineral rights or hunting rights from actual ownership of land."[62] Dene people were not thinking about land as a commodity but rather in terms of their own integrated social and economic practices.[63]

Witnesses like Murphy were caught between divergent understandings of aboriginal title, what it would achieve, and for whom. For the Indian leadership, pursuing aboriginal title rights was part of a broader expression of peoplehood. Leaders placed great hope in the idea that winning aboriginal title would help them reestablish their local, territorial rights in the Northwest Territories. Testimony presented by some of the older witnesses seemed to evidence a distinct understanding of their territorial rights. For instance, Landry had claimed that he "figured it was his own land" before the "white men came," expressing a sense of territorial authority. In a similar vein, Alexis Arrowmaker explained to the court that "when the first treaty was signed they had an agreement that the whole land belongs to the Indians, so we called it our land, and we lived there, and that is how we lived."[64] This phrasing indicated the transformation and loss of authority that colonization had wrought and an attempt to reassert such power in the present. When Baptiste Cazon marked a distinction between those who came from "this" country and those who came from "overseas" in order to emphasize the presence of his people on this land from time immemorial, he was clearly gesturing toward a kind of Dene nationalism in opposition to Canadian assumptions of territorial authority.

However, the political aspirations that Dene leaders held for aboriginal title rights was challenging to wider settler society and to the settler state in particular. The idea that Dene people maintained territorial rights undermined the belief of "perfect" settler sovereignty, or a notion that the state had complete authority over all territory within Canada, and the people who lived on it.[65] Morrow played down this challenge to the sovereignty of the settler state by emphasizing instead how Dene stories of their relationship to the land provided the Canadian nation with access to an indigenous past. For him, hearings in support of aboriginal title claims were a "bridge" to an early colonial world when authentic Indian life was still intact.[66] Or, as he put it, the court was a zone of encounter where the history of the frontier could be re-lived. "I think almost every member of the Court party felt that for a short moment the pages of history were being turned back and we were very privileged to re-live the treaty-negotiating days in the actual setting," Morrow observed in his decision.[67]

Historical reenactment, where one could experience the past unmediated, served to reestablish Morrow's narrative authority as judge, and it drew in the wider audience for the case. His metaphors obscured the fact that anthropologists and others had already begun to build an archive of oral traditions in the region, from which he quoted but did not cite, instead presenting the voices of Indian witnesses as if they had been spoken directly to him.[68] The concept of aboriginal title placed a legal "straitjacket" around oral testimony in terms of what constituted authentic tradition and memory and what did not.[69] In this sense, the "bridge" that aboriginal title built to the indigenous past only allowed for one-way traffic. Settler Canadians could go back and "relive" treaty negotiations, for instance, but indigenous witnesses could not show that they made the reverse journey into the present. They might appear in court in the same moment as the judge, but they were of a different time.

Denying coevalness was how the Dene history presented by witnesses could be turned into the "stuff of Canadian history," as the reporter Steve Hume put it. The hearings for the caveat case were, he wrote in the Canadian oil industry magazine *Oilweek*,

> an historical drama in their own right. The history in this case deals with human beings, not the interpretations of scholars writing after the fact. These old men, whom the court is seeking out in the settlements down the 1,200 mile length of the Mackenzie, are the very stuff of Canadian history. In them lies the origin of what the North is today and what it will be tomorrow, and in their memories rests first-hand knowledge of the wilderness Canada was and will never be again.[70]

Dene witnesses contested the terms of representation and asserted their own sense of peoplehood. However, to have that history authorized as a set of rights, they had to submit to the rules of an institution of the Canadian state. Moreover, their political demands and territorial traditions presented a challenge that had to be managed in such a way as to make them possible of incorporation into the extant state's own narrative. The gesture redeemed the state by demonstrating how it could recognize indigenous peoples' rights. The honor of the country could be restored without a constitutional crisis. And not only was the state redeemed. The recognition of aboriginal title gave Dene people a new role in the making of the state, as co-founders. By emphasizing how Dene history could be incorporated into the tradition of the frontier, Morrow also gave them a limited role in a core national story. However, the cost for Dene people in this compromise was high. In becoming co-founders on the nation's frontier, their coevalness was denied again.

ON 7 SEPTEMBER 1973, Morrow issued a caveat over the lands in question. According to the report in the *Native Press*:

> Tension was high when word came that Judge William Morrow was ready to read his decision on the Indian caveat. After his first few con- clusions were read out, smiles broke out on the faces of the Indian people sitting in the Yellowknife courtroom. Judge Morrow recog- nized the Indian Chiefs and their people as the descendants of the first owners of the land and concluded that the Indian people have never given up their rights to this land.[71]

The caveat case had demonstrated how important Indian accounts of their own histories were for establishing aboriginal title rights and, more broadly, the status as "first owners" of the land. Dene people emphasized some dif- ferent aspects about their history from Yolngu claimants, focusing more on hunting, fishing, and gathering practices than on notions of the sacred. The fact that they had entered into treaty negotiations in the past was also differ- ent from the Australian case. As treaty partners, they asserted their coeval and distinct rights in the present. The assertion of rights had two purposes: to force the Canadian government to consult with them directly about the use of their lands; and, more broadly, to fashion a history that would bind Dene communities together in the pursuit of self-determination and peoplehood. However, the Dene history that was formulated for the court was not inclu- sive of all voices. This history foregrounded the storytelling and experiences of elders and men.

Justice Morrow added a further purpose to the elicitation and recording of Indian testimony. He wanted to demonstrate to a national audience the importance of preserving a non-exploitative subsistence way of life, free of de- pendence on Britain or on the United States. As championed by Morrow and reporters like Steve Hume, the story of Dene land rights complemented and even reinforced rather than challenged Canadian sovereignty. This complex and paradoxical process presented the Indian Brotherhood with a new pre- dicament. In constructing an alternative account of Dene rights and present- ing that account to the law, witnesses and others unexpectedly took on the task of rewriting a history of the settler state. To be successful, the history of

Dene peoplehood needed to re-legitimate the settler state. Dene leaders could claim a distinct status as "first people" and a historical role as co-founders of the state, having negotiated treaties of "peace and friendship" with settler officials. But the role obliged them to tell an origin story that would settle the Canadian nation into an indigenous past. It was a role that represented Dene people as being of the past, but not necessarily of the present too.

Morrow's decision on aboriginal title would not prove to be a binding one. It was overturned in 1974 on the matter of whether a caveat could be filed on unpatented Crown land. Nonetheless, by going to court, Dene leaders and the judge had put more pressure on the federal government to do something about indigenous peoples' distinct rights in Canada, and in the Mackenzie district in particular. Within a few months, the government had decided to create a special commission of inquiry to investigate the impact of the proposed pipeline on the north.

4

Commissions of Inquiry and the Idea of a New Social Contract

When you got your sacred site, you get your country back.
—WENTEN RUBUNTJA, *"Talking about land rights"* [ca. 1976]

[Native] claims must be seen as the means to establishing
a social contract based on a clear understanding
that they are distinct peoples in history.
—THOMAS BERGER, *Northern Frontier, Northern Homeland (1977)*

THE LEGAL ACTIVISM of indigenous peoples laid significant challenges to the settler states of Canada and Australia. These emerged at three levels of claim: that of the legal (in terms of citizenship and rights); the political (in the form of treaties and discussions of sovereignty); and the moral (in terms of justice for dispossession and loss). Once these challenges had begun to win traction in the courts, governments could no longer ignore the significant conceptual and political problems that recognizing indigenous rights presented. However, while the courts had made important findings on evidence and procedure, they could not create new laws or recommend different policies. By the mid-1970s, indigenous activism had forced a broad political consensus that something needed to be done. In response, Australian and Canadian governments created a number of commissions of inquiry that could take a broader and more flexible approach to the issues at hand than the courts could.

This chapter excavates the work of three commissions: the Indian Claims Commission in Canada (1969–1976) which preceded the *Re Paulette* case; the Aboriginal Land Rights Commission in Australia (1973–1974) that was created directly as a response to *Milirrpum v. Nabalco Pty. Ltd.*; and finally the Mackenzie Valley Pipeline Inquiry (1974–1976) which was established following Morrow's decision in *Re Paulette*. Examining the work of the three commissions together draws attention to connections across national borders that commissioners, activists, and others, traveling between Australia, Canada, and New Zealand, began to forge. These transnational participants in the making of indigenous rights saw common challenges and used similar terms to discuss the problem of recognizing the distinct land rights of indigenous peoples in the settler states. Significantly, they also highlighted differences in each country's history of state-indigenous relations. These differences presented commissioners with particular problems and possibilities in recognizing indigenous rights. The comparisons that commissioners and policymakers identified lent further weight to their sense that the issues they faced in each country had to be dealt with at a national level. These issues could not simply be addressed at a local level, nor would international organizations be much help in finding domestic solutions given the particularity of each country's history.

A common feature of Anglo common law jurisdictions, commissions of inquiry were originally used in early modern England to punish opponents of the monarchy. They came into their modern form as inquisitorial aids to policymakers in the nineteenth century, frequently to investigate the violence perpetrated against colonized peoples in British colonies. In colonial contexts including Jamaica and South Africa as well as Australia and Canada, scholars have argued that these institutions were used to legitimate the state in moments of profound social conflict.[1] Commissions also became the object of intense activity in vying for influence over British imperial policy. For instance, metropolitan humanitarians and local colonial authorities competed to win the attention of traveling commissions of the 1820s and 1830s, as these bodies examined problems of governing British colonies, for and against the recognition of local indigenous rights.[2] However, these paternalistic inquiries avoided or deferred addressing the grievances and political demands of colonized peoples themselves as commissioners instead focused on reconciling metropolitan concerns with the expectations of the colonial state and white settler society.

The commissions of inquiry created by settler governments in the 1970s were continuous in some respects with those of the nineteenth century. For instance, none of the commissions examined in this chapter supported indigenous separatism. Nor did they recommend that settler states grant sovereign statehood to indigenous nations. Rather, they aimed at balancing the interests of various levels of government, access to the public domain, the interests of mining corporations, rights of freehold or leasehold settler pastoralists, concerns of conservationists, and the demands of indigenous peoples. However, unlike earlier commissions, those of the 1970s took the task of restoring indigenous rights seriously, using the flexibility that an inquisitorial rather than adversarial approach allowed them. They drew on a broad range of evidence from experts as well as laypeople and consulted widely with local indigenous communities and national leaders.

Although they were given specific terms of reference, these commissions produced reports, created archives, and provoked public debates in each country that went far beyond the technical legal problems of recognizing indigenous rights. Commission reports raised the question of how indigenous peoples could be incorporated into the settler state according to terms they themselves had some capacity to define. Most significant was that indigenous peoples would be incorporated as members of distinct communities with their own cultures, rather than as individual citizens who were to become just like other settlers. The commissioners discussed in this chapter were fully aware of the critique of assimilation and wanted to find a way for the settler state to enhance collective indigenous self-determination. They walked a fine line between critiquing the history of settler colonization and ongoing racist structures, and suggesting reforms that would satisfy some of the demands of indigenous activists without threatening the national political consensus about the extent of those rights.

Debates about the recognition of indigenous peoples as distinct nations in the settler state fractured an older notion of the social contract in Australia and Canada in the mid-1970s. The story of inevitable colonization that had previously justified dispossession was no longer tenable.[3] In its place, stories of indigeneity—that is, stories about the deep connections of specific peoples to specific places—that were discussed and authorized in commissions of inquiry gained credence and power. However, the act of recognizing some groups as traditional owners who were, as first peoples, acknowledged as co-founders of the settler state could entrench ideas about the ahistorical nature of indigenous societies. Moreover, the focus on traditional owners excluded others who could not prove ongoing attachment to land. The completely dispossessed could not win land rights and nor were they considered to be founding members of the state.

CRITICISMS OF THE limits of commissions of inquiry began as soon as they were created. The Canadian Indian Claims Commission (CICC), established in 1969 and the first contemporary commission concerning indigenous peoples' rights in the Commonwealth settler states, was met with considerable reproach from some Indian leaders. George Manuel, president of the National Indian Brotherhood and a Shuswap leader from British Columbia, argued that to obtain the full assent of Indian people to the commission, its ambit needed to be much broader than that determined by the Canadian parliament. The CICC was the first ever nationwide commission of inquiry into treaty breaches in Canada. Its terms of reference gave it power to examine grievances relating to treaty claims and claims about the administration of monies and lands under the Indian Act that "related to accepted Canadian juridical concepts." However, the Privy Council decided that aboriginal title claims could not be examined. Following the logic of the 1969 White Paper, which proposed dissolving Indian treaty status and was viewed by many Indian leaders as dangerously assimilationist, the Council argued that aboriginal title claimants should instead be encouraged to "participate fully as members of the Canadian community."[4]

Manuel firmly believed that the CICC should "deal with the territorial rights" of Indian people, recognized for instance in imperial proclamations, such as the Royal Proclamation of 1763. Lawyers in *Calder v. Attorney-General* were arguing in court at the time for the importance of the proclamation in Manuel's home province of British Columbia. Born in 1921, Manuel had been sent to an Indian residential school and as a young adult, in the 1950s and 1960s, he had begun to work on community development programs among his own people and then rose in the political ranks, becoming president of the North American Indian Brotherhood of British Columbia in 1959. Like other Indian leaders, he was pushed to take action at the nationwide level by the White Paper proposals of 1969, which he opposed.

In criticizing the terms of reference establishing the CICC, Manuel argued, as did the lawyers in the *Re Paulette* case in the Northwest Territories, that the treaties themselves "may be considered as an express recognition of the territorial rights" of Indian people.[5] Other leaders agreed, demanding that the commission discuss the "total concept" of aboriginal rights—that is, their right to self-government that they argued was recognized in the process of treaty-making.[6] The commissioner's role, which was to "inquire into, study and report" on how treaty claims and possible breaches of the trust relationship between the Canadian government and status Indian bands might be "best adjudicated," was far too limited according to these critics.[7] Furthermore, the CICC was only inquisitorial and lacked the power to make monetary awards as did the United States Indian Claims Commission, created in 1946 and a source of influence for the Canadian commission.

Another criticism of the CICC concerned the appointment of a white man, Dr. Lloyd Barber, as commissioner. Barber was vice-president of the University of Saskatchewan and a former member of the Northwest

Territorial Council, but he was not at the time a leading figure in matters concerning Indian affairs. The Union of British Columbia Indian Chiefs expressed its concern that as a single person was appointed to the role, he might have too much "discretion" as to how claims would be classified and adjudicated. The minister of Indian Affairs and Northern Development assured the Union that Barber was "in effect" a co-commissioner, since he was expected to consult with various Indian bodies.[8] Skeptical that such consultation would take place, the National Indian Brotherhood portrayed Barber as a "valuable asset" for the government who would carry out research for its purposes, while Indian organizations conducted their own research. The National Indian Brotherhood warned that the process was therefore likely to become adversarial.[9]

Responding to these criticisms, Barber defined his role as that of a facilitator of discussions about how Indian claims might best be inquired into, prior to being negotiated or adjudicated by another body. He focused in particular on what he explained to parliament was the job of "foster[ing] native research" rather than carrying out research into potential claims on behalf of Indian communities.[10] Significantly, the CICC took up the issue of funding for research carried out by Indian organizations. In July 1970, only seven months after the commission had been established, Barber submitted a budget to the Privy Council Office so that the commission could fund research programs. The budget, he argued, "must make provision for an amount which is sufficient to enable the vehicles chosen by the Indian people of Canada, the National and local research committees, to make a *comprehensive identification, analysis and report on the rights and recourses which the Indian people, bands and individuals of Canada have today* [emphasis in original]."[11]

In 1972, the federal government agreed to provide a set amount of annual funding to "Treaty Rights and Research" programs plus additional awards for specific projects. With quite generous funds for the period, indigenous organizations could plan documentary and oral history research projects and hire researchers and fieldworkers. Between 1972 and 1976, the Research Division of the Department of Indian and Northern Affairs provided $7.5 million to associations for rights and treaty research, although what kinds of projects could be funded continued to be a contentious issue.[12]

Barber also negotiated with the department to make their files more easily accessible to Indian organizations and their researchers. He hired historians to write general reports on Indian claims in Canada and the interpretation of treaty principles; and he even carried out some formal (although not judicial) "hearings" in Saskatchewan and Alberta to record the testimonies of elders in those provincial communities and preserve them for future use, explicitly drawing on the evidentiary precedent and protocols set by Justice William Morrow in the *Re Paulette* case.[13] In his role as "facilitator" and "fosterer" of research, Barber earned approval and even considerable praise from a number of Indian organizations and leaders over the six years of the CICC's operation. The Federation of Saskatchewan Indians in Barber's home province pointed out the considerable achievements of his office when defending him from further criticisms made by the National Indian Brotherhood in 1973.[14]

The CICC came to play a central role in the production and dissemination of new "treaty histories" like those being expounded by the Indian Brotherhood of the Northwest Territories. Making these histories was a political activity according to Indian leaders, one that expanded the archive of the settler state. It was key to providing a new story that would underpin the idea that Indians were co-founders. In arguing for the broadening of their research activities and increased funding, the Federation of Saskatchewan Indians explained that their researchers could not rely on

> papers of the white men who have in large part been responsible for the grievances dealt with below. Traders, missionaries, government officials, and the government have preserved many of their records, but the reliability of these sources is often questionable since many of the persons who have left these records, have written this material to justify their actions, and in the process have distorted what actually happened. Therefore, whenever possible we have sought to supplement these sources and to bring forward our side of the story by drawing on the oral traditions and old people's memories of what happened to them. By comparing the information and interpretations from these sources, we hope to be able to piece together an accurate account of the government's relations with the Indians.[15]

The Federation, like other organizations and activists, argued that the making of the official archive was itself an act of power, one that had marginalized and even discounted Indian understandings of treaty agreements. The racial bias of this archive ("papers of the white men") could only be countered by the new research being undertaken by local and provincial organizations. The research entailed creating a new documentary archive based on the "oral traditions" and "memories" of community elders that could then be compared with the official documentation.

This research countered the ways in which Indian people had been marginalized in social and economic terms and therefore relegated to the footnotes of Canadian history. It also supported claims for Indian self-determination. The highly self-conscious intentions behind the construction of Indian archives would help organizations produce a more "accurate account" of relations between the government and Indians, precisely because it would represent different and contending political perspectives. Even more significantly, accounts based on archives collected from Indian communities, these researchers hoped, would reveal agreements and compromises between polities, rather than (re)constructing a homogenous and unidirectional story of the settler state in which indigenous peoples were left behind. Thus, the writing of new treaty histories, resourced by the CICC, opened up the possibility of writing a new national history as the story of negotiation between founding peoples.

Under Barber's leadership, the CICC fostered transnational connections, particularly with leading figures involved in indigenous rights activism and legal process in New Zealand and Australia. Barber visited both countries in March 1972, a year after an official Canadian delegation led by Minister for Indian Affairs and Northern Development Jean Chrétien had made a similar trip. According to an official communiqué, the purpose of the earlier trip had been twofold. In New Zealand, officials were to focus on "how the Maoris [*sic*] and the other segments of the population of that country have been able to develop a social and economic relationship which is considered among the most successful in the world." In Australia, where mining development on remote frontiers echoed that in Canada's north, the party studied "the government's programs for native people."[16] George Manuel was one of those invited on the trip and it made a strong impact on him. He later claimed that he met people just like his own who had experienced similar things. The "Maoris could help us and we could help them!" he realized.[17]

Barber's trip to New Zealand left him with a strong impression of the successful integration of Maori people into national society. Having met with key Maori leaders, Barber explained to an interviewer on Canadian television on his return that New Zealand was "light-years ahead of Canada in its treatment of native people." According to Barber, the Maori maintained "their own cultural identity and their own racial identity to the extent that they want and make a significant contribution to the cultural mosaic of New Zealand." Many Maori activists in the country at the time would have disagreed with Barber's portrayal; and indeed the image of integration that he depicted was premised on the fact that Maori tribes had barely any land base left and no "reserves" as did Canadian Indians as he pointed out.[18] Nonetheless, the comparison—however inaccurate—served to shore up Barber's argument for the ongoing right of Canada's Indians to choose their own identity on their own land.

In stark contrast, the situation of Aborigines in Australia appeared much worse than that of native peoples in Canada. There, Barber explained to the Canadian press, Aborigines, who had a more "fragmented tribal structure," suffered from lack of unity. "The aboriginal case," he was reported in the *Montreal Star* as saying, "has been confused by state and federal jurisdiction, political pressures and guilt reactions about stealing property."[19] Despite his firm views on the comparative differences between the settler states, Barber was advised against making such comparisons while he was in Australia, as the issue of Aboriginal rights had become a matter of heated political debate during the elections taking place.

While he was there, he met and developed a friendly correspondence with Ted Woodward, one of the lawyers for the Yolngu plaintiffs in the Gove land rights case. Woodward would soon be appointed by the new Labor government to head up the first ever commission of inquiry into Aboriginal land rights, a position that Barber would later congratulate him on receiving and also commiserate with him about, since such work was often an "impossible and thankless task."[20]

AS WAS THE case with the CICC, the creation of the Australian Aboriginal Land Rights Commission was a federal government response to political pressure exerted by indigenous activists and others. More specifically, it was a direct outcome of Justice Blackburn's decision in *Milirrpum v. Nabalco* in 1971, which went against the native title claim of Yolngu people. The decision was galling not only for the Yolngu claimants but also for other Aboriginal leaders and activists around the country. Yolngu leaders and other activists demanded that the federal government do something to recognize Aborigines' land rights.

Aboriginal activists and sympathetic commentators viewed the decision in the Gove case as another example of the racism of Australian law and as an opportunity to increase pressure on the federal government to pass land rights legislation. The Liberal-Country (conservative) coalition government's response to the decision—a proposal extending a system of conditional land leases—drew the ire of activists. A radical group established the longest-running land occupation by Aboriginal people in Australia. In a "swift and brilliant" response to the government's proposals, activists erected a "tent embassy" on parliament grounds in Canberra on Australia Day, 26 January

1972.[21] It put Aborigines' demands front and center in national debate and international scrutiny.

Tent embassy activists connected demands for land rights to their political autonomy. One of the ambassadors at the embassy (which has continued to occupy land on parliament grounds over the past forty years) was John Newfong, an Aboriginal journalist from Queensland. According to him, the recognition of Aboriginal land rights was the door to a new political future for Aborigines across the country. He imagined that in the Northern Territory a pan-Aboriginal political identity could be forged in broad territorial terms once land rights had been recognized. In this state-within-a-state, Aborigines from across Australia would to be able to elect their own representatives in a majority Aboriginal government. Such a political future should not, he advised, be any cause for concern: "like black men in Africa," Newfong wrote in July 1972, "who fought so hard for the right to decide their own destiny, black men here will be quick to reject those of their own who fail them."[22]

National political leaders did not take up the pan-Aboriginalist cause espoused by Newfong. But the idea that land rights might provide a limited kind of self-determination for Aborigines did become a platform in the opposition Labor party's election campaign under the leadership of Gough Whitlam later that year. Whitlam advocated a "new nationalism" for Australia, shifting the country's economic and strategic focus to Asia and the Pacific. While acknowledging Australia's British heritage, Whitlam sought to place the country firmly on an international stage alongside other British Commonwealth countries such as India and Canada. These countries, he claimed, had the most "advanced international co-operation" and were "nations with a secure and distinctive national identity of their own."[23] According to Whitlam, Australia also had to undertake a domestic accounting. He promised that the racial injustices of the past could be overcome, and (some) Aboriginal land rights would be recognized.

No longer were Aborigines to be considered wards of the state. As Whitlam announced in a stump speech just prior to the 1972 election, the Labor Party if elected would "legislate to give aborigines [*sic*] land rights—not just because their case is beyond argument, but because all of us as Australians are diminished while the aborigines [*sic*] are denied their rightful place in this nation."[24] The rights of Aborigines was a long-term cause of his. As a member of the Royal Australian Air Force stationed on the Gove peninsula, Whitlam had campaigned in 1944 for constitutional change that would have given the Commonwealth government, among other things, special power in Aboriginal affairs.

In February 1973, the newly elected Labor government appointed Ted Woodward as commissioner to investigate "the appropriate means to recognize and establish the traditional rights and interests of the Aborigines in and in relation to land." The terms of reference also obliged the commissioner to examine how title might be vested in Aboriginal groups; to look at the effect of existing Crown leases on the "traditional rights" of Aboriginal people; and to propose draft legislation for land rights recognition.[25] There were two significant differences between the ambit and operations of the Woodward commission and Barber's commission in Canada. First, the geographical remit of the commission was limited to investigating how the land rights of Aborigines might be recognized only in the Northern Territory, not across the whole country. Second, it focused on recognizing land rights in a context in which no national precedent existed, and where no treaty claims could be made.

Underscoring the importance that Whitlam attached to land rights, Woodward later recalled that setting up the commission was one of the first orders of business for the new government: "[Whitlam] rang me on his first day in office indicating that he was intending to set up a Royal Commission and asking if I'd be free to conduct it. . . . It was obviously one of the things that was uppermost in his mind."[26] However, Woodward's appointment was met with reproach by some Aborignal organizations. The *Australian* newspaper reported that the National Aboriginal Consultative Committee, which had recently been established to advise the government on Aboriginal matters, called for him to be removed. The committee demanded that six Aboriginal people should be elected "by their fellows to evaluate land rights" and reported widespread discontent that the land rights inquiry would be conducted "solely by a white person."[27]

Despite the criticism, Woodward pressed ahead with proposals for land rights legislation. He issued reports in 1973 and 1974 that laid out many of the parameters of what would become the first legislation to recognize land rights in Australia, the Aboriginal Land Rights Act (Northern Territory), passed into law in 1976. The legislation defined who could apply for recognition and what they would need to prove to win their land rights. It marked a radical shift away from the expectations of the late 1960s when activists had been mostly focused on equal rights for Aborigines and it had complex consequences on the ground for Aboriginal communities in the region. The passage of the legislation demonstrated that some Aborigines would be considered, at least in symbolic terms, as founding members of a new Australia. Others, however, would be excluded from this special role.

Small and larger communities in the Northern Territory appealed to the Woodward Commission for recognition of their rights, with high expectations. In June 1973 a group of dispossessed Larrakia people in Darwin who had formed an association, Gwalwa Daraniki, to assert their land rights in the Territory's capital city, invited Woodward to visit their encampment at Kulaluk. They had mobilized support for a nationwide petition in 1972, signed by more than 1,000 people across the country, which they presented to Princess Margaret when she visited Darwin. Noting that the British Crown had signed treaties with "Maoris and Native Americans," the petition stated:

> The British settlers took our land. No treaties were signed with the tribes. Today we are REFUGEES. Refugees in the country of our ancestors. We live in REFUGEE CAMPS—without land, without employment, without justice [Capitalization in original].[28]

The Larrakia at Kulaluk were worried about imminent residential development and asked Woodward to "freeze" rights to the land as Morrow had done in the Northwest Territories of Canada. Woodward replied that it was not in his power to do so. According to one account of this struggle, "This Justice Woodward took part in the Yirrkala case for land rights—and the Larrakia saw what the Yirrkala got [i.e., nothing]. So the letter didn't surprise them." [29] However, he referred specifically to the demands of Larrakia people in both his first and second reports. Asserting that he had "no doubt that the Larrakia people were the traditional owners of what is now the whole Darwin area," he nonetheless questioned how many Larrakia were "still left" and argued that those who remained could not now be considered traditional owners, with a special land title vested in their organization.[30]

Aboriginal organizations, including regional land councils created by the Woodward commission, urged that he should consider the claims of such groups. While the land councils agreed that such groups did not constitute traditional landowners, they argued that those groups may have had a long association with the areas in which they now resided and deserved some kind of recognition. Woodward therefore recommended that land be set aside as "living space" for urban dwellers who may have "lost" their traditional lands and their "sense of Aboriginal identity caused by their mixed ancestry."[31]

In his 1973 report, Woodward recommended the creation of two regional land councils in the Northern Territory that would take central responsibility for the process of research for and administration of land rights claims. The Northern and Central Land Councils—which began operating the following year—drew on the examples of indigenous Brotherhoods and Associations in Canada,[32] although other Aboriginal leaders remember the land councils as emerging from discussions among themselves, indicating a degree of ownership over them.[33] According to Woodward, these councils would be led by and for Aborigines. Moreover, he thought that such councils should be given support by the Commonwealth government, along the lines of the research funding provided to Indian organizations in Canada. So, like the CICC, the Woodward commission played a significant role in the development of Aboriginal organizational capacity, and it helped to establish new ways of mediating the relationship between local Aboriginal communities, larger regional bodies, and the federal government.

However, not all Aboriginal communities were happy with the arrangement. Roy Marika, the Yolngu leader, demanded a separate "East Arnhem Land Land Council" that would represent only the people in that area. "We all understand each other and connect with each other," he wrote to Nugget Coombs and the Council for Aboriginal Affairs in 1975. "We can only talk for people in eastern Arnhem Land, about what we know for the clans, each bit of land. . . . We can't talk about the country in western Arnhem Land because that country doesn't belong to us."[34] Marika's concerns notwithstanding, both Land Councils made extensive submissions to the commission in 1974, including proposals about the Larrakia, and Woodward took careful note of them in his report, although he admitted he could not "reconcile" all of their demands.[35]

Woodward was mostly focused on the demands of those Aborigines he considered to have maintained ancient, spiritual connections to the land, despite the effects of colonization.[36] Recalling his time on the road as commissioner some years later, Woodward wrote of visiting the Docker River community in the south of the Northern Territory. There he was confronted with the effects of ongoing colonial interventions in Aborigines' worlds, yet he was impressed by the capacity of some of those in remote areas to maintain distinct attachment to their lands. He met Yami Lester, a blind Yankunytjatjara man who was prominent in land rights activism and had worked, among other roles, as an interpreter for the courts. "As we travelled from the airstrip towards Docker River settlement," wrote Woodward,

squatting in the back of a ute, we splashed through a little creek—not much more than drain. "Ah. That must be Docker River," said Yami.

"Well, no Yami," I said. "It's just a small creek." He looked towards me sadly and said, "I was only joking." I found in the course of the day that he often joked about his blindness. "As I see things . . ." or "I see what you mean as clearly as I can see that hill over there."[37]

Lester had become blind as a child during the 1950s as a consequence of fallout from British nuclear testing at Maralinga in nearby South Australia.

In the same essay in which he recalled meeting Lester, Woodward described his "most haunting memory"—a visit to a sacred site in the Yuendumu area. "As we approached the place—a large rocky outcrop—the elders who were taking me called out several times to warn the spirits that we were coming and, I suppose, to explain my presence. It seemed entirely appropriate. The rock paintings at that site were remarkable."[38]

What the event confirmed to Woodward was that the connection of remote Aborigines to land was in the nature of a sacred obligation, as Blackburn had previously defined it in his decision on *Milirrpum v. Nabalco*. Like Blackburn, Woodward believed that traditional Aboriginal communities operated according to their own legal system, highly developed and elaborate.[39] Such communities did not, however, form a recognizable corporate political unit but rather were ceremonial and land-using groups connected by descent.

As Woodward explained in his 1974 report, one of central aims of recognizing Aboriginal land rights was "the preservation, where possible, of the spiritual link with his own land which gives each Aboriginal his sense of identity and which lies at the heart of his spiritual beliefs."[40] This intention framed how Woodward defined "traditional Aboriginal owners" in a draft for proposed legislation that he submitted as part of his report. Such owners were

> a local descent group of Aborigines who have common spiritual affiliations to a site or sites within that area of land, which affiliations place the group under a primary spiritual responsibility for that site or sites and for that land, and who are entitled by Aboriginal tradition to forage as of right over that land.[41]

Some Aboriginal people viewed the emphasis on the sacred and the protection of sacred sites in the definition of Aboriginal land rights as useful and positive. For example, Wenten Rubuntja, an Arrente artist and leader from central Australia, remembered a discussion about land rights and sacred sites among his community thus:

> And they said, "Hey! They're talking about [land rights in a] good way." "What good way—they're talking about?" We been go in there and say, "Talking about *atywerrenge* [sacred object]?"
> "When you got your sacred site, you get your country back."[42]

Under these criteria, however, groups like the Larrakia would find it much harder to prove that they were traditional landowners. Their claim became the longest-running one since passage of the land rights act.[43] In fact, the distinction Woodward drew between two kinds of claimants evoked well-established differences in Australian political and cultural discourse. That was between dispossessed Aborigines (previously regarded as the most assimilable) who were primarily based in country towns and coastal cities, and remote tribal Aborigines who had held on to their traditions on the land and were now being represented as the most authentic. Recalling his work as commissioner, he later explained that, on the one hand, there were those claims based in

> timeless connections with that land and on the other hand claims for general compensation, based on the fact that land is important to all Aboriginal people. In some general sense of land compensation form-ing a basis for other steps by way of social welfare that can be taken, Aborigines have an entitlement to sympathetic consideration. The two kinds of claims are separate.[44]

In Woodward's thinking, however, the distinction between traditional claimants with a purportedly "timeless" connection to land and those in need of "sympathetic consideration" was given new meaning. First, it reversed assimilation-era priorities in which more urbanized and often "mixed race" people were assisted (or forced) to join the national economy. Following the Woodward commission findings, "traditional" Aborigines had the upper hand symbolically. However, as critics of the legislation argued, such a rigid definition of some Aborigines as somehow living in a "timeless" world of tra-dition, effectively de-historicized them. Tradition was posited as antithetical to historical change and, importantly, agency.[45] An idea that traditions them-selves might change and that Aboriginal people themselves might be agents of such change—for instance, in revitalizing artistic production or in adopting anthropological terms for themselves in the pursuit of land rights—was excluded from legal consideration.

Furthermore, those Aborigines considered to be non-traditional, yet in need of "sympathetic consideration" because of the loss of their attachment to ancestral lands, were in effect doubly dispossessed: first of their lands and second of their cultural identities. Despite Woodward's recommendation that the latter group be somehow compensated, the Aboriginal Land Rights Act was only passed once a compensation clause had been removed. This group did not figure as bearing the symbolic value for the nation that "traditional" Aborigines did.

As well as defining who could be considered a "traditional Aboriginal owner," Woodward defined what the nature of that ownership would be. He did not think that Aboriginal communities should be awarded land rights that would allow them to do whatever they wanted with their lands. Successful applicants would be awarded a kind of title that had to be communally held, could not be individualized, and could not be privately sold. According to Woodward, land rights legislation could establish a "trust-like relationship," which he took from "British law" when "you want to get away from strict definition of rights and entitlements and employ something which was more flexible and capable of being adjusted with time."[46] Woodward claimed that this kind of "symbolic" ownership was a more authentic description of how Aborigines regarded their land—not as a commodity that could be bought and sold but rather as something given to them to steward and with which they formed a profound inter-dependency.[47]

In defining the kinds of land rights that successful applicants might be awarded, Woodward explicitly drew on the ideas for collective indigenous ownership, specifically native or aboriginal title rights, being developed in other settler countries. Woodward had already read some legal doctrine on the idea from other jurisdictions in east Africa, the United States, and New Zealand. In 1973, when he made a trip to North America, he was able to see firsthand the possibilities for the recognition of "inalienable" property rights and the difference between such recognition and addressing treaty breaches. He visited the Indian Claims Commissions in the United States and in Canada to compare how those institutions were dealing with indigenous claims with the challenges he faced in Australia. He also met with key Indian leaders including George Manuel. Initially, he noticed strong similarities between the settler states but, like Barber, he noticed most the differences between the nature of claims and claims processes in North America and what he had to contend with in Australia. In particular, the Canadian and US commissions' focus on historical evidence of maladministration was quite unlike the Australian situation where there was no comparable history of "broken treaties."[48]

The recognition of land rights in the Australian case involved a question of how to prove cultural continuity rather than an attempt at accounting for the effects of historical change and dispossession on indigenous peoples. "Paradoxically," as Woodward explained in his 1974 report, "Australia now has an enviable opportunity to give belated recognition to such rights, uninhibited by a history of treaties and statutes by which, in North America, many rights were formally surrendered or compulsorily acquired in return for various forms of compensation."[49] Whereas Barber had reported to the Canadian press on the state of "confusion" in Australian Aboriginal affairs and jurisdictional issues, Woodward instead saw opportunity. The absence of a complex history of treaty-making and claiming provided those working on land rights in Australia, he would later write in his memoirs, with "a virtually clean slate to write upon."[50]

Woodward emphasized a flexible approach in engaging with Aboriginal communities throughout his commission. Instead of holding formal hearings,

FIGURE 4.1 Aboriginal Land Rights Hearing, Yirrkala. Photographer unknown. Photo credit: Northern Territory Library, ABC TV collection, PH 0416/0082.

he traveled around local communities to ascertain the thoughts and desires of Aboriginal people.[51] This was a marked departure from the Gove land rights case, for which all the hearings were held in courtrooms, and it was more akin to the practices of judges like William Morrow in the Northwest Territories and Lloyd Barber in the Canadian Indian Claims Commission.

In his proposals for a land rights act, Woodward included clauses that would further enable evidentiary flexibility, including not requiring testifiers to provide an oath. After the statutory creation of the Aboriginal Land Commission in 1976, the first commissioner, Justice John Toohey, likewise argued for a degree of evidentiary flexibility. All inquiries, he argued, were "to be conducted broadly speaking along the lines of conventional court proceedings, although with much less formality and with a relaxation of the ordinary rules of evidence."[52] Site visits became a normal practice in Aboriginal Land Commission hearings, and commissioners made special arrangements for visits to sacred sites that claimants wished to keep secret. For instance, the commission might choose not to record or transcribe a performance at a sacred site in specific detail, but rather ask an anthropologist to write a report in general terms about the nature of the claimants' attachment to it.[53] Commissioners also observed the gender norms associated with particular sacred sites. Male or female court personnel and lawyers could be excused from discussions of "women's" or "men's business," for example.[54]

Respecting the secrecy of certain ritual performances created an archival quandary for commissioners. On the one hand, they recognized that land rights records had great "importance in historical and contemporary terms," as Justice Toohey put it.[55] On the other hand, such evidence was presented to commissioners under strict conditions about who was allowed to witness ritual performances. Toohey's compromise was that records of sacred practices should be made available for commission inquiries into adjoining lands but that such records should be stored under the authority of the land councils that represented the groups concerned: "it should be appreciated that circumstances giving rise to the secrecy of the material are not likely to be affected by the passage of time," he explained. "This puts the material in a different category from political documents and the like where the reason for confidentiality may disappear over the years or at any rate be outweighed by the advantages of making information public."[56] The Aboriginal Land Commission thus became an institution in which aspects of indigenous norms and customary obligations took effect on non-indigenous others. Even in the seemingly technical questions of how and where land rights records might be stored, notions of the rights of indigenous people to their own cultural records took hold.

The respect given to Aboriginal traditions and practices was a sign for some Aboriginal people that their law was being recognized as distinct from that of Australian law. As Wenten Rubuntja put it, "We gotta find out from our culture country and you got to find out from your law. See? That's the Land Rights Act: your law and my law is standing as one. Two different, different laws standing as one."[57] In the early years under the act, claimants were proud to "assert their rights," as recalled by Toni Bauman, an anthropologist who lived in the Katherine area of the Northern Territory (south of Darwin) and was hired by the Central Land Council in the late 1970s. They hoped that "in showing the 'judge' their places and singing their songs and painting up their bodies in the designs which they inherited and which marked them as the rightful owners of country, then he would 'believe.'"[58]

However, Bauman critiqued the evidentiary burdens placed on claimants to the Aboriginal Land Rights Act, which demanded a high degree of proof of authenticity. Ongoing demands for site visits and ritual performances led to claimant fatigue, and over time Central Land Council claimants' hope that the performance of their histories would help land commissioners come to "believe" in their rights began to fade. Their efforts to instruct commissioners did not appear to have been effective.

Over the years, the evidentiary value of cultural performances became less clear as commissioners came to rely on written documents. They began to use pre-land claim-era ethnographic records, as well as the transcripts of previous hearings for evidence of attachment to corroborate—or dispute—Aboriginal oral testimony.[59] In 1995, anthropologist Deborah Bird Rose therefore cautioned against a rosy view of the record, one which she argued was "highly biased" in failing to represent women as landowners and managers of country, and that reflected the "male dominance of the legal profession."[60]

The land rights legislation won the approval of many Aboriginal people in the Northern Territory, who even came out on the street to ensure its passage in the Commonwealth parliament. In 1976, a thousand Aboriginal people marched on Alice Springs demanding its immediate enactment, following the Northern Territory government's attempts to undermine it.[61] The legislation raised high expectations of what it would achieve culturally and politically. Some Aboriginal people, including Wenten Rubuntja, saw the land rights act as securing their ability to maintain their spiritual obligations to particular areas, and even as recognizing the inherent value of their own law. Others, such as the Larrakia people in Darwin, who were also organizing for a nationwide treaty with Aboriginal people, hoped that land rights would offer them security for housing developments in urban areas. Still others saw the recognition of distinct land rights as promising a new political future for Aborigines across the country, in which Aboriginal people would be able to govern themselves in their own territories.

The Woodward commission enabled the realization of some of these expectations, but not others. "Traditional Aboriginal owners," as Woodward defined them, would indeed be able to lay claim to areas of spiritual significance but dispossessed groups would not be awarded relief. Woodward demonstrated the importance of supporting limited self-determination under the auspices of the Land Councils whose consent should be obtained before political change could be made. He believed that the "steps which ought to be taken [should] involve Aborigines in the solution of problems."[62] However, he foreclosed the more radical political potential of land rights imagined by John Newfong: that such rights would make a pan-Aboriginal state possible on territories recognized as Aboriginal land. Woodward effectively redefined self-determination as a local process in which indigenous peoples were to represent themselves as "timeless" subjects continuously bearing their traditional attachments to specific parcels of land.

The remarkable shift, in the space of ten years, from equal rights to distinct land rights in national political discourse entailed not only changes in Australian law but also in the framing and formation of identities at the local and significantly at the national level. Civil rights arguments—premised in a commitment to racial justice—sought to bring Aborigines out of a condition of wardship and into equal citizenship. Arguments for land rights gave a new symbolic weight to the identities of some of the recently enfranchised. Those Aborigines who could prove they were "traditional Aboriginal owners" were, at the same time, giving substance to the idea that Australia was formed by two founding peoples, the "first peoples" and settlers. Providing a new role to some Aboriginal people, this new story reworked the older basis of a social contract in Australia.

IN ANOTHER COMMISSION of inquiry, the profound question of negotiating a new social contract in the settler state was raised explicitly. The Mackenzie Valley Pipeline Inquiry in the Northwest Territories of Canada was created in March 1974 just six months after the decision in the *Re Paulette* case that drew attention to the threats the proposed oil and gas pipeline posed to Dene people. The presiding commissioner, Thomas Berger, interpreted his terms of reference very broadly. Berger, who had worked as a lawyer for the Nisga'a claimants in *Calder v. Attorney-General*, was charged by the government with investigating the potential environmental, social, and economic impacts of the pipeline on what he came to call the "northern homeland" of Indian, Inuit, and Métis peoples. In his final report, Berger recommended that a moratorium be placed on the building of the pipeline until those claims could be settled. Going beyond the specific ambit of his commission, he also called for the negotiation of a new social contract in Canada.

The Berger Inquiry, as it became known, was large in scale, costing CA$5.3 million and producing more than 40,000 pages of text. A much wider array of people appeared before the Berger Inquiry than came to the more restricted hearings that Morrow coordinated; these included environmentalists, representatives of pipeline companies, political scientists, legal scholars, and other academics, as well as Indian leaders from around the country. The hearings were beamed into Canadians' homes by the television network of the Canadian Broadcasting Company (CBC) and discussed widely in the print media; they provoked national and even international concern about northern issues and the claims of remote Indian people in particular. Unlike the reports produced by the CICC or the Woodward commission, Berger's two-volume report, *Northern Frontier, Northern Homeland* (1977), became a national bestseller.[63]

The spectacle of the Berger Inquiry provided a platform for Dene leaders to articulate their claims to nationhood and self-determination and critique imperialism in highly effective ways. A young Dene chief, Frank T'sleie, protesting the actions of the pipeline company in dramatic terms, directly attacked the chief executive of an oil and gas pipeline construction company, Bob Blair, in a hearing that was broadcast on CBC television news on 5 August 1975. T'sleie accused Blair of being "like the Pentagon . . . planning the slaughter of innocent Vietnamese." He continued, "You are the twentieth century General Custer. You have come to destroy the Dene Nation." The room, a hall in Fort Good Hope filled with local community members, journalists, lawyers, the presiding commissioner, and others working for the inquiry, was quiet. Blair twisted in his seat, visibly uncomfortable.[64]

During the Berger Inquiry, Dene leaders turned local issues into matters of national importance. Indeed, the claims of Dene people came to stand in for a discussion of the relationship between Aboriginal and non-Aboriginal Canadians. As the hearings circulated around the North, attracting increasing national attention, the Dene declared themselves a "nation," following a meeting between the Indian Brotherhood of the Northwest Territories and the Métis Association at Fort Simpson. "We the Dene of the N.W.T.," proclaimed the declaration, "insist on the right to be regarded by ourselves and the world as a nation." Demanding their right to self-determination, the declaration explained that the Dene

> find themselves as part of a country. That country is Canada. But the government of Canada is not the government of the Dene. The Government of the N.W.T. is not the government of the Dene. These governments were not the choice of the Dene, they were imposed upon the Dene.[65]

Borrowing language from human rights discourse and the recent history of anti-colonialism,[66] Frank T'sleie's confrontation with the pipeline executive made it clear that the Dene associated their situation with the fate of other colonized peoples. But their experience of colonialism was also peculiar. The Dene Declaration was not issued as the culmination of violent resistance to the state in which the Dene now "f[ou]nd themselves." Indeed, as the declaration put it, "we the Dene" did not resist but insisted on their nationhood, a verb that coordinated a sense of persistence and survival with the fact of being here, in this place.[67] The Dene insisted on the recognition of their peoplehood not because they had violently asserted their distinctiveness but because they, the first people of the land, had persisted despite the violence inflicted on them. They had not disappeared.

Dene people framed their collective identity as members of the "Fourth World." This was a term coined by George Manuel, who was by then president of the World Council of Indigenous Peoples that he helped to found in 1974. He testified at the Berger Inquiry, in support of the Indian Brotherhood of the NWT, where he explained his notion of the "fourth world." The term referred to the fact that indigenous peoples, who maintained a special relationship to the land, were nations in their own right but they existed "within" larger state structures, and were unlikely to achieve a separate nation-statehood.[68] Manuel coined the term the "Fourth World" in order to mark the commonality between minority indigenous peoples and their difference from peoples of the first and third worlds. He claimed to have thought up the term in conversation with Julius Nyerere when he visited Tanzania in the early 1970s as he differentiated the struggles of indigenous minorities from those of peoples in the "third world" who were achieving independence.[69] While the members of the "fourth world" might not achieve full political independence, Manuel argued that they made a particular claim to political distinctiveness as first peoples within the settler state. He connected this to indigenous peoples' distinctive land rights, as such were already being given recognition through the concept of native title: "The lands that belong to us by native title, and the compensation for our aboriginal rights," he averred, "are our birthright as the aboriginal peoples of North America."[70]

The Dene Declaration gained widespread attention and was discussed in the Canadian parliament. Despite its moderate claims and the limited demand for self-determination that those like Manuel were promoting, the declaration was interpreted as an example of overzealous revolutionary rhetoric. Minister of Indian and Northern Affairs Judd Buchanan explained his reaction in the House of Commons in no uncertain terms: "Two nations in the Northwest Territories is no more acceptable than two nations in any other part of Canada." According to the record of parliamentary debates "some honorable members" then shouted, "Hear, hear!"[71] Just a few months earlier, however, a senator from Toronto, speaking in the Senate in March 1975, had lamented that "Many of us are aware of that unhappy situation in which we Canadians find ourselves in holding two territories (the Yukon and the Northwest Territories) actually close to half of our whole land area, under what is 'neo-colonialism.'"[72]

The Dene Nation continued to articulate the aspirations of northern people as held in common with those of others, even non-indigenous others. In "A proposal presented to the government and people of Canada on 25 October 1976," the Dene Nation reiterated the commonality of the Dene struggle with that of other "oppressed and colonized people." The proposal demanded the recognition of the Dene people's aboriginal title rights to their traditional lands. The document made it clear that the Dene leadership was considering the pursuit of Dene rights as a "basic human struggle" that also required Dene people to come to understand how "the Dene struggle affects the rights of others," particularly those who lived around them. The set of proposals ended with a commitment that "the Dene recognize that there are non-Dene who have come to live among the Dene and the Dene wish to be fair to them." The proposal further observed that "while Territorial Council and municipal councils are governments in the non-Dene tradition, the non-Dene have the right to evolve more democratic forms of institutions based on democracy and equality and the representation of the interests of the masses of non-Dene, not an elite." The Dene Nation thus invited the non-indigenous constituency of the Northwest Territories into its political domain, so long as those guests respected the political authority of the Dene.

In further promoting the idea that indigenous and non-indigenous demands and concepts were parallel rather than constitutively opposed to one another, others argued that aboriginal title actually dovetailed with concepts in "British law." Leroy Little Bear, a member of the Blood Indian Tribe in Alberta who had recently earned a law degree from the University of Utah, explained to the Berger Inquiry that the distinctiveness of Indian peoples' attachment to land was not so different from the principles underlying Anglo property rights. "An underlying premise of the British property system," pointed out Little Bear, "is that no one can own land in the same way that one can own a book." In both British and Indian legal systems, he suggested, ownership was "symbolic" since all individual estates could be traced back to the idea of the Crown in the British system, or to the Creator in the Indian worldview. In making such a comparison between founding traditions, Little Bear posited Indian and British "systems" as equivalent rather than as hierarchically ordered.[73]

Like other activists and intellectuals, Little Bear also pointed out the paradox of treaty-making by which governments claimed to have extinguished indigenous land rights. Indians never could have surrendered their land, he argued, since they did not ultimately own it. However, they could share their land with fellow beings according to terms "not unrelated to the concept of social contract that has been forwarded by some philosophers."[74] In working out the terms for how to "share" common lands, Little Bear and other leaders including Harold Cardinal, who also spoke to this idea in the hearings, gave weight to the importance of aboriginal title. To these leaders, the fleshing out of the concept was crucial, for it would enable the larger project of recognizing and establishing indigenous peoples' rights to peoplehood. Aboriginal title was not simply a distinct kind of property right but rather something that affirmed the profound sense of belonging that indigenous peoples had to their lands. If this sense of belonging was fully recognized by the state—and the settler public—then indigenous peoples could make a more meaningful claim to self-determination.

Dene assertions of nationhood made a considerable impact on Berger. He recognized in this assertion a challenge to the older social contract, which was premised in the forgetting of indigenous peoples and their claims. In his report, he argued that taking Dene claims to distinct peoplehood seriously required the negotiation of a new social contract in Canada. Picking up on the language of the Dene Declaration and the submissions of Manuel, Little Bear, and others he argued, "The native people of the North now insist that the settlement of native claims must be seen as a fundamental re-ordering of their relationship with the rest of us." The Dene had successfully persuaded Berger that they were entitled to recognition as a distinct people within the larger nation-state. "Their claims," he asserted, "must be seen as the means to establishing a social contract based on a clear understanding that they are distinct peoples in history."[75]

However, rethinking the social contract was not a priority for many local people. In "community hearings" that encouraged the participation of a wide a range of local people including hunters, trappers, community workers, and far more women than Morrow's circuit court had listened to, individuals raised more basic concerns. As pointed out by Phoebe Nahanni, director of Land Claims Research at the Indian Brotherhood, local people "have a lot of questions such as, who gives the leases to the people who are out there on the land doing drilling and moving around in helicopters and everything. They are concerned about the regulations, who draws up the regulations."[76] Revealing the gap between discussions of high political theory and social needs on the ground, an anonymous speaker, interrupting proceedings, put it like this:

> Poor people, I'm talking about, the trappers and hunters don't understand what the pipeline is about . . . the people that are living off the land, they don't understand a single thing even though there are people coming in there and having meetings. You know, they don't go to meetings, trappers–hunters don't go to meetings, they're living off their land, they got to think about next winter's stock feeding, next winter, you know, get ready preparing for the trapping.[77]

TASKED WITH EXAMINING how indigenous land and treaty rights might be recognized, commissions of inquiry in Canada and Australia in the 1970s went far beyond their remits. They began to broach questions of the relationship between distinct indigenous nations and the settler state. They did this in a number of ways. For instance, they fostered research into the histories of treaties that emphasized indigenous interpretations of those agreements. They identified how "traditional owners" of lands could prove their rights, processes that led to the creation of new archives concerning indigenous attachment to land. And they even created a platform for a nationwide discussion of what indigenous nationhood comprised and broached the question of what indigenous consent to incorporation into the settler state might entail.

These commissions, therefore, were different from their nineteenth-century predecessors. By engaging with and consulting indigenous peoples, commissioners showed how it might be possible to reconcile some indigenous demands with the ongoing sovereignty of the settler state. In effect, they modeled a kind of negotiation that could be emulated on a nationwide scale, as the prospect of a new social contract between settler and indigenous nations seemed necessary and even attainable.

However, these exciting possibilities did not include all indigenous peoples. The definition of traditional owners excluded those who could not make the mark because of how effectively they had been dispossessed. That definition also laid the ground for ongoing competition for the symbolically valuable status of "first peoples." Land rights processes created new assymetries of power and access to the redistribution of resources between indigenous groups vying for the benefits of recognition.

Furthermore, making real the idea of a new social contract was dependent on the political sympathy of the settler majority and their elected representatives in federal parliaments. Commissions of inquiry might make radical and far-reaching recommendations, but not all of those would be turned into legislation and policy. In the decades to come, changing political dynamics between federal and provincial or state governments, shifts in economic priorities, and the increasing power of mining corporations as well as debates about multiculturalism significantly impacted the negotiations between indigenous peoples and the state.

In Canada, the realization of a new social contract seemed possible and even likely. Provoked by the threat of Québécois secessionism, the Canadian government made a new constitution in 1982 that sought to balance various political interests. Indigenous leaders exerted extensive pressure to be included in constitutional negotiations, wanting to ensure that the rights of what were now being called "First Nations" were given explicit recognition. In late 1980, a prominent group of leaders including George Manuel mounted a new protest. Calling themselves the "Constitution Express," they traveled across the country by train from Vancouver to Ottawa and then on to the United Nations in New York to publicize their demands for constitutional recognition.[78] They had considerable success. Section 32 of the 1982 constitution did indeed recognize the "existing aboriginal and treaty rights of the aboriginal peoples of Canada." However, the actual scope of these rights— their "hidden strata of meaning"— was left up to the courts to decide.[79] This meant huge expenses in time and energy as well as finances for indigenous communities who had to continue to press for their rights in legal avenues. Other groups decided to take direct action. Opposing the expansion of a golf course and the building of luxury condominiums on their land, which had not been recognized as theirs by the state despite long protest, Mohawk people at Kanesatake led a seventy-eight-day stand-off in the summer of 1990, which received widespread media attention, nationally and internationally.[80]

In the wake of this protest, the federal government created a new nationwide Royal Commission on Aboriginal Peoples. Its 1996 report took up where the Berger Inquiry left off, considering what should be the terms of fair and honorable dealings between the state and First Nations. Its far-reaching recommendations were not fully implemented.[81]

In Australia, where native title was still not recognized across the continent following the Woodward commission, indigenous leaders continued to push for such through the 1980s. Finally, following the well-known finding by the high court in *Mabo v. Queensland (no. 2)* in 1992 that the Meriam Islander plaintiffs in the case did indeed continue to have native title rights, the Commonwealth parliament passed nationwide legislation. The *Native Title Act* (1993) was regarded as a revolution in Australian law. However, following the rigid definitions of "traditional owners" established by the Woodward commission, the *Native Title Act* required claimants to mount a high degree of proof in showing continuity of attachment to the land or waters under claim.[82] There have been notable successes and some high-profile failures of this test. As Yorta Yorta native title claimants in the southeast of the country found to their detriment, a failed claim had repercussions beyond the law. Their claim was dismissed in 1998 because they could not show continuity of attachment given the extensive settlement of their tribal lands in the nineteenth century. They were left feeling as though their identity as Aboriginal had been delegitimated.[83]

Outside the legal domain, Aboriginal activists pursued their quest for the making of a modern treaty that would give symbolic recognition of their status as first peoples and co-founders of the country. A treaty movement that included Yolngu leaders involved in the 1971 Gove land rights case gained considerable public support in the mid-1980s. In 1988, the year of the bicentenary celebrations, Labor Prime Minister Hawke committed to making one. He did not follow through on this promise, nor did his successors in parliament. In the 1990s, as was the case in Canada, the idea of reconciliation with indigenous peoples took precedence over formal political negotiations. A movement for the distinct constitutional recognition of Aboriginal peoples' rights continues today.[84]

5

Making a "Partnership between Races"

MAORI ACTIVISM AND THE TREATY OF WAITANGI

A landless Maori is a lost Maori.
—PROTEST POSTER, *1970s*

THIRTY-YEAR-OLD PROTESTOR HANA JACKSON stood behind a leading politician at the annual celebration of the Treaty of Waitangi in northern New Zealand on 6 February 1971, dressed in a Victorian mourning skirt and coat with a bodice woven in Maori design and carrying a black parasol. As the politician, Robert Muldoon, addressed the official attendees, she clapped, slowly and mockingly. Behind her, other members of the protest group Nga Tamatoa (the Young Warriors) chanted, "Shame! Shame!" while police wrestled Jackson off the ceremonial grounds.[1] Jackson performed what Nga Tamatoa had declared: the day was one of mourning not celebration. Officially, the treaty (signed in 1840) was being commemorated by the settler state as the founding of a unified nation. Nga Tamatoa challenged the myth of racial harmony that the treaty symbolized and the idea of nationhood that it commemorated.

At the same time that indigenous activists in Canada and Australia were confronting the settler state, Nga Tamatoa pushed their claims of injustice to the forefront of national debate. This was a critical moment in the history of the Commonwealth settler states, and all the more so for New Zealand. The country's dissolving economic ties to Britain had a greater effect on New Zealand's primary agricultural export market than was the case for Australia and Canada, and it provoked a rethinking of cultural ties. In a moment of national uncertainty, settler leaders sought to assert an independent identity by reenacting a mythical founding moment: the signing of the Treaty of Waitangi.

The representation of this event in nationalist terms was quite distinct from the ways in which indigenous peoples were represented in, or erased from, the founding stories of Canada and Australia at the time. Official celebration of the Treaty of Waitangi was unlike the marginalization of treaties with Indian groups from national discourse in Canada by the late 1960s. Whereas in Australia Aboriginal people were excluded from the national memory, in New Zealand, Maori protested not how they had been forgotten but how they were being incorporated by the state as symbolic co-founders.

Celebrations of the treaty, Maori activists argued, glossed over what they had lost as a consequence of settler colonization and the wrongs committed against their people. Celebratory nationalism emphasized the good relations between Maori and Pakeha (white settlers) and foregrounded a benign story of colonization. It ignored the dispossession of land and culture that Maori had suffered and the contemporary racism to which they were subject. Young protestors demanded redress.

Over two decades, from the emergence of new "treaty activism" in the late 1960s to the return to the courts by leaders in the 1987 "Lands case," Maori radically shifted the terms of their representation. Regarded as co-founders in celebrations of the treaty, they were nonetheless subject to policies of assimilation, which activists viewed as hastening the loss of culture and language. Activists wanted to bring the policy of assimilation to an end and expose the hypocrisy of official discourse about racial harmony. Using an argument akin to that of "citizens plus" for the right to maintain their distinctive identity, Maori established themselves as "first among equals."[2] By the end of the 1980s, Maori were being recognized as coeval treaty "partners," and the Treaty itself had gained constitutional significance beyond a symbolic story of origins. Maori language was officially recognized. Using the symbolic cachet of the Treaty of Waitangi, Maori activists forced settler power-holders to enter into a new set of negotiations with them.

SYMBOLIC PROTESTS AT the official celebration of the signing of the Treaty of Waitangi are now an anticipated part of Waitangi Day, which was made a national public holiday in 1974. In 1971, Nga Tamatoa's protest was novel in local and global terms. Influenced by global activism for national liberation, including that of Black Power in the United States, these young activists argued against policies of assimilation that would make them equal citizens. While they protested racial discrimination, like indigenous activists in Canada and Australia, they did not see the attainment of civil rights as the answer to the unique problems they faced.[3]

Referring in particular to anti-Vietnam War and anti-Apartheid protests, activists in New Zealand exposed the contradictions in official discourse. Being represented as co-founders of a homogeneous and harmonious nation concealed how Maori had been dispossessed as a consequence of large-scale wars in the nineteenth century and ongoing state actions in the twentieth century. Symbolically incorporated as museum pieces, young activists protested how they were being further dispossessed of culture and language through the policy of assimilation.

In a context of rapid demographic change in the post–World War II period, Pakeha policymakers insisted on the importance of full integration of the Maori minority into wider New Zealand society, just as those in Australia and Canada did for their indigenous populations. In New Zealand, this entailed doing away with various legal distinctions—termed a policy of "amalgamation" by the historian Alan Ward—that had been imposed on Maori by the nineteenth-century settler state purportedly for a temporary period but that had lasted into the twentieth century. Those distinctions, including a separate electoral roll and land title system, had come to shore up a sense among Maori of their racial and cultural difference.[4]

Between 1945 and 1966, the Maori population underwent two significant demographic shifts. The mortality rate declined and the growth rate of the population climbed exponentially, doubling that of non-Maori, at around 4 percent. By 1966, there were around 255,000 people of Maori descent, 8 percent of the total population (by 1996, the number of people claiming Maori descent had increased to over 500,000 or about 14 percent of the total population). This young population was also rapidly urbanizing.[5] In 1945, 75 percent of the Maori population lived in rural areas; by 1966, 60 percent were urban-based, drawn to the cities by state-sponsored programs, although many maintained rural ties.[6] In cities, they often faced informal segregation in housing and frequent racism. Some critical commentators saw this as a structural problem, akin to the structural disenfranchisement suffered by black Americans.[7]

Government policymakers did not address racism and inequality but instead advocated assimilationist policies that envisaged the ultimate dissolution of Maori identity into a hybrid but unitary New Zealandness. The "problem" was considered to be a Maori one of lagging behind rather than one of structural exclusion. In 1961, a report written about the Department of Maori Affairs advocated the integration of Maori people into a "modern way of life." Known as the Hunn Report after its author, it endorsed the Department of Maori Affairs' policy of "pepper-potting," or dispersing individual Maori families among those of Pakeha in the suburbs. Such might result in the "combining" of Maori and Pakeha in order to "form one nation wherein Maori culture remains distinct," as J. K. Hunn wrote in the report.[8] Like Trudeau and the compilers of the White Paper in Canada, Hunn argued for a kind of equality for individual Maori citizens that presumed the eradication of differences and downplayed the importance of tribal and collective identity.[9]

In rural areas, Maori faced renewed threats to their lands as policymakers pursued further reforms. In 1967, the incumbent National (conservative) government passed the Maori Affairs Amendment Act. The legislation was meant to make "better use" of the small amount of rural lands still in Maori hands, which by the late 1960s was less than 5 percent of the original land base. The legislation made it easier for the government to compulsorily acquire land known as "Maori freehold" that was held by Maori owners but considered by state authorities to be under-utilized. It was promoted by Minister of Maori Affairs J. R. Hanan as a "progressive reform" that was based on a proposition of equality. The legislation would, he claimed, remove "many of the barriers dividing our two people."[10]

Maori leaders and intellectuals immediately demanded repeal of the 1967 amendment. Deeply concerned that it threatened the small amount of land remaining in Maori hands, protestors dubbed the act the "last land grab." The rhetoric referred both to the paucity of remaining Maori land and the wars of the 1860s which, in the 1960s, were usually referred to as the "Maori wars" or the "Land wars." The nineteenth-century wars were provoked, in the first instance, by highly controversial land purchases and the efforts of some tribes and pan-tribal organizations (notably, the "Kingitanga" or King Movement) to halt the sale of land to the Crown. The settler government eventually won out, although only with the aid of imperial troops. As a punishment, it confiscated huge areas of tribal lands, even from those who had not fought against the colony.[11] Tribes also lost landholdings through a specially designed Native Land Court that began operating in 1865. By 1900, more than 60 million acres of Maori land had been confiscated or sold, and by 1920, Maori holdings were less than 5 million acres.[12] The use of "last land grab" therefore sent a warning to the government: Maori would not allow any further forced appropriation of their remaining lands.

Criticism of the legislation concerned the process by which it had been drawn up, as well as the outcome. Maori leaders were particularly incensed that the government had passed the act despite trenchant criticism from Maori organizations. As stated shortly afterward to the parliamentary Maori Affairs Committee by one of several provincial organizations that represented local Maori concerns to government, "It is surely preferable that development should proceed with the co-operation and goodwill of the Maori people, rather than be rammed down their throats against their passive or active objection."[13]

In arguing for direct consultation about matters of importance to their communities, Maori leaders reasserted the fact that in crucial ways their political distinctiveness and not just their symbolic role as founders had been affirmed by the colonial state. Notably, they believed the Treaty of Waitangi recognized some kind of ongoing Maori authority as well as providing them the rights of British subjects. Furthermore, despite the considerable undermining of and direct attack on tribal autonomy from the 1850s onward, the settler state was not able to entirely absorb Maori people into its realm. As was the case in Australia and Canada, administrative distinctions imposed by the settler state did marginalize Maori people in some serious ways but they also provided a basis for reclaiming distinct rights in the late twentieth century.

While older leaders in traditional areas were focused on the economic problems related to land loss, young activists saw in the opposition to the amendment act an opportunity to make a larger protest about the majority's complacent attitude toward the Maori minority. They addressed the question of national identity symbolized in official celebration of the treaty. Writing in the left-wing journal *Comment* in early 1968 to mark Waitangi Day, Koro Dewes, a Maori student activist, was forthright. The proposed land reform, he argued, showed that the treaty was not "worth the paper it is written on." Since the treaty had never been ratified, Dewes argued that the colonial imperative in drawing it up was "from the beginning to *annex* New Zealand; that consultation with the Maori chiefs was to pacify both them and the humanitarian elements in England and in New Zealand." Dewes argued that Maori had always contested the Crown's monopoly of power to define Maori customary practices such as land ownership and succession. He demanded that New Zealand recognize the "bi-racial" constitution of its history in terms of ongoing contestation between Maori and the state.[14]

Like activists in Canada, spokespeople such as Dewes used the symbolic cachet of the treaty to draw attention to the dispossession and social alienation of Maori people, although in different terms. Whereas Cree activist Harold Cardinal located treaty-making in an idealized political time of good faith negotiation in order to critique Trudeau's "just society," Dewes and other activists argued that the Treaty of Waitangi was a "fraud."[15] This interpretation contested official representations of the treaty. A constant feature of the official celebrations, as one historian has put it, was the "legendary good relationship between Maori and Pakeha. . . . The common theme was the forming of one nation from the partnership of two races."[16] The theme of unification was commonly associated with the apocryphal saying attributed to Lieutenant Hobson, the representative of the British Crown in 1840, as he shook hands with the signatories, "he iwi kotahi tatou" (now we are one people). Such nationalism was given a favorable gloss by some scholars.[17]

These arguments did not sit well with young, university-educated Maori, who were self-conscious of what they did not have access to in cultural terms. This sense of alienation from their own traditions, scholars have argued, drove the formation of Nga Tamatoa in 1970 after a Young Maori Leaders conference held at the University of Auckland.[18] As well as protesting at the official treaty celebrations, they wanted recognition of the Maori language. In 1972, they brought a petition to the steps of the New Zealand parliament in Wellington, signed by 30,000 people, which demanded that Maori language be taught in schools.[19] Following this protest, one of the activists, Tame Iti (whose first language was Maori), established the first "tent embassy" on parliament grounds, taking his cue from the Aboriginal protestors encamped at parliament in Canberra. Like Aborigines, Iti later recalled, Maori felt like "foreigners" in their own land.[20]

The next step for young activists was forging a connection with the rural and traditional leaders around issues of common concern. This was not straightforward. Many Maori elders were critical of the young activists who, they believed, did not properly understand Maori cultural practices and protocols and were rude to Pakeha elites. Activists thought that many elders were too polite, and talked endlessly about problems rather than finding solutions to them.[21]

Like activists in Australia and Canada, those in New Zealand drew together issues of land rights and identity to protest what they had lost and to forge connections between rural and urban leaders. As one protest poster put it, "A landless Maori is a lost Maori."[22] Slogans such as these intimated what needed to be done: young urban Maori could find themselves in their rural ancestral homelands and begin to fight alongside their elders for land rights.

The full effect of this new-forged solidarity was felt in 1975 when older, Maori leaders and young activists joined forces on a nationwide "Land March." Early in the year, Maori leaders formed an organization to lead a land march to parliament, along the lines of the "Trail of Broken Treaties" undertaken by Native American activists in the United States in 1972. Their cause was the retention of the last remaining lands in Maori hands and redress for dispossession. According to one historian, "Setting up Te Matakite [the Land

March organization] was practically as great a feat as the march itself. It was a synergy of old and new ideologies and methods, which unified a range of groups and interests: kuia, kaumātua [female and male elders] and rangatahi [youth], young urban activists and older conservative traditionalists."[23] On 14 September 1975, the first day of the recently established Maori language week, the march left Te Hapua in the far north and began to wend its way down the length of the North Island to parliament, about 700 miles away. Led by a northern elder, Whina Cooper, and her granddaughter, marchers used the slogan, "Not One More Acre." The small core of walkers was joined at different moments by up to 40,000 supporters.

The march was highly publicized and demonstrated how widespread the discontent was among Maori people. Young leaders, including Joe Hawke who would later lead the longest running land occupation in Auckland city in 1977, took on prominent roles. Once they reached parliament grounds, the marchers presented a "Memorial of Rights," signed by 60,000 people, insisting that no further legislation be passed alienating or confiscating Maori land and demanding the repeal of previous legislation that enabled such. The memorial complained of the injustices suffered by the Maori people, and it set the expectation that Maori assent to laws affecting them should be sought as a matter of due process.[24] A small group of activists erected the second tent embassy on parliament grounds. This time, an Aboriginal delegation from the tent embassy at Canberra visited the Maori protestors.[25]

Although the Memorial of Rights did not explicitly mention the creation of an institution to investigate Maori grievances, the Land March was timed to put pressure on the government to do so. The Labor government was considering the Treaty of Waitangi bill, which would establish a tribunal to investigate grievances stemming from promises made in the treaty. This was the first time that a nationwide commission of inquiry had been seriously discussed in the country's parliament. Debates around the bill and proposed tribunal raised a number of issues that were also discussed in relation to commissions of inquiry in Australia and Canada. Were those involved in the bill's passage moved by moral claims of injustice, and what did they think could be done about that? What was feasible in terms of redress? What would the electorate support? What could actually be proved in evidentiary terms? Finally, would Maori demands for securing their political assent to changes affecting them actually be met?

THE TREATY OF Waitangi bill had first been introduced to parliament by Minister of Maori Affairs Matiu Rata at the end of 1974. Like Whina Cooper, Rata hailed from the far north, and he had been elected on a Labour ticket as the member for Northern Maori in 1972. Previously a trade union official, Rata made significant changes to the Maori Affairs Amendment act of 1967 and he organized the return of some Crown land to Maori tribes, although he did not publicize this work for fear of a Pakeha backlash.[26]

The system of separate electoral Maori seats was a colonial invention, part of the nineteenth-century policy of amalgamation. Created in 1867, the electorate, which was represented by four "Maori seats," was intended to be a temporary measure to bring Maori into the settler political process in the aftermath of the New Zealand wars.[27] The Maori seats enabled Maori men who were otherwise excluded from the national franchise because of the property qualifications but who were nonetheless taxpayers to vote in general elections (Maori women gained the vote in 1893, along with settler women). In 1876, the electoral provisions were extended indefinitely and the Maori electorate continues to this day, despite criticisms from some that it permits a racial separatism in the country.[28] Maori politicians holding these seats had access to political power that indigenous leaders in Australia and Canada did not. To outsiders, including indigenous leaders and intellectuals, this system was worth emulating. George Manuel, for instance, thought that the existence of the Maori seats helped to explain why Maori people were better off than Canada's Indians.[29]

Rata's attempt to have Maori grievances redressed by parliament were supported by some of his new Labour colleagues. In its 1972 election campaign, Labour had used the slogan "It's Time"—the party had been out of office for twelve years—and it took up popular causes of the moment. Labour leader Norman Kirk, like his contemporary Gough Whitlam in Australia, wanted to pursue new relationships with African and Asian nations. He opposed sporting links with South Africa, and he promised to reform Maori land law.

In fact, politicians on both sides of the house acknowledged that Maori people had suffered injustices. However, Rata's proposed bill provoked considerable debate about how historical grievances could be ascertained with any certainty and whether new grievances might be created in the process of redressing the old. The debate was as fierce within the Labour caucus as across the benches.[30] Minister of Forests Colin Moyle, whose area of concern would likely be most affected by historical claims considering that substantial land confiscated from Maori tribes had been turned into state-owned forests, admitted that there were "undoubted injustices to the Maori people that occurred in the last century." Much of state forest land, he pointed out, "must necessarily have been acquired by a Crown action inconsistent with the principles of the treaty and that Maoris have been prejudicially affected."

However, Moyle also warned of "the very real difficulties, if not impossibility in some cases, of determining what actually happened in any of these past actions," and he worried about the "loss of certainty in legal relationships and the inequity to parties who have made their contract within the existing law."[31] Concerns about fairness to all parties, past and present, were magnified in cabinet meetings. Rata offered a compromise: the legislation could refer back to Crown actions since 1900 for which, he assured his colleagues, "there are ample records and evidence."[32]

The Labour government held power only for one term and it was voted out of office shortly after the Land March arrived on parliament's steps. With the groundswell of support for the marchers, the new National (conservative) government decided to implement a version of Rata's plan. The Treaty of Waitangi Act (1975) established what was commonly referred to as the Waitangi Tribunal, which could "make recommendations on claims relating to the practical application of the principles of the Treaty" (preamble), "determine [the] meaning and effect" of treaty principles (s. 5), and determine whether a claim showed Crown acts or omissions to be inconsistent with those principles (s. 6). Notably, the second sentence of the preamble emphasized the difference in meaning between the English and Maori texts of the treaty. Like the commissions of inquiry in Canada and Australia, the Waitangi Tribunal was not awarded binding powers.[33] Despite Rata's extensive efforts, the tribunal was not enabled to inquire into claims that related to events prior to the passage of the act and was limited to what occurred after 1975. The extensive grievances about land and resource loss would not be addressed. For its first few years, the tribunal was effectively moribund. As one historian put it, the tribunal "was not expected to hear many claims, to meet often or to cost much."[34]

The first case the tribunal heard concerned customary fishing rights in Auckland, New Zealand's largest city. It was brought by Joe Hawke of the Ngati Whatua tribe, who was at the time also leading a long-term land occupation of land the tribe claimed as theirs in central Auckland and that was slated for a high-income housing development. The tribunal dismissed the claim, having convened in the ballroom of a large hotel in downtown Auckland to hear the evidence. This was an entirely inappropriate venue as David Williams, a white anti-racist activist, academic, and lawyer who was working for Ngati Whatua, pointed out to the minister of Maori Affairs afterward. Williams recommended that any future hearings be held on a marae (tribal meeting place) or at least in a community hall and that the tribunal encourage the use of the Maori language. "There should, at least, be a short mihi [greeting and introduction] before a hearing commences," he argued. "Waitangi should be pronounced according to the Maori manner."[35] Williams's suggestions for introducing more Maori cultural practices into tribunal hearings went unheeded for the time being.

In the late 1970s, the National government began to undertake large development projects under a policy framework known as "Think Big." These included building hydroelectric stations that affected many of the waterways where more remote Maori communities were located. With their resources threatened anew, Maori leaders sought out legal recognition of their rights and began to bring more claims about present-day grievances to the tribunal. New claims made in the early 1980s were well received by the new chairperson of the tribunal, Edward (Eddie) Taihakurei Durie, who was also appointed as chief judge of the Maori Land Court in 1979. Under his leadership, the revived tribunal began to issue important and politically astute recommendations on present-day issues to wide public acclaim. These mostly concerned the effects of development schemes such as sewage plants on rivers and the ocean foreshore that were of economic and cultural significance to local tribes.

Durie was born on 18 January 1940, just a few days shy of the centenary celebration of the signing of the Treaty of Waitangi, as he has subsequently pointed out. The first Maori to be appointed chief judge, he became one of the central figures in transforming the Waitangi Tribunal in the 1980s and developing the conceptual and practical implications of an official policy of biculturalism in New Zealand. Durie grew up in rural Manawatu, in the central North Island of New Zealand, and is affiliated with several tribes in that area including Ngati Kauwhata and Rangitane. After studying law at Victoria University of Wellington in the early 1960s alongside a few other Maori students, several of whom went on to become prominent leaders, Durie clerked and then took up private practice in Tauranga. He admitted to mostly avoiding Maori clients at that time since he thought they never seemed to pay, but he did take some cases about Maori land title disputes and tried to secure loans for a Maori-led kiwifruit initiative in the early 1970s that would supply new markets in Japan.[36]

In 1974, Matiu Rata approached Durie to accept an appointment as a judge on the Maori Land Court. Durie recalled feeling quite ambivalent about the offer, since judge's salaries at the time were much lower than what could be earned even in small-town private practice. However, the effects of the global oil crisis were beginning to be felt and he worried that lean times might be ahead. Rata, a "total visionary" according to Durie, wanted to overhaul the court and turn it from a colonial institution premised in the rule of the "great white father" to something more responsive to Maori needs. Rata had already established Maori Land Boards that were carrying out some interesting research into land dispossession, despite the assertions of government ministers that historical grievances could not be accurately evidenced. Durie was persuaded that he should take the job and began as a judge in Rotorua.[37]

If Rata awakened an idealistic streak in Durie, it was one also born from formative racial experiences at a young age. In an interview in 2001, Durie recounted an early childhood memory of attending a hearing at the Native (now Maori) Land Court with his grandmother about a block of land that had been sold without her knowledge. A senior and well-respected woman in her community, she was abused by the judge and told never to set foot inside the court again. Durie recalled feeling her humiliation "all through me and I felt so angry with that chap on the bench there."[38] And in his work as a lawyer he became critically attuned to the resignation of some Maori plaintiffs who were used to the "all-wise and all-knowing" Pakeha judges who told Maori applicants what "the best thing to do" was so that they "had come to expect that."[39]

While rejecting the label of activist in talking about his work, Durie undertook extensive reforms as a judge. He was particularly motivated to make the land court more hospitable to Maori practices and understandings, for which he drew on international innovation and local precedent, including the community hearings of the Mackenzie Valley Pipeline Inquiry in the Northwest Territories which he had visited in person. Once Durie took over the reins of the Waitangi Tribunal in 1980, he established new protocols that were intended to help Maori claimants feel more comfortable with the process of inquiry.

Durie relocated hearings of Maori evidence to tribal marae (meeting places), and permitted Maori witnesses to speak in the Maori language providing there was a translator available. Witnesses were not necessarily sworn in. Both the location of hearings on marae—urban and rural—and the use of Maori language are now standard practice in tribunal hearings. In fact, there was already an extensive legal precedent in New Zealand for the admission and evaluation of Maori histories, particularly in evidence of land tenure in land court hearings, which made the country's legal history quite distinct from that of Australia.

Outside the formal process of addressing Maori grievances in the late 1970s, young Maori activists used tactics of civil disobedience and at times violence to draw attention to continued racism. When white engineering students at the University of Auckland dressed in grass skirts and performed a mock haka (dance) in 1979, a group of Maori and Pacific Islanders who called themselves He Taua (the war party) interrupted the show. Some of the students laid complaints with the police that they had been assaulted, and members of He Taua were later charged.[40] Then, in 1981, much to the anger of anti-Apartheid activists and others, the South African "Springbok" rugby team toured New Zealand despite the international boycott against them.[41] The tour provoked large and violent protests around New Zealand and brought increasing attention to racism within the country.[42]

In the volatile environment of the early 1980s some Maori leaders argued that reconciliation premised on the acknowledgment and redress of Maori historical grievances was an imperative for stabilizing New Zealand society. In 1980, the Member of Parliament for Southern Maori who was a member of the Labour party in opposition, Whetu Tiraketene-Sullivan, sponsored a Treaty of Waitangi Reconciliation Charter Bill that would ensure the return of Maori land that had been compulsorily taken and provide for historical claims.[43] Toward the end of 1981, after the Springbok Tour protests, Durie began to press the Minister of Maori Affairs for a commitment to the resolution of what he called "Maori grievances." Stressing that the tribunal must begin investigating historical claims, he rejected other demands for stronger, judicial-type decision-making powers. "The significance of the Treaty of Waitangi for many Maori," he wrote, "and the emphasis that they would place upon it, should not be understated. It would be bad however if it were now to be used to put us all in a bind."[44]

Durie and the many others protesting the tribunal's disempowerment had to wait until 1985 for a significant expansion of the tribunal's jurisdiction and operation. By then, the incumbent National government had lost office, replaced by the fourth Labour government, under the charismatic leadership of Prime Minister David Lange. Soon after the election, the minister of Maori Affairs and the Crown Law Office went to work amending the Treaty of Waitangi Act and a bill was introduced to the House of Representatives at the end of 1984. This included a provision to extend the tribunal's jurisdiction retrospectively so that it could investigate claims going back to 1840. Government ministers attended a national hui (meeting) on Waitangi Day in 1985, to discuss the proposals with Maori leaders and organizations.

As was the case with commissions of inquiry in Canada and Australia in the mid-1970s, Maori leaders in 1985 recognized this as a moment to exert pressure on the government for institutional change. They demanded that the Waitangi Tribunal be given the power to make binding recommendations and made a range of demands about Maori representation: that the chief judge of the Maori Land Court, and hence chairperson of the tribunal, be of Maori descent by law; that there be a Maori member at all hearings; and that at least 50 percent of tribunal and staff be Maori women. Maori leaders demanded that the Treaty of Waitangi be recognized constitutionally, and they emphasized that it provided both for Maori self-determination and a partnership between "Maori and the Crown."[45]

Others, however, viewed the demands of Maori leaders as unreasonable because they were premised in racial preference. In one submission on the bill, P. J. Southern, on behalf of "70 NZ born citizens in Ponsonby and Grey Lynn [neighborhoods in Auckland]" disavowed the historic rights that Maori leaders and activists had been claiming and went on to "emphatically reject the notion that present-generation Maoris are entitled to special rights simply because their ancestors (not themselves) lived in New Zealand during the 17th–18th centuries [*sic*]."[46] The charge that the Waitangi Tribunal furthered a system of "apartheid" in New Zealand was frequently made at this time.

This opposition notwithstanding, the Treaty of Waitangi Amendment Act was passed in 1985 and the tribunal was finally provided retrospective jurisdiction. The extension of the tribunal's jurisdiction to include historical grievances was more the consequence of moral and political pressure than a forensic argument for historical evidence. Whereas politicians in the 1970s had expressed concerns about whether the tribunal could find out what "actually happened" in the past, by the 1980s, the investigation of historical grievances seemed imperative to offering some kind of racial conciliation in the present. Changes in procedural norms were also important in gaining the support of Maori themselves, who were beginning to see the tribunal as a place more hospitable to their cultural protocols as well as their needs.

The amendment increased the number of tribunal members to seven including the chairperson, at least four of whom were to be Maori, and it provided for the establishment of an office that would register claims, commission research, and hire counsel. There are now up to sixteen members of the tribunal at any one time, appointed on the recommendation of the minister of Maori Affairs in consultation with the minister of Justice but there are no requirements as to the number of Maori and non-Maori members.

Maarire Goodall, the first director of the tribunal's office appointed in 1986, recalled the heady period following the expansion of the tribunal's jurisdiction and its research capacities. The work involved in setting up the tribunal office ran the gamut from relocating archival files from the Department of Maori Affairs, appointing junior research officers, and negotiating budgets, to strategizing about the tribunal's wider public importance. Goodall was determined to ensure that the tribunal would win the respect and under-standing of government departments, ministers, and the general population. With a number of supporters Goodall formed what he described as an "invis-ible army . . . approving, supporting, advising, and defending" the tribunal. That "army" spent time and energy speaking about the tribunal process to a broad range of interest groups including lawyers' associations, engineering societies, and Returned Servicemen Associations, as well visiting schools and universities and providing commentary to the press. As Goodall reiterated, the tribunal's success depended on affecting the "climate of opinion."[47]

A large part of this work of explaining the tribunal's work to the public was demonstrating the importance of the activist demand that New Zealand had a "bi-racial" history. Tribunal reports emphasized that the nation was constituted in the relationship—conflictual and otherwise—between the two parties to the Treaty of Waitangi, Maori chiefs and the British Crown.[48] As Goodall emphasized, "the Tribunal by definition has to be bicultural, bi-historical, bi-legal."[49] This meant that the tribunal attributed considerable weight to Maori protocols, customary practices, and cultural concepts, both in proceedings and in its reports.

Indeed, in the late 1980s the tribunal became a central institution for the development of biculturalism, an official policy in New Zealand created by the Labour government. The policy was given legislative authority, for in-stance, when a law commission established in 1985 to review and make rec-ommendations on New Zealand law was to take "into account te ao Maori (the Maori dimension)" and the "multicultural character of New Zealand society."[50]

Biculturalism is distinct from its better-known cousin, multiculturalism, in the New Zealand context. It gives primacy to Maori "values and perspec-tives" in matters of policymaking, especially around issues of culture and lan-guage. In the vein of "citizens plus" it recognizes that Maori have a distinct status as founding peoples and are entitled to distinct rights. They are "first among equals."[51] As Goodall's comment attests, in the tribunal setting, "bi-culturalism" entailed recognizing two different (yet founding) histories in New Zealand, and the operation of two different systems of law—bases for the recognition of distinct nationhood. This political meaning of "bicultur-alism" emerged from the discussions of the meaning of the treaty in the 1970s, particularly as more attention was paid to the difference between the Maori and English language texts than had been done in the past. Activists began to look more closely at the Maori version, which guaranteed the retention of "rangatiratanga" or chiefly authority.

Discussion about the historical interpretation of the treaty documents was provoked by the publication of a scholarly article by historian Ruth Ross in 1972. Making explicit references to present-day claims to land and fishing rights, Ross examined the problems and the politics of the translation of the English-language treaty into a Maori text at the time of the treaty's signing in 1840. In Ross's opinion, although the treaty acknowledged Maori tribes' political authority and their land rights, it was "hastily and inexpertly drawn up, ambiguous and contradictory in content, chaotic in its execution."[52]

In the English version of the treaty text, Maori ceded their sovereignty to the British Crown, retained their "full exclusive and undisturbed possession" of their lands and resources, and became British subjects. In the Maori version, tribes retained their "rangatiratanga" or chieftainship, referred to elsewhere as their "mana" or political authority and power, and ceded governorship (translated via the neologism "kawanatanga," which had little significance for the chiefs). Both versions made it clear that by recognizing the authority of Queen Victoria they would become British subjects, and many chiefs hoped that this would further secure their rights to trade in imperial networks in which they had become extensively involved.[53] Following the precedent established in the 1763 proclamation in North America, the British Crown acquired for itself the right of preemption, that is, it became the sole purchaser of Maori land.[54]

Ross was the first scholar to examine in depth the history of the (mis) translation of the treaty carried out by the prominent missionary Henry Williams and his son, both of whom also had extensive land interests in the north. "Even if the treaty were all that Williams claimed it to be," she pointed out, "it does not seem from his own account that this was something which those who had signed it could perceive for themselves." Five years before the Treaty of Waitangi had been signed, a confederation of northern chiefs had, at the suggestion of the British resident James Busby, issued a Declaration of Independence that had been recognized by the British Colonial Office. In it, the notion of sovereignty was translated by the much stronger terms of "mana" and "rangatiratanga." The use of the weaker term, "kawanatanga" in the treaty seemed designed to mitigate against the signatories understanding the full intent of their cession of sovereignty and the terms of Crown preemption.

Ross's argument made an immediate impact and was quickly taken up by activists and circulated in government departments.[55] It added weight to the depiction of the treaty as a "fraud." However, rather than delegitimating the treaty entirely, Ross's argument about the Maori text was used by activists as leverage to argue for their ongoing "rangatiratanga" over their lands, forests, and fisheries. The historical politics of translation laid bare in Ross's analysis of the treaty texts guided arguments by Maori activists for self-determination, or as some put it, "Maori sovereignty." Some argued for separate authority and imagined a distinct Maori state, recalling political arguments and innovations in nineteenth-century Maori history. Others saw their ongoing rangatiratanga as a constitutional matter for the existing state. They demanded that their language, culture, and ways of life on the land should be respected and even protected, not simply because the settler state valued diversity but because such protection was constituted in the recognition of Maori "rangatiratanga."[56]

The difference between the two texts was also made a matter for tribunal investigation. The preamble to the 1975 Treaty of Waitangi Act observed that "the text of the Treaty in the English language differs from the text of the Treaty in the Maori language." The act also tasked the tribunal with determining the "meaning and effect" of treaty "principles" by which Crown actions that negatively affected Maori could be measured.[57] Thus, like the Indian Claims Commission in Canada, the tribunal was given the task of treaty interpretation. The issue of linguistic translation became one of conceptual translation into legal and political terms. Indeed, in the case of the Waitangi Tribunal, the clause enabled an unexpectedly radical rethinking of New Zealand's political constitution in the 1980s.

The first principle defined by the tribunal was that that the Crown and Maori were in a "partnership" that acknowledged the ongoing political authority of Maori people, mainly as they were represented by tribal leaders. The second was that the Crown was obliged to "protect" Maori interests and identity.[58] Crucially, Durie recognized that the principles had to be given practical effect. By turning the tribunal into an institution that Maori felt comfortable in, Durie demonstrated *how* the political negotiation key to a "partnership" might be conducted. Further, he showed that a state-funded institution like the tribunal could be a place in which Maori practices were protected and could thrive.

The tribunal also developed a distinctive method of treaty interpretation in its early reports that showed how principles gained meaning in practice. Notably, it drew on legal practice concerning the interpretation of international treaties. This was a critical move, since it demonstrated that the tribunal considered the Treaty of Waitangi to be an international agreement. Referring to the British legal scholar Lord McNair's work on treaty interpretation, the tribunal argued that in the event of ambiguity, treaty provisions should be interpreted broadly, "in light of the surrounding circumstances."[59] The tribunal also referred on several occasions to the *contra proferentum* rule, which establishes that ambiguous clauses in international treaties be construed a-gainst the drafters.[60]

The tribunal therefore gave "considerable weight" to the Maori version of the treaty, which made sense since most Maori chiefs had signed this version.[61] This was not simply a historical claim, however. To some degree, the tribunal's approach to took the lead of Maori activists who had emphasized the importance of the Maori version, particularly the guarantee of their ongoing rangatiratanga, in order to recuperate historical recognition of their political authority. Rather than considering the Maori version an inadequate translation of the English, Maori activists read the English version as a misrepresentation of what Maori chiefs had understood in agreeing to the treaty's terms. The Maori version was, according to this interpretation, the authentic and even original account.

However, the tribunal was careful in the early reports to argue for the importance of both texts. Although it gave weight to the Maori version, it would not always privilege it. Nor would the tribunal argue for or recommend political separation. According to article three in both texts, the tribunal emphasized, Maori had become British subjects. Rather, it interpreted the Maori version of the treaty and the guarantee of continued rangatiratanga as a limit on Crown power as well as an opportunity for political dialogue and enforcing consultation.[62] But how would recognizing Maori political authority actually change, in any significant sense, how state power was conceived and exercised? Despite the increasing references to the Treaty of Waitangi and to Maori culture and language in government policy and political debate in New Zealand in the 1980s, the treaty itself was not ratified by the New Zealand parliament—that is, made into law; nor has it been since.

HOW MUCH POWER Maori had in directing state policy came to have real and immediate importance in 1986, when the Labour government began a radical experiment restructuring the domestic economy. Proposing to turn state assets, including forestries and coal mines, the delivery of electricity, the national postal service, and the telephone company, into corporations, the government turned a highly protected economy into a very open one. In the State-Owned Enterprises bill, it sought to privatize assets affecting 52 percent of the land area of New Zealand, worth NZ$11.1 billion, and employing more than 10,000 workers. The bill also affected lands and resources that could potentially be used for the redress of Maori grievances. Part of a raft of reforms that came to be known as "Rogernomics," after Minister of Finance Roger Douglas, the reforms went beyond those taking place in the United States and the United Kingdom in a similar period. They made the New Zealand economy highly vulnerable, but the Labour government promoted its far-reaching economic changes as increasing the "efficiency" of the market and the delivery of state services, and thereby enabling a new kind of "equity" in New Zealand.[63]

When the State-Owned Enterprises bill came before parliament in 1986, the Waitangi Tribunal was sitting to hear the Muriwhenua fisheries claim in the far north. The claim was led by Matiu Rata, who was no longer in parliament. Concerned that land and other resources, including access to commercial fisheries that was the subject of this claim, would be privatized before the tribunal could make recommendations, the body sprang into action and issued an interim report on the bill. "The honour of the Crown is at stake," avowed the tribunal. "We think it inconsistent with the principles of the Treaty of Waitangi that the particular relationship of the Maori and the Crown should in any way be diminished, or even threated with compromise. We do not think in particular that the Crown should dispose of lands that are the subject of claims and risk thereby some prejudice to the Claimants' position."[64]

In response to the tribunal's objections, the government added two clauses. One stipulated, "Nothing in this Act shall permit the Crown to act in a manner that is inconsistent with the principles of the Treaty of Waitangi." Another provided that land under a claim already submitted to the Waitangi Tribunal on or before the passage of the act would continue to be subject to that claim, and therefore the registrar of land titles would not be able to issue title for it. On 16 December 1986, a week after the interim report, the government passed the State-Owned Enterprises Act with the new sections added.

However, the act did not clarify which actions would be considered inconsistent with the principles of the treaty—especially since those principles had neither been defined statutorily nor in the common law. Of greatest concern to Maori leaders, the legislation did not explain what would happen to future claims over formerly Crown land if that land had already been transferred to state-owned enterprises and could potentially then be alienated to private buyers. Because of the far-reaching implications of the asset sales, the New Zealand Maori Council decided to submit the legislation to judicial review, a provision that allows those who consider themselves to be adversely affected by a law to seek a recommendation by the courts on the exercise of the law or principles underlying it. The council was led by Sir Graham Latimer, a leader from northern New Zealand, who became the first named appellant in the case, which he also underwrote financially. It was a huge risk since, if the case should fail, he would become responsible for all costs.[65]

New Zealand Maori Council v. Attorney-General (1987), often referred to as the "Lands case," is regarded by legal scholars as a seminal moment in the identification of treaty principles and the explication of how those principles should guide the exercise of state power.[66] Indeed, the president of the Court of Appeal, Justice Robin Cooke, saw that the case was "perhaps as important for the future of our country as any that has come before a New Zealand Court."[67] Deploying an image of the state as moral actor, the Court of Appeal found that the Crown was obliged to act fairly and in good faith toward Maori, which involved consulting with them on matters of significant concern including the sale of public assets in which they might have a specific interest. This obligation stemmed from principles of the treaty. For the first time in New Zealand law, the court found that the treaty "signified a partnership" which the Crown bore a particular responsibility to protect.[68]

The case marked the return of Maori leaders to the courtroom in pressing for recognition of their rights. Wanting to force a new political negotiation, as other indigenous peoples had been doing in Australia and Canada, they acknowledged that the efforts of activists outside the state, and Maori politicians and judges inside the state, were not enough to secure rights to indigenous land and identity. They needed the force of the nation's law behind them.

In making its case, the New Zealand Maori Council, the named appellant, asserted an indigenous identity as integrally relating people and land. It argued that the nature of the Maori relationship to land was spiritual and ancestral and was the basis of their distinct peoplehood, primarily in the political and social form of the tribe. The definition of indigeneity as an identity with the land was accepted by the judges in the case, despite the fact that so little land was left in Maori tribal ownership and their claims to ongoing attachment were therefore harder to prove.

The case also marked Maori attainment of a new symbolic role and status in the settler state. Maori were awarded the role as stewards of the national estate, as well as being historical co-founders. The way in which the Court of Appeal judges discussed the Maori appellants' "indigeneity" and the emphasis they gave to Maori people's spiritual relationship to the land brought their national role into the present moment. It implied that Maori would protect what was of value to *all* New Zealanders from the neoliberal reforms. Indeed, in a critical turn in the stories that underpinned jurisprudence, the judges repurposed the notion of indigeneity in order to counter the government's efforts at privatization. This echoed arguments in Australia and Canada about indigenous stewardship of the land, but was much more politically significant because it was applied by the highest court of the land and not just at a local level. However, the judges did not provide a clear definition of the authority and power of specific Maori groups, nor did they question the rule of law. The judges conjured a generalized, abstract, and unified "Maoriness," the bearers of which were ultimately subject to state sovereignty.[69]

The case was heard in May and June 1987 in Wellington. At the opening of the hearings on 4 May, Maori elders and young activists led a haka (dance of challenge) outside the court, located across the road from New Zealand's houses of parliament. The hearings primarily involved legal submissions and the presentation of documents, including a range of affidavits from Maori leaders and scholarship concerning the Treaty of Waitangi, rather than oral evidence. While the admissibility of oral history and traditional evidence was not at stake in this case, the idea of orality was key to the interpretation of treaty principles. Noting the considerable discrepancies between the Maori and English textual versions of the treaty, the judges agreed that the oral understanding of the treaty at the time of its signing was what mattered. Interpreting the treaty in and for the present, the judges therefore argued that they should affirm a broad "spirit" rather than uphold specific contractual obligations made in the past.

Thus, according to Chief Justice Cooke, the treaty "signified a partnership between races" that had existed since the signing of the treaty and was "on-going." The partnership should be conducted according to "reasonableness" and "good faith." It obliged the Crown to protect a present-day Maori identity and way of life, including the restitution of some of their lands where possible; and it obliged Maori to continue their "duty of loyalty to the Queen, full acceptance of her Government through her responsible Ministers, and reasonable co-operation."[70] The transfer of Crown lands to state-owned enterprises, Cooke argued, "is such a major change that, although the Government is clearly entitled to decide on such a policy, as a reasonable treaty partner it should take the Maori race into its confidence regarding the manner of the implementation of the policy."[71] Notably, Cooke conceived of "the Maori race" in singular terms.

In making this argument, Cooke and the other judges were particularly swayed by some of the written Maori affidavits and reports that were presented to the Court. These affidavits—from leading Maori around the country including Latimer himself, Whina Cooper, a number of Maori academics and lawyers, and Pakeha legal and historical scholars—included "eloquent and moving passages" about the relationship of Maori to their land.[72] Cooper's affidavit made a significant impact on the judges, as one of the counsel who acted for the New Zealand Maori Council recalled:

> At lunch time I was summoned by Dame Whina. She presented me with a photograph which contained in the foreground some unattractive mud flats, in the middle ground some nondescript foliage, and in the background a less than exciting landscape. I puzzled over it as we returned to court. Then the coin dropped. I handed the photograph to the crier to pass up to the President and said "to a European eye . . ." and gave the description I have just recounted and added "But this is what this land means to Dame Whina."
>
> I began to read her affidavit. By the end of the first paragraph the President's familiar handkerchief was out. As it continued his emotion became evident. By the end of the affidavit Dame Whina had taken the case from his head to his heart and we had captured him. His colleagues agreed.[73]

At stake in the hearings was whether individual tribes would be able to claim back specific lands that had been wrongfully taken from them, once those lands had been transferred to state-owned enterprises. As Cooke pointed out, the legislation did not affect the tribunal's power to recommend monetary or other forms of compensation for grievances arising from dispossession.[74] What the New Zealand Maori Council sought to show, therefore, was that the return of specific blocks of land to tribes was what mattered—in other words, restitution and not just redress. If Maori tribes were denied the opportunity for restitution, then the Crown might be in breach of the treaty, now considered a social contract, all over again. In a paper prepared in 1983 and submitted to the court, the New Zealand Maori Council summarized the Maori relationship to land thus:

> [Land] provides us with a sense of identity, belonging and continuity. It is proof of our continued existence not only as a people, but as the tangatawhenua [people of the land] of this country. It is proof of our tribal and kin group ties. . . . It is proof of our link with the ancestors of our past, and with the generations yet to come. It is an assurance that we shall forever exist as a people, for as long as the land shall last.[75]

This excerpt, which was quoted in the judicial decision, echoed the language of indigenous peoples in other settler states. In Australia and Canada, indigenous peoples represented themselves to courts, commissions, and the wider public as having a special relationship to the land—a form of belonging to the natural environment that was integral to who they were as "first peoples." Likewise, Maori appellants in the Lands case emphasized the inextricable relationship between land and their identity. Indeed, according to the New Zealand Maori Council, the connection to the land was itself "proof" of the continuity of Maori peoplehood. In emphasizing this idea, the council drew on the phrase "as long as the land shall last," which was frequently used by First Nations in Canada in reference to treaty promises and may have been directly borrowed from them. It was a risky strategy since the loss of land— which Maori tribes had suffered extensively—could by the same argument be interpreted as resulting in the loss of indigenous identity. In this particular case, however, the judges took the Maori claim to their special connection to the land as something that deserved protection into the future.

Perhaps they did so because the idea of a landed identity spoke to a sense of crisis that the economic policy of the incumbent government had provoked. The idea that indigeneity spoke to something more profound than economics certainly appealed to some judges in the Lands case. As one argued, the "crucial importance of land in Maori culture" cannot be "measured in terms of economic utility and immediately realisable commercial values."[76] As well as establishing the importance of land to indigenous identity and ongoing peoplehood, the statements of Maori leaders countered the ways in which land was being valued in the commercial terms of the market. The spiritual and cultural value they attributed to land stood in stark opposition to the economic value being attributed to state assets in the political moment of privatization. In other words, the idea that Maori belonged to the land, rather than the other way around, was at this historical moment more politically useful in national terms than when Yolngu people had been described in such terms in 1971.

By juxtaposing two sets of values—cultural/spiritual and commercial— this judge implied that Maori indigeneity challenged the ascendant economic ideology. Indeed, the reason that the Court of Appeal judges saw this case as having such great significance for New Zealand as a nation was that Maori grievances raised a broader issue about the protection of the national estate. The judges saw the argument for indigeneity as a moral force that could protect what was left of the national estate, as the government turned away from a commitment to social redistribution and embraced notions of market efficiency. The Court of Appeal thereby attributed a new role to a generalized Maori collective and to the meaning of their indigeneity. Maori, as bearers of non-economic values in regard to the natural environment to which they were ontologically bound, were the real guardians of what remained of the national estate. They could hold the state to account by mobilizing the principles of the treaty and because of their indigenous attachment to the land.

What was much less clear was whether the emphasis on political partnership and the repurposing of indigeneity for the wider public good would mean that the settler state was bound to recognize the "rangatiratanga" or the authority of specific tribes. There was "no precise equivalent" for the term "rangatiratanga" according to the judges, although they all agreed that it was not the same as sovereignty. Instead, they limited its meaning to an undefined (and anachronistic) operation of "chieftainship," which did not substantively challenge the state.

In a paper written in 1983 and submitted to the Court of Appeal during the Lands case by the New Zealand Maori Council, the council defined rangatiratanga exclusively in internalist terms, as a "moral contract between a leader, his people, and his god." It is, continued the paper, "a dynamic not static concept, emphasizing the reciprocity between the human, material and non-material world." Practically, the council explained, rangatiratanga entailed the careful administration of tribal assets and resources; in the present-day the exercise of rangatiratanga was both enabled and limited by statutes of the New Zealand government.[77] The council did not explain how rangatiratanga operated inter-tribally nor how it served to regulate relations between the tribe and the state.

The Court of Appeal judges did not refer to this definition nor to the respective spheres of interest and power of the state and the tribe. They assumed, rather, that the Maori and the Crown would reach agreement on matters of importance to each of them. Yet other Maori leaders have interpreted the relationship between the Crown and Maori tribes differently. Reflecting critically on the Lands case and its implications for tribal authority and citizenship twenty years later, Tipene O'Regan, a Ngai Tahu leader, wrote in no uncertain terms about the principle of partnership, which he regarded as a political "anaesthetic" used by the state to placate Maori dissent, rather than a useful tool for the tribes. According to him, the state

> is the ultimate enemy of the tribe because it is always trying to create a formula to control the tribal citizen. There is a continual tension of conflict and co-operation between the tribal citizen and the State [*sic*]. This, in short, is the history of Māori politics. I think it is helpful to conceive of the State, like God, as an ocean. It displays neither grief

nor malice. It is neither good nor bad. It's just there. And if you're not careful, it will get you.[78]

IN THE 1970S, Maori activists broke apart the nationalist story of benign colonization and racial harmony in New Zealand. They forced a reinterpretation of the Treaty of Waitangi, arguing that it was a "fraud." However, they also claimed that the Maori language version's promise of continued rangatiratanga could be recuperated to reestablish their identity. By the mid-1980s, Maori leaders and activists had changed the orientation of government policy away from assimilation to biculturalism. This acknowledged a distinct collective basis for Maori identity.

Within institutions of the state, Maori leaders helped to bring to the fore new political principles for framing their relationship with the Crown. The principle of partnership, first discussed in the specially designed, nationwide Waitangi Tribunal and then given greater legal force in the Lands case decision, was a novel and significant invention. It went beyond recognizing Maori as co-founders in a story of origins and awarded them a potentially significant role in the politics of the present. The idea that Maori and the New Zealand Crown were in a political partnership even suggested that a renegotiation of the terms of consent to state sovereignty might be under way. Specifically, the power of governments to carry out widespread reforms might be limited to the extent that they must take account of distinctive Maori rights.

Yet the policy of biculturalism and the principle of partnership exposed rifts among Maori tribal leaders and activists, as well as between Maori and the state. These engendered new struggles. Significant differences of opinion existed as to what partnership obliged the partners to do. For many tribal leaders, partnership entailed the recognition of distinct tribal authority as that had been affirmed in the treaty's promise of ongoing rangatiratanga. For some Maori activists, the guarantee of rangatiratanga amounted to the recognition of Maori sovereignty, which was, or should be, a unifying force across the Maori world in order to resist the state. According to the judges in the Lands case, partnership obliged the state to consult with a generalized, abstract grouping of Maori, and it obliged Maori to recognize their primary obligations as citizens within the New Zealand state. The court was silent as to how conflicts among tribes and between individual tribes and the state should be negotiated. It avoided the question of whether a broad-based Maori sovereignty existed and, if so, whether it contested the absolute authority of the state.

What the Court of Appeal did do was to bring a new figure of indigeneity into national discourse. This was the figure of Maori as guardians of the national estate. Being represented in this way potentially provided Maori with a unique opportunity to criticize government reforms. But it also burdened them with a new historical role, as bearers of an indigenous past for the enduring settler state's postcolonial future.

The Pacific Way

The Whanganui River retains and, maintains the *Spiritual Elements, and, Tribal Cultural bondage of our Māori People together*, that can be described within the Terms and, Practical Observances of: *Ihi, Tapu,* and *Mana.* [emphases in original]
—HIKAIA AMOHIA, *ca. 1991*

It is only when we appreciate that it is not possessions that most count but how we relate to, and respect the mana of, each other and the environment that we will understand the contribution that Māori thinking can make to a better society, and can develop a philosophy of law that is more in tune with the Pacific way.
—WAITANGI TRIBUNAL, *Whanganui River Report (1999)*

ANALYZING THE SEA change in Māori relations with the state in the 1980s, a number of scholars argued that the creation of the Waitangi Tribunal, the policy of biculturalism, and the principle of partnership enhanced state sovereignty and deferred Māori political desires. The judgment of the Court of Appeal in the Lands case, political theorist Andrew Sharp explained at the time, "reasserted the sovereignty of the state."[1] Legal scholar Jane Kelsey claimed that the creation of the Waitangi Tribunal and the policy of biculturalism were attempts to further incorporate the Māori into existing state hegemony rather than constituting a real acknowledgment of pluralism.[2] Both of those arguments suggest more continuity than change in the 1980s and they echo other criticisms of indigenous-state relations made in Canada and Australia. However, a significant change did take place in constitutional ideas in New Zealand in the late 1980s. Constitutionalism not only consisted of political principles and administrative structures but also the rethinking of history and national identity. Māori claims for indigeneity provoked a considerable reimagining of national identity, which in turn ushered in renewed struggles by Māori and non-Māori over the terms of their representation.

The claim of Whanganui leaders to their river, one of the country's longest, brings these different struggles into sharp relief. The claim, which leaders had pursued for over a century, addressed notions of indigeneity, debates about

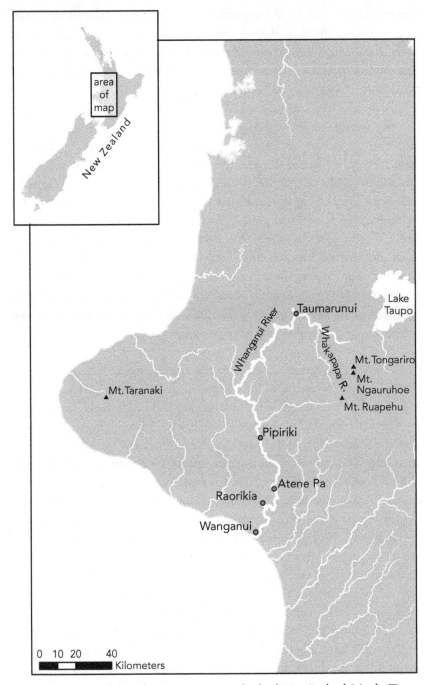

FIGURE 6.1 Map of the Whanganui River, North Island, New Zealand. Map by Tim Stallmann.

national identity, and the representation of indigenous historical agency. Examining how the claim shifted over a century against a changing historical background shows how in New Zealand, perhaps more intensively than in other settler states, ideas about Māori survival and revival served to re-found the nation in a postcolonial "indigeneity."

Located in New Zealand's central North Island, the Whanganui River was significant economically to the tribe and, more important, they considered it to be their eponymous ancestor. In a series of legal cases in the mid-twentieth century, they had argued that the river and its people were inextricable from one another and that the tribe should be at least compensated for its use by outsiders. These claims were made to little avail.[3] In the 1980s, Whanganui Māori engaged in renewed protests at the local, national, and international levels. They brought their claim to the Waitangi Tribunal, which finally heard it in 1994. By this time, transnationally circulating notions of indigeneity, land rights, and international law concerning indigenous peoples had gained some degree of moral and political acceptance in New Zealand. Rights based on identity with and belonging to the land—and potentially with waterways too—were now claimable with wide-ranging effects.

IN THE LATE summer of 1994, Māori who lived along the Whanganui River in New Zealand's North Island and further afield gathered for the first hearing of a claim they had lodged with the Waitangi Tribunal in 1990. The hearings were held over four non-consecutive weeks at local marae (meeting places), a motor inn, a town hall, and even under a tarpaulin beside the river. The claimants sought recognition of the unextinguished "customary and common law rights and title" of the Whanganui tribe to the waters and lands alongside the river.[4] Tribal leaders brought the claim because they were concerned about the depleted water levels in the river due to the diversion to the Tongariro power scheme. They were also angry about the appropriation of much of the area by the government for a national park, which made little provision for their rights to the river. The claim raised some novel issues for the tribunal to consider but it was not the first time local tribes had come together to seek recognition of their rights to the river and its environs.[5]

The Waitangi Tribunal hearings were part of a long legal battle that generations of Whanganui leaders had undertaken seeking recognition of their rights. The longevity of the claim and its repeated assertions in a number of legal and political forums was evidence for the tribunal of the depth of Māori attachment to the river. That depth of attachment was also evidence, for the claimants' lawyers and the tribunal, of the connection between the river claim

FIGURE 6.2 The Waitangi Tribunal hearing evidence at Tieke on the Whanganui River, April 1994. Sitting at the table, L-R: Fergus Sinclair (Crown lawyer), Sian Elias (lawyer for claimants, face obscured), Tribunal members John Kneebone, Eddie Durie, Gordon Orr, Mary Boyd, Keita Walker (wearing life jacket), and Makarini Temara, and unknown. Photographer: Paul Hamer. Photo courtesy of the photographer.

of the Whanganui iwi (tribe) and the broader history of New Zealand. As the claimant counsel explained in opening submissions in 1994, the tribe's claim was a matter of national importance. It was

> almost as old as the history of New Zealand. The petitions to Government, protests, and litigation from the end of last century through the barren middle years of the twentieth century and into the present day indicated the bonds between the people of the Whanganui and their River and their grief."[6]

Even prior to the late nineteenth century, when significant conflict emerged between Whanganui Māori, local Pakeha, and the state over river rights, the Whanganui River had already been a site of inter-tribal contestation. As one historian has explained, "The question of exercising mana, or authority, and creating and maintaining aukati, or barriers to passage, was inevitably bound up in tribal, hapū [sub-tribe] and even whānau [family] relations with the newcomers."[7] Considered by Whanganui Māori not simply a waterway but an ancestral body that connected communities along its banks, by the late nineteenth century it had become an important highway in the central North Island for the transportation of goods and the servicing of farms. In 1891, the government established a Whanganui River Trust authorized to both pre-serve the natural scenery and improve navigation. Later, the trust was em-powered to remove sand, boulders, and other impediments from the riverbed and its banks that were then deposited in other parts of the region.

Beginning in 1873, Whanganui Māori protested the loss of fishing weirs for which they said they were not compensated and the extraction of gravel and other river resources. By the turn of the twentieth century, the river had gained value in settler society as one of the most scenic rivers in the country. Indeed, it was referred to as the "Rhine of Maoriland" in tourist marketing campaigns.[8] In 1916, the government established the Whanganui River Reserves Commission, which was charged with assessing the scenic value of different parts of the river and deciding which areas should be reserved and placed under the Scenery Preservation Act passed in 1903. "We have here scenery equal to or better than any in the world, an asset which is not fully realised by the average individual and therefore I think it is the duty of the state, to take every care and means to safeguard against its destruction," asserted H. Lundius, a Crown Lands ranger, convincing the commission to ingore the Whanganui people's demands.

Following two more petitions sent to the government in 1927 in which leaders demanded specific terms of compensation for loss of fisheries, Minister of Māori Affairs Apirana Ngata recommended that the Native Land Court hear an inquiry into the demands of Whanganui Māori. However, no inquiry eventuated and so a prominent Whanganui leader, Titi Tihu, began to go around villages seeking funds so that the tribes could mount their own legal case. Tihu was the grandson of Te Kere, a prophet, tohunga (holder of esoteric or specialist knowledge), and key supporter of the King movement—the major, inter-tribal political force that fought against the colonial government in the 1860s. Like his grandfather, Tihu was recognized within and beyond his tribe as holding special powers in relation to the river.[9] Despite the impoverished state of most Māori villages along the river, Tihu gathered enough money to hire King's counsel D. G. B. Morison from Wellington to bring their case to the Native Land Court. It was finally heard in 1938.

The Whanganui claim that was lodged with the Native Land Court sought recognition of the tribe's ownership of the riverbed, "from the tidal limit at Raorikia to its junction with the Whakapapa River," rather than the river as a whole entity.[10] The claim to the riverbed followed English common

FIGURE 6.3 Elders and other representatives of Whanganui River tribe in Wellington for a hearing of the Maori Appellate Court of their claim to ownership of the bed of the Whanganui River, 1945. Hekenui Whakarake is in the middle row, second from left. On Whakarake's left is D. G. B. Morison and next to Morison is Titi Tihu. Photographer unknown. Photo credit: Margaret A. Maynard, photographs of Judge D. G. B. Morison and representatives of the Whanganui River tribes. PAColl-2427-1, Alexander Turnbull Library.

law practice in which the bed is separated from the waters; that is, the claimants were arguing that they had a territorial interest in the river. The claimants further argued that they held a unique customary interest in the bed, based on take tupuna (ancestral right), a right recognized in New Zealand common law.

Customary rights had more commonly been applied to land than to waterways, and so the court parsed the river claim in terms of customary territorial rights. They claimed that such rights reflected Māori practice at the time of the signing of the Treaty of Waitangi. "Every foot of land in New Zealand," [they] explained,

> apart from such as may have been alienated, belonged to some Maori tribe or hapu. The boundaries of the land of each tribe or hapu were well defined and the members of that tribe or hapu [sub-tribe] had the

exclusive right in common to everything within those boundaries including rivers and lakes.[11]

Bodies of water were thereby treated by the Native Land Court as geographical features occurring within "well defined" territorial boundaries. A claim to a riverbed was, the court found, quite appropriate in a legal context in which a river was considered by the court as land that happened to have water running over it.

The Whanganui tribes' customary right to the river had not been recognized by the Crown and European inhabitants of the region, the court argued, who had "indiscriminately . . . destroyed or done away with" the eel weirs and fishing traps of the "natives" in extracting gravel from the river and using the river for steamship travel. Yet the tribe's customary right to the river had never been explicitly extinguished, the court asserted, and, in fact, may have been guaranteed by the Treaty of Waitangi. Therefore, the court upheld the claim of Whanganui Māori to customary rights in the river.[12]

However, in recognizing these rights, the court distorted the ways in which claimants explained the history of their rights to the river. The court assumed that the ancestral right of Whanganui Māori to the river was based on descent from ancestors who had "well defined" rights to blocks of land alongside the river. This reasoning drew on English common law practice rather than the law and tradition of the Whanganui people. In the English common law, rights to riverbeds are usually determined according to the extent of land boundary along the banks of the river and can continue to the middle of the river's flow. The judges in the Native Land Court applied the reasoning of such a rule to the ancestral rights of the Whanganui Māori claimants to their river. However, when Morison was finally allowed to examine a prominent Whanganui elder, Hekenui Whakarake (whose evidence was given in Māori although only the translated English version appears in the Native Land Court minute book), a more complicated picture emerged. Whakarake, in fact, suggested that it was the ancestors of the river itself that bestowed different kinds of rights on the peoples who lived beside—and in relation to—the river.

MORISON: Who are the tipunas [ancestors] in the river?
HEKENUI:[13] Hinengakau up the Taumaranui end, Tamaupoko the middle portion of the river and Tupoho the lower regions of the river.
JUDGE: Have the descendants of these ancestors exercised the rights of ownership?

HEKENUI: Yes. Tamakehu [the father of Hinengakau, Tamaupoko, and Tupoho] is the great ancestor for the Wanganui people.

MORISON: Are these tipunas the same tipunas as were set up for the land adjoining the river?

HEKENUI: No. They did not get into the land.

JUDGE: None of the descendants of Tamakehu got into the land.

MORSION: You mean they did not get in on these tipunas?

HEKENUI: They did not get in themselves but their descendants did.

JUDGE: That is a different thing altogether. They may not have been included in the claim but their descendants may have been included.

HEKENUI: Yes.

MORISON: Can you tell the Court whether the tipunas of the river are different for the blocks of land adjoining the river?

HEKENUI: Yes. When our ancestors arrived in New Zealand some of them went to the hills where they lived on the birds, some of them lived on the banks of the river and some of them lived on the seacoast. Those who lived on the coast lived on what they could get from the sea. Those who established themselves on the banks of the rivers built for themselves eel weirs and other traps for catching fish. Those who lived on the hills and land lived on what they could catch from their snares and built snares on various trees. They did not bother what others were catching from the rivers or seas. . . .[14]

In establishing the Whanganui claim to the river, Whakarake referred to the founding tradition of Whanganui people, "te taura whiri a Hine Ngakau," or the plaited rope of Hine Ngakau. The tradition refers to the genealogical relationships and obligations between the three hapu (sub-tribes) along the river who trace their descent from one of three children of Tamakehu, himself a descendant of Te Atihaunui who arrived from the ancestral homeland of Hawaiiki on the waka (canoe) Aotea.[15]

Whakarake's evidence emphasized the bonds between Whanganui people and with other descendants of the first canoe arrivals as well as recognizing the differences between them. Related through common ancestry, the three hapu of the river nonetheless held rights of occcupation to distinct regions of the river and particular food gathering and hunting rights. Implicitly, in Whakarake's testimony, the kinds of rights held by different groups signified from whom they were descended. So, the knowledge of ancestors and genealogy could not be divorced from the material and economic practices of individuals and families. The founding tradition of the plaited rope and resource-gathering practices confirmed and elaborated each other. The Native Land Court decision, although favorable to the claimants, distorted the basis of their claim by misrecognizing the inextricability of the founding tradition with material or economic rights. According to the court, it was not the tradition of the plaited rope that gave rise to customary title in this case but, rather, the extension of the territorial rights of Māori owners along the river's banks to its bed.

The Native Land Court's decision troubled the national government since it opened up the possibility for tribes across the country to lay claim to waterways. So the government immediately challenged the court's decision. A series of complex legal hearings followed. The Native Appellate Court upheld the Native Land Court's decision but it was then overturned in a 1949 Supreme Court ruling. A 1950 Royal Commission disagreed with some of the Supreme Court's findings and recommended that the tribe receive compensation for gravel extraction. The government then enacted special legislation so that it could appeal this decision. The Court of Appeal asked the newly reconstituted Māori (formerly Native) Appellate Court to answer some evidentiary questions, in particular whether the tribe could claim an ancestral right in the river that was based in a different authority from their land rights. The Māori Appellate Court cast doubt on there being a substantial difference between ancestral rights to the river compared to the land. This helped the Court of Appeal decide, in the final legal decision on the river, that any customary river rights had been extinguished when adjoining lands had been sold in 1962.[16]

Throughout these hearings, Māori witnesses (including Whakarake who appeared several times in later hearings) reiterated the tradition of the plaited rope as the basis for their ancestral claim. Just as frequently, some judges and lawyers dismissed that tradition as merely "mythical" and unnecessary to understanding the evidence presented about resource harvesting. Sometimes those dismissals of the evidence entailed disparaging the witnesses themselves. Justice Adams, in a dissenting opinion in the Court of Appeal case in 1953, for instance, questioned Whakarake's "mental calibre" and suggested that previous Land Court judges believed too much of what they were told by Māori witnesses. He wondered how a tribe could claim a property right over large bodies of water "where a somewhat refined mental process has to come into play before the bed can be envisaged as a possible subject of ownership."[17] To Judge Pritchard of the Māori Appellate Court, who reheard evidentiary issues in 1958, traditions such as that of plaited rope were simply "background," giving a sense of "the general and cosmogonic [sic] conceptions which the ancient Maori had towards his property." Pritchard further explained that such conceptions were unnecessary to the case because the court viewed "the claims made to it for inclusion in a title to be tied more to the foundations of practical realism rather than to those of mere symbolism."[18] Even the lawyers working for the Māori claimants emphasized the material nature of the claim, wary of claiming a "cosmogenic" source for the Whanganui tribe's riverine authority.

In 1962, the Court of Appeal issued the final decision on the river claim: where blocks of land adjoining the river had been investigated and issued with individual titles, the English common law rule applied which gave title to the middle of the river's flow. Therefore, the tribe as a whole could not claim rights to the riverbed as a whole. The legal claim could go no further.[19] From this point on, national government, businesses, and individual Pakeha assumed that waterways like the Whanganui were publicly owned. In 1971, water from the mountains in the central North Island began to be diverted away from the river to the Tongariro power project. Titi Tihu, who had pursued the claim for rights to the river through its winding passage in the higher courts and commission, in the later years aided by his nephew Hikaia Amohia, now sought recognition of the tribe's river rights through political means.

Once again, they petitioned the New Zealand government and even the Queen. In an oblique retort to those judges who had dismissed tribe's claim as "mere symbolism," Tihu and Amohia presented a petition in 1975 to Minister of Māori Affairs Matiu Rata that demanded that "the title to the bed [be] restored to us to preserve our sacred symbolical right to the River. This is far more important to us than any question of money, because what was done was a direct attack on religious ritual and custom and such an attack is forbidden by law."[20] Thus, like many indigenous leaders, Tihu and Amohia employed a range of strategies in pursuing their rights, including appealing to articles of religious freedom.

By the mid-1970s, the distinct rights of Māori to areas of importance to them were beginning to be reconsidered at the level of the state. In 1978 the National government passed the Mt. Egmont Vesting Act, which had returned Mt. Egmont or in its Māori name, Taranaki, to the local tribes from whom it had been confiscated in 1863 during the New Zealand wars. The legislation recognized the mountain's "special significance" to those tribes. In the same piece of legislation, however, the mountain was immediately returned to the Crown as a national park by the tribes "as a free gift and a symbol of love to all the people of New Zealand."[21] In response to further petitions from Tihu and Amohia, the National government's Minister of Māori Affairs Ben Couch proposed a similar solution to that negotiated with the nearby Taranaki tribes: he agreed that the government could meet "the spirit of the petition . . . without transferring material control of the river to the Maori people."[22]

Other members of the tribe, however, argued that they wanted to negotiate their material rights, compensation, and representation on the board of a proposed Whanganui national park. Tihu's lawyers wrote back to Couch explaining that a variety of rights and compensation was being sought. "Our client Mr. Titi Tihu is a Tohunga of the old school, a man to whom matters of spiritual well being are all important, and to whom money or material things are irrelevant. . . . [I]t was put to [Tihu] that his attitude in regard to the Wanganui River and its bed overlooked the rights of other persons whose attitude to material possessions resembles that of the average New Zealander rather more closely than the attitude of our client." Government officials suggested that the government might recognize the tribe's "spiritual sovereignty"[23] or a "nominal" ownership.[24] Neither possibility was taken up by the tribe. And neither Tihu nor Amohia lived to see the Waitangi Tribunal visit the river in 1994.

In the 1980s, tribal leaders, along with a number of environmental organizations and the Department of Conservation, began to raise concerns about the deleterious effects of reduced water levels on aquatic life, birds, and flora along the river's banks as more water was diverted for the hydroelectric project. The tribe demanded that it be formally consulted about the flow management plan used to measure water levels, without success. It also protested details of a proposal to turn much of the region into a national park that would include a considerable length of the river. In 1986, the recently established Whanganui River Reserves Trust, representing the tribe, demanded co-management rights over the park and $4 million in compensation. Neither of these demands were met in full when, at the end of that year, the Labour government officially recognized the national park. In a later amendment to legislation, the park board was to have "regard to the spiritual, historical, and cultural significance" of the river to iwi and to seek advice from the reconstituted Whanganui River Māori Trust Board.[25]

In 1990, the Trust Board lodged a claim to the river with the Waitangi Tribunal, on behalf of Whanganui Māori. Asserting the tribe's unextinguished "customary and common law rights and title to the lands and waters, fisheries and other taonga [treasures] of the Whanganui River," the written claim observed that those rights had been repeatedly "denied." The claimants demanded restoration of the tribe's "tino rangatiratanga" over the river and "full customary entitlements" as well as various forms of compensation and "the restoration of the River to its full strength."[26]

The claim to the tribunal over the entirety of the river made a different argument from earlier legal actions. Unlike earlier claims for the recognition of the tribe's rights to the riverbed, Whanganui claimants in 1990 made it clear that, for them, the river was an indivisible whole. Their rights to it encompassed something considerably more than use and access. Indeed, since the river was what bound the different Whanganui hapu together, it could not be divided into different kinds of "products" as Hikaia Amohia, the first named claimant, explained:

> The Whanganui River has a Significance to the Māori People of this Region beyond its use as a Commercial/Resource Product. The Whanganui River retains and, maintains the *Spiritual Elements, and, Tribal Cultural bondage of our Māori People together*, that can be described within the Terms and, Practical Observances of: *IHI, TAPU,* and *MANA* [*sic*].[27]

Amohia, who had presented an affidavit in the 1987 Lands Case as part of the New Zealand Māori Council's submission, went on to explain these concepts: "Any interference with NATURE, including the RIVER, breaks the LAW OF TAPU; breaks the IHI or Sacred Affinity of our Māori People with the river; and reduces the MANA and Soul of the Whanganui River."[28]

In order to protect and maintain the interconnectedness of the river and riverine people, Whanganui Māori demanded recognition of their tino rangatiratanga, or distinct political authority—not just access and harvesting rights to parts of it. As chair of the Whanganui Māori Trust Board and tribal leader, Atawhai (Archie) Taiaroa stated in his submission to the Waitangi Tribunal,

> What we are talking about here is the river in its wholeness, Te Mana, Te Mauri, Te Ihi, Te Tapu, Te Wehi [again referring to the power, spirit and sacredness of the river]. Its waters, its fish, its bed, its water life, its tributaries and *the tino rangatiratanga of the iwi of Whanganui over the river held by them since first occupation, never ever relinquished and repeatedly asserted* [emphasis in original]."[29]

In making their claim to authority over the river, Whanganui leaders drew on various ideas circulating at national and international levels and they connected those ideas with their spiritual relationship to their ancestral river. The assertion of tino rangatiratanga drew on the contemporary activism about and political discussion of the Māori text of the Treaty of Waitangi. In the demands of Whanganui Māori, rangatiratanga meant more than "chieftainship" as the Court of Appeal judges in the Lands Case had translated it. Taiaroa's use of rangatiratanga conjured the body of the people and their inextricable identity with the river, not simply a limited exercise of leadership implied in the notion of cheiftainship.

Moreover, Taiaroa emphasized that his people had "repeatedly asserted" this authority—for instance, in the litany of legal cases they had pursued through the mid-twentieth century as well as in the numerous petitions they had sent to the New Zealand parliament and the British monarch. They had not intentionally ceded authority or let it lapse. As prior occupiers who had maintained a continuous authority over the river (even if this authority had not always been acknowledged or respected by settlers), Whanganui Māori could thereby assert their native title rights to the river, which they did.

The concept of rangatiratanga as Archie Taiaroa deployed it also resonated with the new global discourse of indigenous rights. Taiaroa claimed that Whanganui Māori had held authority over the river since "first occupation." As we have seen, this was a frequently made claim by indigenous peoples in establishing their rights. Even more significantly, the ideas of Taiaroa and others about their authority over the river was expressed in terms of the right to self-determination for indigenous peoples. At the time that the Whanganui claim came before the Waitangi Tribunal, this right was being discussed at the highest levels, in discussions among the Working Group on Indigenous Populations at the United Nations in which Whanganui people took part.[30]

Archie Taiaroa explained to the Waitangi Tribunal that in 1993—the United Nations' International Year of the World's Indigenous People—the Whanganui Māori Trust Board had issued a charter on "tino rangatiratanga and iwi (tribal) water rights." The charter "reaffirmed" these rights, pointing out the "inalienable right" of Māori communities to "care for, protect, manage, and use their waters."[31] The meeting out of which the charter was created included representatives from other tribes across New Zealand and North America, among them Dene people from the Mackenzie River region in Canada. According to Taiaroa, this charter was submitted by a Whanganui delegation to the United Nations Working Group for Indigenous Peoples when it met the following year at Geneva. That working group had recently produced the "Draft United Nations Declaration on the Rights of Indigenous Peoples," article three of which asserted the right of self-determination.[32]

Indigenous peoples' assertion of the right of self-determination differed substantially from that of other anti-colonial activists. Most indigenous peoples in settler states were not demanding separate statehood but, rather, to be recognized as distinctive nations with local territorial rights within larger state federations. The basis of their self-determination was premised on their distinctive relationship to the land which pre-dated the creation of the settler state. Central to the discussions of self-determination in the Working Group was the notion of indigenous place. Indigenous peoples at this forum frequently argued that they lived in deep interconnection with specific places under environmental threat of destruction or significant degradation. The rights they claimed to those places were as much moral as political and positioned their own struggle to survive alongside that of the survival of particular ecosystems. This was certainly true of the ways in which Whanganui claimants expressed their rights: as political claims to authority over specific territories, and as moral claims about the inextricability of their peoplehood from their environment.[33]

Whanganui claimants argued their rights to the Whanganui River specifically and in generalized terms of indigeneity that enhanced their local and long-standing traditions about their identity. These arguments were particularly convincing to the majority of the tribunal members, since they were local and global at the same time. In marked distinction from the earlier legal cases, Whanganui claimants made their sense of identity with the river and belonging to it, as well as the founding tradition of the plaited rope, core to their argument for tino rangatiratanga in respect of the river and their tribal right to self-determination. The significance that the tribunal attributed to that evidence demonstrated the break with the legal past in which such testimony had been dismissed as "mere symbolism" or ambient background to the material rights of Whanganui Māori.

Much of the evidence that the Whanganui claimants presented to the tribunal sought to establish the inextricability of their belonging to the river in personal and collective terms. In a careful shift in rhetoric, one that echoed the assertions of Yolngu and Dene people, claimants stated that they did not "own" the river but rather that they belonged to it. The river, those witnesses explained, was not simply the property of the tribe but rather a "tupuna awa" or ancestral river, as they demonstrated in stories and songs. One song that the claimants performed particularly struck tribunal members—it was one of the "Tribunal's enduring memories" as the report puts it.[34] The words to the song followed the well-known proverb:

> *E rere kau mai te awa nui nei*
> *mai te kahui maunga ki Tangaroa*

> *ko au te awa*
> *ko te awa ko au*
>
> *The river flows*
> *from the mountains to the sea*
> *I am the river*
> *the river is me.*

Whanganui people often use a version of the proverb, or at least the phrase "ko au te awa/ko te awa ko au" in their mihi (formal introductions). It is a simple phrase, but one that produces its meaning to great effect.[35]

Claimants also referred extensively to the founding tradition of the plaited rope and the relationships between various peoples that the tradition establishes. Indeed, relationships between hapu (sub-tribes) along the river extend outward—for example, to hapu such as Ngati Rangi who are more closely associated with the mountain region in the central North Island but who, nonetheless, consider themselves and are recognized as belonging to the river and its people. As one Ngati Rangi elder, Matiu Mareikura, explained to the tribunal in the first week of the hearings in 1994, the maintenance of relationships between the various hapu was a matter of health and well-being for all: "It's no good for Hinengakau to be okay when Tamaupoko is not okay. It's important that we all know this. We need one another for strength, we need one another to be able to hold ourselves together as a people, as a tribe. Without that, we become individuals."[36]

Mareikura's submission was notable for the way he wove the life of the river and the life of the people together. Not only did he represent the river as a place of belonging, but he called the river an ancestor itself, or a "tupuna awa." Likening the river to an umbilical cord, Mareikura argued that the illness of individual Whanganui Māori, and the tribe as a whole, was in direct relationship to the health of the river. He blamed the pollution of the river, as well as the inability of Māori to secure loans for farming earlier in the century, on the depletion of the Māori population along the river and the migration of young people to towns and cities.[37]

Claimants frequently expressed the ancestral bond between the river and its people as sacred and the obligations that the bond entailed as spiritual. As such, the bond and its obligations, claimants explained, were beyond the grasp of ordinary language. In English-language submissions, Māori terms were usually used to denote the spirituality of the river in conceptual terms. Further, the sacred traditions and practices of belonging to the river, which combine Christian and Māori beliefs and are known as the "maramatanga," are esoteric, and the claimants and Trust Board were careful to maintain the secrecy of this knowledge.[38] Presentations to the tribunal hearing that concerned the maramatanga were kept off the public record; and the nature of this knowledge was, according the Trust Board's website, not up for negotiation or comment in the settlement of the claim in the twenty-first century.[39]

The Whanganui claimants argued that they retained customary rights to the river as first people and prior occupiers. They provided evidence of that occupation as continuous both in terms of their use of the river's resources and in terms of how they had long asserted their rights in respect of the river in court cases and petitions. Claimants argued that their rights in the river were not precisely those of property, in the sense of having an alienable interest, but stemmed rather from their tino rangatiratanga, their political authority as recognized in the Treaty of Waitangi, which denoted more than mere possession. Their political authority, they then argued, was founded in a different order from the authority established by the Crown but it had been recognized by that entity. Moreover, the authority of Whanganui Māori in respect of their river was not only temporal and political. Their tino rangatiratanga denoted rights and obligations in relation to the river that they considered a founding ancestor: the river was the origin for the Whanganui tribe as a people and it bound them together in the present and for the future.

THE WHANGANUI CLAIM to the Waitangi Tribunal in the 1990s did not signify the incorporation of indigenous dissent into settler state hegemony. In fact, arguments within the hearings brought new conflicts and terms of struggle to the fore. In particular, the claimants and Crown lawyers engaged in a struggle over history and historical representation which had important political implications.

According to the claimants, their long and historically consistent claim was evidence of their distinct authority over it. Crown lawyers and their expert historians challenged this on empirical and normative grounds. They conceded that some property rights of the tribe might have been violated—and that indeed such violations formed the initial provocation for the legal cases that Whanganui Māori had mounted. However, they disputed the argument that Whanganui Māori had "long" demanded their rights according to their "spiritual relationship" to the river. Indeed, they suggested that the claim was a recently invented one. In so doing, they challenged the assertion of Whanganui peoplehood as premised in narratives of belonging and practices associated with the river that, leaders claimed, were at the foundation of the tribe's identity.

In their submissions to the tribunal, Crown lawyers pointed out that a variety of different rights had been claimed by Whanganui leaders in different forums. The territorial rights to the riverbed that Titi Tihu and other leaders had claimed in 1938 were not rights of a sacred nature that encompassed the river in its entirety, they argued. Moreover, the claim for material rights of use and access were not the same as making a claim to a political authority over the river.[40] Customary rights of usufruct were capable of being recognized as a form of native title right but not as the exclusive right to decide how the river could be used by others.

In supporting their argument that Whanganui Māori might have had specific and limited title rights to the river that were subsequently lost, Crown lawyers made a larger argument about history and the nature of Māori historical agency in the context of the settler state. They argued that in order to be acknowledged as coeval and equal citizens, Māori must be represented as secular historical agents drawn into the economic and political world of colonial settler society. Like other citizens, they mobilized legal claims to establish some economic security for themselves. By situating Māori actors within changing economic and political realities, historians could show both how Māori had pursued the recognition of their customary rights and how they had been dispossessed of them. Perhaps unexpectedly, Crown lawyers and historians made broader arguments about the importance of historicizing Māori actors in a nuanced manner. Telling the history of Māori political and legal engagement, Crown lawyers suggested, was a project that helped "to expand knowledge through research."[41] But such an argument also dismissed the history of distinct rights that indigenous peoples were intent on showing.

Crown lawyers agreed that Whanganui claimants were entitled to a degree of historical redress for what they had lost, including cultural traditions. However, precisely because they were eligible for redress, these lawyers argued that claimants could not be recognized in the present moment as bearing an ongoing, continuous, and sacred attachment to the river. Acknowledging Whanganui Māori as coeval, historical agents meant that, according to these lawyers and historians, the tribe could not also claim to have maintained a spiritual and sacred relationship to the river. This proposition was, Crown lawyers argued, a new foundation for the claim, not an old and continuous one. "While the issue of spiritual significance has been highlighted in recent years," the Crown lawyers observed in closing submissions, "and advanced as the foundation or wellspring of the claim, it is clear that other concerns are involved. In the most general sense, the claim has become the expression of a mixture of aspirations. Not all of these . . . are easily reconcilable."[42]

The idea that the common law could recognize a "right" to a sacred relationship to place was a fallacy since this could not be proved using usual historical methods. Indeed, Crown lawyers claimed that historical truth could not be reconciled with the "spiritual truth" that Māori claimants ascribed to their traditions. Those traditions were based in "fixed" knowledge that was "by definition, untestable or beyond analysis," they argued. The kind of inquiry that professional historians practiced, in contrast, was one in which "no knowledge is fixed by higher authority." It established historical facts that were tested through critical, rational debate such as that emulated in the legal practice of cross-examination to which those providing evidence of the spiritual relationship to the river had not been subject.[43] The fact that Whanganui leaders had sought to keep some of their esoteric tradition off the public record showed that they did not want those traditions to be subjected to such truth-testing.

Recalling the paradox of indigenous peoples as at once inside and outside the space of law, Crown lawyers argued that Māori claimants could claim the violation of customary rights and have those rights recognized by the settler state. But they could only do so insofar as those rights were compatible with the common law. The recognition of customary rights did not enable the recognition of a distinct spiritual or political authority, they suggested, for they were not derived from a tribal history, in this case, the ancestral tradition of the plaited rope and the sacred relationship of Whanganui Māori to the river. In an argument similar to that made by Justice Blackburn in the Gove land rights case, Crown lawyers thus asserted that New Zealand common law could not recognize a spiritual relationship as a property right. Whanganui Māori might belong to the river, but if this was the case then the river did not belong to them.

In light of the foregoing arguments, the tribunal became tasked with the job of mediating disputes about historical representation as well as legal rights.[44] Following its established practices of interpretation that had been developed in relation to defining treaty principles, tribunal members, particularly chairperson Eddie Durie, established at the outset of the proceedings that they would pay attention to the ways in which the claimants themselves expressed their attachment to the river. "To get inside the Māori world," as explained by the report that the tribunal issued in 1999, "one must set aside preconceived notions of State-like territories and concepts of private ownership or rights."[45] According to the tribunal, a "Māori world" existed that was organized around principles and norms distinct from those of the common law world of the settler state.

During the course of the proceedings, Justice Durie made it clear that he disagreed with the arguments and assumptions of Crown lawyers and experts. He gave considerable attention to the idea that alternative founding orders existed in New Zealand, which required rethinking what was meant by Māori historical agency. The more Crown experts represented Māori as involved primarily in terms of their engagements with the settler state, the more they diminished the possibility of an alternative world that had survived colonization and that was being revived in the contemporary moment. Thus, rather than viewing Māori as agents who were subject to constant change (and therefore loss) in a secular and materialist history of national progress, Durie proposed another periodization of Māori history. This was a cyclical one that emphasized the revival of tradition and represented Māori as agents of that revival. In his cross-examination of an expert historian who appeared for the Crown, he offered his alternative version of this history:

> I would like to suggest there could be three phases [of Māori history] and the first is a pre-contact stage when Māori social and political beliefs, whatever they were, must have prevailed and the second would be a colonial period when Māori are adapting and responding to a new set of beliefs and of social and political beliefs and that we might describe in very broad terms as 19th century. And we come to the 20th century, or modern period, in which Māori might be seen to be reviving social and political beliefs that were submerged during the colonial period. Now if that were a correct scenario, then some things said in the 20th century about the ownership of the river, for example, might not in fact be modern but might in fact be very old.[46]

Durie called into question the assumption of Crown lawyers and historians that the historical inquiry they pursued was purely empirical. Was it not the case that the notion of Crown domain also operated as a "belief system" and one that, in a court of law and in everyday life, was also beyond critical assessment? As Durie put it:

> It has always struck me for example that even amongst English people in talking, what they say is not necessarily what their own society as a body politic believes in, for example, I don't know whether you own your own house, but if you did and I asked, "*do you own your own*

house?" you would probably say *"Yes, I own my own house"* . . . Yet the underlying belief system is that you don't, you hold it in fee simple. . . . [Y]ou in fact hold it in fee from the Crown which has a larger authority over you, you have the right to use it but you don't absolutely own it, it is not an allodial title. . . . There is something bigger above you.[47]

In this oblique reference to the story of the social contract, Durie questioned the insistence of Crown lawyers that theirs was a purely "empirical" argument and did not itself rely on a higher authority. Positioning Māori within a materialist history, Durie suggested, depended on a certain forgetting. That is, the Crown's argument rested on an assumption that members of the body politic often forgot the very principle of the social contract they had consented to— that in awarding to the state the capacity to govern on their behalf according to the law, they also ceded an absolute right to their property.

As Durie was well aware, however, such forgetting was not as easy for colonized people to undertake. In their day-to-day lives, the Crown's higher authority marked the usurpation of indigenous peoples' own tribal authority. From the confiscation of lands, to the use of resources for development projects, to the fact that they had to seek permission from state or regional governing bodies to harvest resources, Māori were reminded that the exercise of their tribal authority was diminished. It was the usurpation of the normative political and legal order of Māori life, as premised in alternative founding traditions of tribes, that constituted the full extent of the historical injustice that Māori people had suffered. Thus, the tribunal had to seriously address, as a matter of political principle, the fact that tribal traditions had survived and could be revived if the idea that Māori were partners to the Treaty of Waitangi was to have substantial meaning.

Durie's approach to history-making sparked further criticism by scholars outside the institution. Arguing that the history the tribunal was producing was "juridical history" in which facts are related to "a body of known rules that govern [the judge's] judgment," some scholars charged the institution with presentism.[48] Or, as one historian put it, the tribunal produced history based in "a historical mentality less concerned to recapture past reality than to embody present aspiration."[49]

ARGUMENTS ABOUT THE terms of historical representation, whose history was being recognized within the tribunal, and for what purpose, spilled out into public protests for years after the hearings. The Waitangi Tribunal concluded the hearings at the end of 1994, after which followed a report-writing phase. Tribunal members met among themselves to discuss the story they wanted to tell and the recommendations they would make to government. They had to consider whether Whanganui Māori did indeed have rights over the river, what such rights might allow, and whether any compensation was owed to the tribe. This was a time-consuming process as it has been for most claims that have gone to the tribunal.[50] The final report on the Whanganui River claim was not issued until 1999. Frustrated by how long the tribunal was taking, some members of the Whanganui tribe undertook a new public protest in the year following the hearings. The protest attracted nationwide attention and revealed considerable hostility to Māori claims on the part of Pakeha locals in the town of Wanganui/Whanganui[51] and many others in the nation-at-large.

On 28 February 1995, a group of Whanganui Māori activists, old and young, occupied a park in downtown Wanganui—the major town at the mouth of the Whanganui River. Officially the park was known as Moutoa Gardens and it memorialized a battle in the New Zealand wars of the 1860s. A plaque at the park reads: "To the memory of the brave men at Moutoa, 14 May 1864, in defense of law and order against fanaticism and barbarism."[52] The activists who lived in the park for seventy-nine days referred to the place by its prior name, Pakaitore, when it had been the site of a fishing village. Activists argued that their ancestors who signed a land deed covering what was now the park had no intention of permanently alienating the land. Now, the activists explained, "we've returned [to our land to] celebrate our Whanganui-tanga [way of being Whanganui]." Not only did activists protest the misunderstanding of their ancestors' intentions but they also countered the terms by which their own actions were represented in the present. The "occupation" was in fact a "reclamation" of their land, and the "protest" was actually a "celebration" of their peoplehood.[53]

Key to the action was the presentation of counter-histories of the river and region and the assertion of tribal sovereignty. Activists frequently referred to oral histories as the authoritative source for their understanding of land dealings between chiefs and settlers in the nineteenth century. Those oral histories proved, according to activists, that nineteenth-century land deeds were "not worth the paper [they were] written on."[54] Both activists and journalists covering the Pakaitore occupation/reclamation drew on Waitangi Tribunal research into the Whanganui River claim, which corroborated the facts of injustice about which local Māori complained, and added weight to the assertion of their rights—although the research did not clearly evidence the rights of Māori to the specific site of Moutoa Gardens/Pakaitore.[55] The research produced for tribunal claims served a double purpose of enhancing indigenous expressions of peoplehood and evidencing a particular legal claim.

In the first week of the reclamation, leaders sent out a statement about the sovereign rights they were "re-establishing" at Pakaitore. "There are rituals that have been performed here," asserted one activist, "and it means we cannot just walk off the land."[56] The statement was published in the *Dominion*, a nationally circulating newspaper, and it made clear that the spiritual bond that characterized the relationship of Māori to their lands and waters was definitively a legal one. The exercise of laws by the Whanganui iwi, the authors of the statement explained, was what made them sovereign in places to which they claimed an ancestral relationship.

The "tangata whenua [people of the land] are born of and with the land, they live not under but with the law of the land," the authors emphasized, pointing out too that, in the Māori language, "whenua" is the word for both land and the umbilical cord. The ritual of burying the child's placenta in the land of his or her ancestors was a "defining act of *law* which gave public notice of the legal status and place of the child." The legal status that the authors referred to was that attributed by the tribe, not by the settler state, demonstrating that the tribe's legal capacity that had survived the imposition of Crown sovereignty. Thus, only the tribe could determine what was right for the land and for the people of the land.[57] Continuity of their tribal sovereignty led some activists to refuse to further engage in the Waitangi Tribunal process. As one leader put it: "We've got a long history of going to the courts on both our river and the land. We're not going to the tribunal because we say we own the land."[58]

However, according to the Wanganui District Council and the national government, the occupation was illegal. In May, the council sought an injunction in the High Court that would affirm their rights over the gardens and authorize them to remove the protestors. Extensive documentary evidence was presented to the High Court justice who declared it unlikely that the specific site of Moutoa Gardens had in fact been the exact site of a Māori village. The evidence, the court found, confirmed that the council owned the land on which the gardens were now located; and indeed Whanganui Māori had not previously claimed possession of the particular site, unlike their long-standing claims about the river. The protestors left the site before force was used. Notably, three leaders of the protest who were named in the High Court case did not appear, since they declared their action a matter of politics, not something to be resolved in the courts.

Although they left the park, members of the tribe did not stop protesting. They demonstrated against aerial dropping of poison to kill possums in the river environs and the use of the river for tourist ventures. On 14 December 1997, protestors tried barricading the river to stop a tourist riverboat operator from navigating it. According to some hyperbolic journalism that editorialized the conflict, the tourist boat operator Winston Oliver was subject to a "savage attack of rocks, stones and abuse." Oliver claimed that although he had sought permission to use the river, he was giving up his enterprise since "one of us could have been killed." Oliver was hurt and disappointed by the "attack" and had no way of responding. "It's not for me to argue," he said. "I'm a Pakeha and I don't have a claim."[59]

As the tribe continued to wait for the tribunal's report, Archie Taiaroa explained to the press later that year that Māori along the river would continue to protest in order to assert their control over the river and its environs. "It sounds like a threat," he observed in 1997. "But really it's just a statement of fact." Acknowledging the limits of the legal process, he continued,

> We've fought this through Parliament and the courts for more than
> 150 years and we haven't got anywhere. We're at the end of our tether
> in energy, time and money. Our young people are telling us we should
> step aside and let them take over, which means more of the protests
> we've had lately.[60]

The dispute over the Whanganui River also offered an opportunity for Pakeha who had a long association with the river, as well as representatives of environmental and outdoor organizations, to express the important role the river had in their lives. They made submissions to the Waitangi Tribunal and in other public venues. Although Winston Oliver said that, as a Pakeha, he lacked a "claim" to the river, many non-Māori did indeed claim the river, often using terms they appropriated directly from Māori claimants.

Notably, Pakeha argued for a settler indigeneity. A number made oral and written submissions to the tribunal expressing strong sentiments of attachment. "I came to the banks of the river as a young school-boy in 1932," said Jock Erceg, who later became a friend of Titi Tihu's. "The water of the river, the force and power of the singing rapids, and the most beautiful of all, the native forests which lined the banks. The preservation and the protection of all these became my main interest." Hugh Barr appeared for the Federated Mountain Clubs of New Zealand and expressed a similarly strong sentiment. "This land makes those of us who feel this way in a very real sense the tangata whenua, the people of the land, whether we are of Māori descent or not," he argued.[61]

This was not the first example of Pakeha making their own claims to indigeneity to the Waitangi Tribunal. High country farmers in New Zealand's South Island had appeared at the hearings of the extensive Ngai Tahu claim, arguing that they were the "indigenous people of the pastoral lease land," as one of the farmers put it. In his testimony to the Waitangi Tribunal, this farmer continued, "The lessees themselves . . . are the only people in New Zealand to have actually settled on and worked the land in question. My people, regardless of race or creed . . . have the indigenous feeling of the high country."[62] Also echoing indigenous claimants' submissions, the lessees argued that because of their distinctive knowledge as well as their history of care for the land, they were guardians of it. Further, they boasted about having helped to preserve it "for the benefit of all New Zealanders."[63] This assertion of guardianship on behalf of the nation was intended to trump the claims of Māori tribes to indigenous belonging and stewardship, which had been given such prominence in the 1987 Lands case. So whether indigeneity was ritually performed, related in historical narratives, or expressed as deeply held sentiment, it was something that non-indigenous people living in settler states regarded as central to their identities too.

Another risk in defining indigeneity in terms of belonging to the land became clearer. Pakeha high country farmers, however distinctive their cultural identity, were able to represent the interests of the nation precisely because their "indigenous feeling" for the land existed irrespective of their "race or creed" and tribal affiliation. Pakeha suggested that their indigeneity was something that could be subject to liberal governance, rather than the implicitly illiberal authority of the tribal chief. For instance, Hugh Barr argued that "commonly owned resources" such as the Whanganui River should be vested in the state rather than the tribe, or "under a democratic rather than a chiefly authority" as he put it.[64]

Pakeha claims to indigeneity challenged neither the unity of the nation nor the authority of the state to represent them. They did not claim "special" rights premised in racial or cultural difference, and they were perfectly compatible with democratic rule and national sentiment about care for the environment. In fact, such claims actually lent further legitimacy to settler power.

The indigeneity asserted by Pakeha farmers, environmentalists, and others diverged from that asserted by Māori on the crucial issue of authority. For Māori, the assertion of indigenous feeling and belonging, premised in long-standing attachment to and knowledge of particular areas, helped them to establish a political demand for self-determination in its local conceptualization as rangatiratanga. Their indigeneity was, as the New Zealand Māori Council had put it to the Court of Appeal, "proof" of their peoplehood and demonstrated that they were nations within the larger settler state. Pakeha who asserted indigeneity did not need to make such a demand. Their version of indigeneity did not challenge the historical or geographical boundaries of the settler state. They were not "first people," nor were they trying to establish rights to tribal territory.

THE LONG-AWAITED REPORT of the Waitangi Tribunal on the Whanganui claim was finally published in June 1999. As had become customary in tribunal practice, members of the tribunal and staff launched the report on tribal grounds—at the Putiki Wharanui marae in the town of Whanganui—on Saturday, 26 June, the day after it had been delivered to the minister of Māori Affairs. Claimants welcomed the tribunal members and staff back on to their grounds and, in exchange for the report, presented each of the tribunal members with gifts of mounted riverstones.[65]

Almost 400 pages long, the report included an extensive discussion of the history of the river and the tribe's relationship to it. It canvassed settlers' historical use of the river and its significance in local and national terms. The report discussed the mid-century litigation brought by Titi Tihu and others in depth, and it provided a detailed outline of what the tribunal considered to be the major treaty breaches in respect of the tribe's ownership of the river.

In failing to recognize the rights of Whanganui Māori to their river, the tribunal found that the Crown was in breach of the Treaty of Waitangi in at least two major respects. The English version had guaranteed the rights of the signatories to maintain their extant possessions, which had not occurred in the case of Whanganui Māori. Moreover, the Crown had failed to protect the tribe's rangatiratanga over the river, as promised in article two of the Māori version. These breaches now needed to be rectified. Once out in the public domain, the report quickly earned considerable national attention because of its potentially far-reaching recommendations.

In a reversal of Justice Blackburn's reasoning in the Gove case in Australia and the decision of the New Zealand Court of Appeal regarding the river in 1962, the majority of the tribunal found that the tribes had distinct rights of possession of and authority over the Whanganui River. The tribunal argued that these rights existed because of the strength of the tribe's "unique" spiritual attachment to it. The tribunal was convinced by the Whanganui people's assertions that they belonged to the river and that therefore the river belonged to them. Moreover, the distinct rights of indigenous peoples to their properties were recognized in the "established" doctrine of aboriginal title in New Zealand.

The tribunal dismissed the arguments of the Crown lawyers that the Whanganui tribe's interest in the river could not be translated into property rights. It argued that theories of property rights could be broadened to accommodate the inextricable belonging of Whanganui Māori to their tupuna awa. The tribe's "right of ownership" of the river could be recognized as a right to the river as a whole entity, rather than according to the "English legal conception of river ownership in terms of riverbeds." As the report explained, this acknowledged what was important in Māori legal practice and principle, that "the lands of the people ... are defined not by boundaries but by relationships. The identifiable lands of a group of Māori people are the lands of their history, the places where their tupuna are buried, all those lands that they could occupy or defend, or on which they could keep their fires alight."[66] The tribunal further proposed that that the river be vested in "an ancestor or ancestors representative of Atihaunui, with the Whanganui Māori Trust Board as trustee." Such an arrangement had direct practical implications. Among other things, it would mean that resource consent applications would have to be first approved by the board.[67]

As a commission of inquiry established under the authority of the New Zealand state, neither Durie, nor the tribunal as a whole, contested the right of the New Zealand government to govern, nor did they seek to overturn Crown sovereignty. But the tribunal report did, like other legal decisions in settler states in the late twentieth century, bring into question a conception of Crown authority as unitary or "perfect." Indeed, quite radically, as some commentators pointed out, the tribunal recommended that the Crown and the Whanganui tribe should become equal partners in control, management, and use of the river. Going beyond the Court of Appeal's finding in the 1987 Lands case that the Crown had a duty to consult with Māori, an equal partnership gave much more authority to Whanganui Māori over the river, without, the tribunal claimed, jeopardizing public access and use.

Not all the tribunal members agreed with these recommendations. John Kneebone, a former president of the advisory body Federated Farmers, dissented since, he argued, water was not something that could be owned by anyone. The vesting of authority over the river in the Whanganui tribe could not be a "universally acceptable" solution. Kneebone's opposition echoed with the claims of other Pakeha to their indigeneity in respect of the river, although he did not stake out a strong conservationist claim. He sought to uphold the status quo. Māori, he argued, had to face the realities of modern industrialized life, however "brutal" those realities might be. In Kneebone's interpretation, like that of the Crown lawyers, Māori had already submitted to the settler state and the rule of law and they had to accept, as did other citizens, that the state had the prerogative to manage the river flow and control its use. Kneebone therefore countered the idea that Māori were "citizens plus" and "first among equals." Similarly, other media commentators argued that resources such as rivers (and air and radio waves) were public assets, and that the tribunal's findings would set dangerous precedents, conferring, as one commentator opined, ownership and management to groups "based on their ethnic origin."[68] For this writer, the idea that Māori could be considered guardians of the national estate was unacceptable.

The tribunal report was clear that the recommendations were not based in "special" rights for one ethnic group or race. They were founded in law, the Treaty of Waitangi, and a bicultural respect for and appreciation of the Whanganui tribe's depth of attachment. They were, in other words, constitutional rights. Moreover, this form of attachment and the rules and obligations it gave rise to, the tribunal further emphasized, was something that non-Māori New Zealanders could also learn from. As the report argued,

> It is only when we appreciate that it is not possessions that most count but how we relate to, and respect the mana of, each other and the environment that we will understand the contribution that Māori thinking can make to a better society, and can develop a philosophy of law that is more in tune with the Pacific way.[69]

The tribunal borrowed the term "the Pacific way" from the decolonization discourse of Pacific Island leaders of the 1970s and 1980s. Notably, Ratu Sir Kamisese Mara, the first prime minister of Fiji after the country won independence from Britain in 1970, spoke of "the Pacific Way" in 1975. According to Mara, the postcolonial future of Pacific Island nations was markedly different from others that had gone through decolonization. In the Pacific, a tradition of tolerance and friendly exchange between Pacific Island peoples provided a foundation for interdependency in the present, he claimed.[70] The tribunal's reference to the Pacific Way reminded New Zealanders that their country was located in the Pacific and founded in a human history of interactions between different peoples of the region. The use of the concept further emphasized how New Zealand might be indigenized through a reimagining of the country as founded in two traditions.[71] It expressed hope for respectful and tolerant interaction between different groups in New Zealand in the present and into the future. Indeed, the idea of re-founding New Zealand in the Pacific Way called for Māori and Pakeha to create a new, mutually beneficial, and peaceful postcolonial nation.

AFTER GENERATIONS OF protest, litigation, petitions to governments and the Queen, extensive fundraising, and the deaths of three leaders (Titi Tihu, Hikaia Amohia, and Archie Taiaroa), had Whanganui Māori finally received a fair hearing? Many members of the tribe were happy with the settlement that had been negotiated on their behalf by the Whanganui River Māori Trust Board, even if it was so long in coming. The deed of settlement was finally ratified by the tribe in July 2014—seventy-six years after Titi Tihu and other leaders brought the first legal claim. Some of the activists who led the protests at Pakaitore in 1995 had even become signatories to the settlement on behalf of the tribe. The deed included provisions to develop a unique form of legal recognition for the entirety of the river, "from the mountains to the sea," and the enhancement of the tribe's mana in relation to the river.[72]

In bringing their claim to the tribunal, Whanganui people had not resisted state power or reasserted full political autonomy. But neither had they simply been incorporated into existing state hegemony. The Whanganui claim brought to the fore new and complex struggles between the settler state, indigenous peoples, and settler society. The idea that Māori had distinct rights to their lands and waters based in spiritual attachment and deep identification with place gave them the opportunity to assert a new status in New Zealand. It prompted a rethinking of historical agency and the telling of history. However, according to Crown lawyers and historians, acknowledging Māori as coeval historical agents actually undid the claims of Whanganui Māori in particular to a distinct, sacred relationship to the river. The Whanganui people's claim for indigeneity also prompted local Pakeha to assert their identity in similar terms of connection to place. These were claims that could shore up or undermine tribal authority.

The tribunal's argument that New Zealand should be re-founded in the "Pacific Way" was itself, perhaps, an attempt to bring an end to those struggles and reestablish the fragile truce between indigenous peoples, settler society, and the state. This marked a timely aspiration and it was one that recognized the efforts of those who had spent many years arguing for the importance of Māori tradition and history. The tribunal's serious consideration of an alternative Māori history demonstrated that institutions of the state were, finally, taking real notice of and giving proper appreciation to the first peoples of the land. Their history seemed to have become a usable past for the settler state. But in wider settler society, many disputed the relevance of Māori history to their sense of nationalism. Moreover, this aspiration to a postcolonial indigeneity for the settler state placed a new burden on Māori, as "guardians" who were now asked to make a "contribution" to the country. The irony of asking Māori to do so, in the very moment in which the injustices that they had suffered were supposedly being redressed, was surely bittersweet.

Epilogue

TRUCE UNDONE

BY THE TURN of the twenty-first century, the fraught and fragile truce between indigenous peoples and settler states seemed to be unraveling. Indigenous claims had, unexpectedly, made a significant impact on social democratic governance in the settler states in the 1970s and 1980s as those countries sought out new postcolonial futures while holding on to principles of equality and justice. Activists persuaded national governments that recognizing their distinct rights was a matter of fairness. However, by the 2000s, with income inequality increasing and governments providing fewer social services in all three countries, the activist arguments of the 1970s had lost the influence they had then. Immigration from Asia and the Middle East, official multiculturalism, and the unpredictabilities of the mining boom, inspired widespread discontent among sections of white settler society. Extensive neoliberal reforms had broken the commitments of earlier governments to equality and some ideas of social justice seemed to have less purchase. Leading politicians and white commentators argued that the "special" rights being awarded to indigenous peoples did not sit well with the principle of individualist "user-pays." The once-radical idea that these settler states had a much longer indigenous past was now being taken for granted.

Fueling the flames of an acrimonious and sometimes hysterical backlash against indigenous rights, these politicians mobilized a new set of uncertainties in the settler states. They argued that indigenous claims, complex and wide ranging, were taking too long to resolve and that they had spawned industries, paid for the by the state, which employed academic researchers and lawyers whose knowledge production was of little use to anyone else.[1] They questioned the success of policies of self-determination, given high rates of welfare dependency among some indigenous communities, and argued that these policies were a further drain on limited government resources. Influenced by scholarship critical of the cultural distinctiveness that indigenous peoples claimed, political commentators questioned whether indigenous peoples really were so different from settlers. Critical scholars launched "history wars" on other scholars they saw as too sympathetic to indigenous demands—in Australia labeled the "black armband historians"—and whose arguments, the critics claimed, were undermining national pride.[2] Some among settler society rejected the idea that indigenous peoples could be guardians of the national estate and mounted counter-protests to protect public access to areas they considered theirs.[3] These arguments against indigenous rights pushed back some of the reforms that had so radically transformed the settler states' indigenous policies between the 1970s to the early 1990s.

Indigenous peoples responded to attacks on their rights and the effects of economic reforms from a wider spectrum of positions and ideologies than was the case in the 1970s. Opposing neoliberal reforms and demanding a "peaceful revolution, to honor indigenous sovereignty, and to protect the land and water," the Idle No More movement in Canada forged connections with anti-globalization movements.[4] It rapidly spread to the United States and Australia in 2012. Activists in this movement contested what they saw as backtracking by governments in the twenty-first century and drew links between the problems facing indigenous communities and the economic disenfranchisement of other social groups.

Pointing out that processes of rights recognition that had seemed to promise so much had generally failed to alleviate social and economic problems, other activists advocated turning away from the state. In this light, some scholars began to theorize a politics of "refusal" as a normative practice that indigenous communities could undertake in rejecting the liberal politics of recognition.[5] The legal reforms that activists spurred in the 1970s to counter the colonial threat of assimilation seem, to this generation of activists and scholars, to have become yet another form of colonization. For instance, Yidindji man, Murrumu Walubara (formerly Jeremy Geia) argued that indigenous peoples in Australia should abandon the national "citizen ship" as he called it, in order to achieve true decolonization. Murrumu left his job as a chief political correspondent in Canberra in 2014, giving up his bank accounts, superannuation funds, and passport, and returned to his tribal territory. "The truth is that we were here before the British," he told a journalist, explaining why he had rejected some entitlements of Australian enfranchisement that earlier generations of activists had fought for. "The truth is that we hold sovereignty and dominion over these lands. The truth is that there've been genocide and multiple crimes against humanity and massacres committed on this land that haven't been brought to . . . justice."[6]

Other indigenous leaders, particularly of tribes that negotiated substantial monetary settlements with the settler state, argued for a focus on economic development. They did not necessarily see a contradiction between indigenous peoplehood and neoliberal reform and their tribal corporations moved into the space left vacant by the withdrawal of state services. Less concerned with asserting political sovereignty, these leaders sought engagement with global markets. The "trappings of sovereignty," were not important for Māori any longer, argued Sir Tipene O'Regan, a leader of the South Island tribe Ngai Tahu, in 1995 on the eve of the signing of the tribe's economic and cultural settlement agreement, which was one of the largest in New Zealand's history. "The only way for Maori to live in the new century," he claimed, "is in the whole world."[7]

Still other leaders focused on the arena of international law. They appealed to the United Nations Declaration on the Rights of Indigenous Peoples, which was finally signed in 2007 after twenty years of difficult negotiations and which recognizes the right of indigenous self-determination.[8] Nonetheless, many indigenous groups continued to engage in legal claims-making at the level of the settler state in pursuit of their rights and to push for further constitutional reforms. Even in a much less sympathetic environment, some groups won remarkable victories in the courts.[9] Moreover, significant symbolic events, such as the Australian Commonwealth government's apology for the suffering of members of the "Stolen Generations" (Aboriginal children removed from their families by agents of the state) in parliament in February 2008, brought the nation to a standstill in a shared mood of regret, mourning, and possibility.[10] Today, the stakes of indigenous claims remain high and far from resolved.

Historians cannot yet definitively assess the long-term outcomes of indigenous claims-making at the end of the twentieth century. What this book has argued is that, over a thirty-year period, indigenous peoples did a remarkable thing. At a moment of the highest stakes of survival, when their collective identities seemed to be most at risk of obliteration by policies of assimilation and the mining boom, they forced the settler state to enter into a negotiation with them about their rights. Indigenous communities in Australia, Canada, and New Zealand had experienced common histories of dispossession, loss of language, and psychic wounds inflicted by state institutions. Perhaps they felt they had nothing more to lose by the 1970s when they made new protests and decades if not centuries of colonization had taken their toll. At the same time, leaders like Harold Cardinal in Canada and Hana Jackson in New Zealand recognized that there was something unique about this historical moment, a moral and political opening that they could widen in pressing for rights that would protect and even help to restore their identities. In a common act of political genius, they realized that they could tie the survival of their own communities to the needs of settler nationalism as Australia, Canada, and New Zealand searched for a postcolonial identity.

The extraordinary achievements of Roy Marika and the Yolngu people in northern Australia, James Wah-Shee and the Indian Brotherhood of the Northwest Territories in Canada, and Archie Taiaroa and the Whanganui people in New Zealand, among many others, are too easily overlooked. This is especially so since scholars working with some indigenous groups today see the raw and violent effects of years of poverty, welfare dependence, substance abuse, and the explosion of diseases in remote communities that have been eradicated everywhere else in the settler countries. The era of land rights recognition and self-determination has not necessarily yielded the widely hoped for social and economic benefits that many thought it would.

Yet, through complex and often personal engagements in the law, indigenous peoples established a new status for themselves in the settler state. Despite the intractability of governments at the time, by pushing for their land rights and tying the recognition of those to their historical relationship to place, they made themselves newly known to settler societies as first peoples. This idea struck at the heart of the settler colonial enterprise, throwing into doubt the rightful sense of belonging to Australia, Canada, and New Zealand that settlers enjoyed in the 1960s. It splintered the assumptions of the social contract in these countries, that the colonization "by a more advanced people" as Justice Blackburn put it in his decision on the Gove land rights case in 1971, was inevitable and relatively benign and mainly the work of white settlers. It forced countries that prided themselves on egalitarianism premised in cultural homogeneity to reckon with difference. First peoples had survived despite, and not because of, the "advancement" offered to them by settler states. By making their history foundational to the settler state, they ensured that governments and wider settler society would acknowledge their histories of loss, dispossession, and persistence and offer some redress.

The Land Is Our History has told a rare story of the disempowered changing the status quo. It is a history that brings into focus the process by which an unequal and unexpected negotiation took place between the powerful and the virtually disenfranchised and through which they worked out a temporary compromise. Given the nature of the asymmetry between the parties, it was not one that always served indigenous peoples well, at the time or today. But it is an achievement, nonetheless, that needs to be recognized and appreciated in all its complexity and contradiction. It behooves scholars to grapple with indigenous peoples' struggles for rights and autonomy not simply as future aspirations nor as watered-down versions of global demands for decolonization. This book has argued that we should cast these struggles as effective political critiques of the intense form of colonization indigenous peoples experienced and as an insistence on their survival as nations. These are stories that can be drawn on and used by a range of actors—indigenous peoples, settlers, and newer immigrants—in the years to come as we undertake and reckon with new, and persisting, injustice.

Notes

ABBREVIATIONS

AEWP   Sir Albert Edward Woodward, Papers, University of Melbourne Archives, Melbourne, Australia

AIATSIS Australian Institute for Aboriginal and Torres Strait Islander Studies Library, Canberra, Australia

ANZ   Archives New Zealand, Wellington

ATL   Alexander Turnbull Library, Wellington

CICC   Canadian Indian Claims Commission, Ottawa

LAC   Library and Archives Canada, Ottawa

NAA   National Archives Australia, Canberra

INTRODUCTION

1. On the rapid expansion of Anglo settler colonization in the nineteenth century and the booms and busts that underwrote its successes and redirected economic efforts, see Belich, *Replenishing the Earth*. On the legal and extra-legal instruments that setters used to take new lands, see Weaver, *The Great Land Rush*. On indigenous struggles and resistance to dispossession in the nineteenth century, see Laidlaw and Lester, *Indigenous Communities and Settler Colonialism*.

2. Ford, *Settler Sovereignty*, 2.

3. On the framing of settler states as politically independent but economically dependent on European metropoles, see Denoon, *Settler Capitalism*.

4. Crosby, *Ecological Imperialism*.

5. For a discussion of the scholarship on assimilation in settler states, see Chapter 1.

6. For a discussion of indigenous claims in earlier periods of settler colonization, see Belmessous, *Native Claims*. On the "unreceptiveness" of Canadian courts up until

the 1960s to Indian leaders' legal challenges, see Harring, *White Man's Law*, 4. On attempts by indigenous leaders to win international attention for their claims from the League of Nations and other organizations, see de Costa, "Identity, Authority, and the Moral Worlds of Indigenous Petitions"; and Niezen, *The Origins of Indigenism*, chapter 1. For the range of issues that indigenous rights claims have raised in the late twentieth century see, for example, Havemann, *Indigenous Peoples' Rights in Australia, Canada & New Zealand*; Knafla and Westra, eds., *Aboriginal Title and Indigenous Peoples*; Ivison, Patton, and Sanders, eds., *Political Theory and the Rights of Indigenous Peoples*.

7. On the emergence of "indigeneity" in relation to late-twentieth century rights claims in Anglo settler states, see Niezen, *The Origins of Indigenism*; and Merlan, "Indigeneity: Global and Local." See also Tim Rowse who argues that the global concept of indigeneity is "non-racial." Rowse, "Global Indigenism." The use of the term "indigenous" is contested by some "indigenous" groups themselves for its lack of specificity. See Arvin, "Anayltics of Indigeneity." Others argue for the term's importance as an "analytic of political resistance" and the work such a term does in creating possibilities for transnational solidarities. See Teves, Smith, and Rahetja, "Indigeneity," 116. See also, Kauanui, "Indigenous." This book elaborates on the idea of indigeneity as a contested term of engagement. Distinctively, I argue that it is also a term that has been taken up by some settler states as they try to "re-settle" themselves into a new, ancient, past. All these arguments, including my own, are centered in political worlds largely produced under Anglo settler colonialism. For origins and meanings of indigeneity in non-Anglo contexts, see the account provided by Alcida Rita Ramos who argues that in Latin American countries, the term refers to a realm of "interethnicity." See Ramos, *Indigenism*. For an argument for a Southeast Asian origin for the concept of indigeneity, see Tsing, "*Adat*/Indigenous: Indigeneity in Motion."

8. See Anaya, *Indigenous Peoples in International Law*.

9. This was a claim frequently made by politicians in the 1960s and 1970s, the period in which indigenous peoples began to make their rights claims. See Chapter 1.

10. As in other postcolonial societies, settler states "invented" new traditions for themselves, as Eric Hobsbawm and Terence Ranger explain. These national traditions "attempt to establish continuity with a suitable historical past" and might emerge "in a less easily traceable manner within a brief and dateable period ... establishing themselves with great rapidity." Hobsbawm and Ranger, *The Invention of Tradition*, 1.

11. In Johannes Fabian's critical account of anthropology, the "denial of coevalness" was a constitutive part of the colonial anthropological enterprise in which native people were represented as inhabiting a time "other than the present of the producer of anthropological discourse." The temporal othering of indigenous peoples can be seen in a range of other domains too, including the political. Therefore, demonstrating coevalness was key for late twentieth-century indigenous activists

in order to engage with public institutions on an equal footing that would force settlers to acknowledge their co-presence. Fabian, *Time and the Other*, 31.

12. Thus, according to Patrick Wolfe, settler colonialism is a "structure" not an "event" that follows a "logic of elimination" of indigenous peoples. See Wolfe, "Land, Labor and Difference," and Wolfe, "Settler Colonialism and the Elimination of the Native." Wolfe's argument has been widely taken up by scholars, particularly those working in North America and Australia. See, for example, Hoxie, "Retrieving the Red Continent." Wolfe's argument has come under increasing criticism for its totalizing claims. See, for example, Ford, "Locating Indigenous Self-Determination in the Marigns of Settler Sovereignty;" and Rowse, "Indigenous Heterogeneity." Following Rowse, this book examines the "contending structures" of the state that were more complex, and also more porous, than an ahistorical "logic of elimination" can allow for. Since the argument in this book is centrally focused on the agency of indigenous peoples in pressing for their rights and the unexpected consequences of their actions, the definition of settler colonialism given by Wolfe, although important, is insufficient. See also Elkins and Pedersen, "Introduction: Settler Colonialism: A Concept and Its Uses," 2–3.

13. See Nettheim, " 'Peoples' and 'Populations.' "

14. Anderson, *Imagined Communities*.

15. On indigeneity and notions of place, see Basso, *Wisdom Sits in Places*. The idea that a historical and ancestral relationship to land is critical to collective identity is now central to heritage practices in New Zealand, Canada, and Australia and is included in the charters of the International Council on Monuments and Sites in each country. See for example ICOMOS New Zealand Charter, http://www.icomos.org.nz/nzcharters.htm; Australia ICOMOS, "The Burra Charter," http://australia.icomos.org/publications/charters/; and Canada ICOMOS, http://canada.icomos.org/bylaws_charters.html. I thank Peter Hobbins for these references.

16. Deloria in Manuel and Posluns, *The Fourth World*, xii. Deloria's argument echoes that of Irish poet James Cousins who argued for a poetics of internationalism through his studies of Indian mythology. According to Viswanathan, Cousins was opposed to "selfish" nationalism which was never "able effectively to ground politics in a goal beyond itself." Indigeneity, in Deloria's rendering, similarly operated as an identity that went beyond the political and was critical of the selfishness of nation-states. Viswanathan, "Ireland, India, and the Poetics of Internationalism," 15.

17. This book takes up Anthony Hopkins's invitation to rethink post–World War II decolonization by incorporating the history of the "white dominions" into it. However, by centering indigenous claims-making, the argument in this book draws out a different story from that proposed by Hopkins and reaches alternate conclusions. According to Hopkins, the claims by indigenous peoples to equality is part of a larger story of the shift to a multicultural labor market in Australia, Canada, and New Zealand, and the concomitant shift away from a reliance on British immigration. Like many historians of empire, Hopkins misses the significance of

indigenous claims to distinct rights, based on specific histories of relationship to the land and agreements forged in treaties, and which inspired new narratives about the origins of the settler state. Hopkins, "Rethinking Decolonization." See also Curran and Ward, *The Unknown Nation*; and Ward, "The 'New Nationalism' in Australia, Canada and New Zealand."

18. In many ways, the colonial history of the United States is quite similar to that of Australia, Canada, and New Zealand. The former country shares a common law heritage with the latter three. As scholars have begun to uncover, there is a similar and, indeed, connected history of indigenous dispossession and subordination to the law in the making of settler sovereignty across the settler states. However, in the United States, a limited notion of tribal sovereignty was recognized by the United States Supreme Court in the nineteenth century and this conditioned possibilities for making larger claims later. Most significant to the argument made in this book, American Indian claims about treaty breaches in the mid-twentieth century in the United States Indian Claims Commission (USICC) did not provoke the same kind of extensive debate about national identity and the origins of state sovereignty that those in the Commonwealth settler states did, at a later period. On indigenous dispossession and subordination to the law in the eighteenth and nineteenth centuries, see Banner, *How the Indians Lost Their Land*, and Ford, *Settler Sovereignty*. On the European intellectual bases for dispossession, see Williams, *The American Indian in Western Legal Thought*. On tribal sovereignty, see Deloria, *Behind the Trail of Broken Treaties*, especially chapter 8; Biolsi, "Imagined Geographies"; and Duthu, *American Indians and the Law*. For a tribal history premised on the idea of ongoing Indian sovereignty, see Wilkinson, *Blood Struggle*. On the history of the USICC, see Rosenthal, *Their Day in Court*, and Lurie, "The Indian Claims Commission." The difference between the USICC and the later claims commissions in the Commonwealth countries is also notable in terms of the lack of indigenous self-representation in the former. One historian who appeared as an expert witness in the USICC later observed that "From the beginning, the absence of any visible Indian participation in the ICC struck me." Tanner, "In the Arena," 187.

19. Pagden, "Fellow Citizens and Imperial Subjects," 29.

20. For example, the Australian Natives' Association, founded in 1871, aimed to cultivate "national feeling, the federation of Australia . . . a white Australia, a strong hand in the Pacific area," and so on. See Blackton, "Australian Nationality and Nativism." See also Lake and Reynolds, *Drawing the Global Colour Line*.

21. See, for example, Haebich, *Spinning the Dream*, 130–131.

22. For a discussion of these challenges in psychoanalytic terms, see Moran, "The Psychodynamics of Australian Settler-Nationalism." Scholars have taken part in these debates too in order to influence policymaking. See, for example, Flanagan, *First Nations? Second Thoughts*; and Waldron, "Indigeneity? First Peoples and Last Occupancy."

23. For instance, the testimony of Aborigines in colonial New South Wales was not usually taken account of since it was not sworn on the Bible. The admissibility of Aborigines' evidence in New South Wales was discussed by Crown Law officers in 1832, as Lisa Ford recounts. See Ford, *Settler Sovereignty*, 174–175. Reginald Good argues that the evidence of "non-Christian Indian witnesses" was not usually admitted in the municipal courts of most of Canada in the nineteenth century. See Good, "Admissibility of Testimony from Non-Christian Indians in the Colonial Municipal Courts of Upper Canada/Canada West." As Heather Douglas and Mark Finnane explain, even legislation making Aboriginal evidence admissible in the mid-nineteenth-century Australian colonies was not seen as a "remedy that would bring Aborigines into equal status with British subjects." Rather, the "long-term task was to transform the Aboriginal person into an individual with the attributes of British subjects like themselves." Douglas and Finnane, *Indigenous Crime and Settler Law*, 57–58.

24. Jean-Francois Lyotard calls this assymetrical situation a case of the "differend," when the "'regulation' of the conflict that opposes them is done in the idiom of one of the parties while the wrong suffered by the other is not signified in that idiom." Lyotard, *The Differend*, 9, 28. In a similar vein, Robert Cover argues that "legal interpretation takes place in a field of pain and death. . . . A judge articulates her understanding of a text, and as a result, somebody loses his freedom, his property, his children, even his life. . . . When interpreters have finished their work, they frequently leave behind victims whose lives have been torn apart by these organized, social practices of violence." Cover, "Violence and the Word," 203. But acknowledging an asymmetry in power does not mean that the stories indigenous peoples told in the law were not signifiable in changing legal idioms. The efflorescence of judicial decisions and legal thinking on treaties made with indigenous peoples in Anglo settler states in the late twentieth century shows that legal idioms can be changed, for the better and for the worse.

25. The effects of indigenous testimony on judges and lawyers discussed in this book contrast sharply with the story told by James Clifford about the Mashpee trial in Boston in 1976. In an essay that is now considered a classic in the field, Clifford argued that what was at stake in the courtroom was a "contest between oral and literate forms of knowledge." In the Mashpee case, the application of a "literalist epistemology" by the judge and jury worked against the Mashpee who were seeking recognition of their tribal identity and sovereignty. Clifford, "Identity in Mashpee," 202.

26. Baragwanath, "Arguing the Case for the Appellants," 29. See also Chapter 5.

27. For another example of negotiation of the law by indigenous peoples, see Norman, *What Do We Want?* See also Scholtz, *Negotiating Claims*. These approaches draw on ideas developed in law and colonialism literature—for instance, that the colonized can use the law, as John Comaroff puts it, to open up "fissures through which the contradictions inherent in colonialism became visible." See Comaroff,

"Colonialism, Culture, and the Law: A Foreword," 312. They take heed of Sally Merry's observation that courts can be "critical sites of cultural production." See Merry, "Law and Colonialism," 892.

28. For a discussion that emphasizes indigenous agency in the making of international treaties, see Borrows, "Wampum at Niagara."

29. On the revival of native title by the Hualapai in the United States, see McMillen, *Making Indian Law*. On the legal history of revival as an intellectual project, see McHugh, *Aboriginal Societies and the Common Law*. See also, McHugh, *Aboriginal Title*.

30. See McHugh, *Aboriginal Title*, chapter 1.

31. The classic statement on "free land" and the frontier was made by Turner, "The Significance of the Frontier in American History."

32. In the nineteenth century, the inalienability of such title effectively excluded indigenous peoples from participating in the property market since they could only sell their lands to the Crown or federal state. In this sense, the doctrine portrayed indigenous peoples as living out of time with settler capitalism. Donald Denoon conceived of settler capitalism as premised on the commodification of land in frontier societies. Denoon *Settler Capitalism*. See also, Belich, *Replenishing the Earth*; and Weaver, *The Great Land Rush*.

33. As Webber explains, the recognition of a collective land title held by indigenous peoples does not mean that within those societies all land is held communally. Rather, native title implicitly recognizes the "political and legal autonomy of indigenous societies" and therefore their capacity to determine land-holding internally. Webber, "Beyond Regret," 71.

34. Although for a treaty made with Kulin people in Port Phillip but not upheld by the Colonial Office, see Attwood, *Possession*.

35. See Chapter 5 for a longer discussion of the use of principles of international treaty principles by the Waitangi Tribunal in New Zealand.

36. See Ford, *Settler Sovereignty*, especially the introduction. Her argument focuses on how settler states imposed territoriality not simply through the appropriation of indigenous peoples' land but also through the imposition of criminal jurisdiction over them, thus denying the validity of their own legal systems. On the territorialization of sovereignty in the nineteenth century, see also Anghie, "Finding the Peripheries."

37. On the making of the Mabo case which focuses on the biography of the lead plaintiff, Eddie Mabo, see Russell, *Recognising Aboriginal Title*. For a discussion of the implications of the discussion, see Ivison, "Decolonizing the Rule of Law."

38. Paul Keating, "Redfern Speech," available at www.antar.org.au.

39. See, for example, Gelder and Jacobs, *Uncanny Australia*.

40. For the creation of this imagination, see Chatterjee, *The Nation and Its Fragments*, especially chapter 4.

41. See Slattery, "Understanding Aboriginal Rights."

42. See Pocock, *The Ancient Constitution and the Feudal Law*.

43. See, for example, Rose, "Women and Land Claims." Women's evidence, particularly if secret in nature, has been the subject of deep legal controversy—for instance, in the Hindmarsh Island case in Australia. See Langton, "The Hindmarsh Island Bridge Affair."

44. Anthropologist Elizabeth Povinelli argues that processes of rights recognition have irrevocably distorted indigenous peoples' self-expression and even harmed indigenous communities. Povinelli, *The Cunning of Recognition*. Other scholars, however, see this critique as unnecessarily pessimistic. Webber, "Beyond Regret," 78–79. See also the debate between John Frow, Meaghan Morris, and Elizabeth Povinelli on Povinelli's article, "The State of Shame," all conducted in *Critical Inquiry*. Frow and Morris, "Two Laws: Response to Elizabeth Povinelli"; and Povinelli, "Critical Response." Povinelli's critical argument against legal recognition does not take full enough account of the radical changes in state practice and national imagining that indigenous claims-making inspired.

45. Kirsty Gover argues that continuity is a "cardinal" principle of indigeneity that is key to the definition of tribal membership. See Gover, *Tribal Constitutionalism*, 211. See also, Gover, "When Tribalism Meets Liberalism."

46. On the oppressive demands for indigenous peoples to perform a rigid image of authenticity, see Sissons, *First Peoples*, chapter 2. On the ways that indigenous peoples helped to construct notions of their authenticity in the late nineteenth century, and used these representations for political ends, see Raibmon, *Authentic Indians*. The trap of authenticity is hard to avoid. For instance, anthropologist Paul Nadasdy worries that in engaging with state processes of rights recognition, indigenous peoples must "learn completely new and uncharacteristic ways of speaking and thinking," implying that this is a bad thing. Yet when white communities, for instance, learn "completely new" behaviors scholars do not judge them by how "uncharacteristic" those are but, rather, try to understand why those behaviors came about and perhaps what their effects were. In representations such as these, indigenous peoples' capacity to define their own terms of belonging and identity in multiple and complex ways may be taken away from them once again. See Nadasdy, *Hunters and Bureaucrats*, 2.

47. Aotearoa literally means "land of the long white cloud." It began to be used nationally to refer to the bicultural nature of New Zealand society in the 1990s. See Fleras and Spoonley, *Recalling Aotearoa*.

CHAPTER I

1. Petitions of the Aboriginal people of Yirrkala 14 August and 28 August 1963, Parliament House, Canberra. NAA, *Documenting a Democracy: Yirrkala Bark Petitions 1963 (Cth)*, www.foundingdocs.gov.au.

2. For a brief discussion of the petitions in a longer Aboriginal political history, see Morphy, "Art and Politics."

3. See NAA, *Documenting a Democracy*.

4. "Aboriginal Petition on Bark," *Canberra Times*, 15 August 1963, 3. The author of this article called the petitioners the "Yirrkala group." Yirrkala was the name of the mission village where some members of Yolngu-speaking clans lived, but it was not the name of a linguistic or ethnic community. The petitions were signed by leaders from a number of different clans. A later report questioned the status of the petitioners as too "young" to be representative. See "Status of N.T. Tribal Petitioners Queried," *Canberra Times*, 21 August 1963, 3.

5. Mining and resource extraction had long been important to the economies of Australia and Canada. However, in the 1960s operations markedly intensified and expanded into new areas. In Australia, corporations began to undertake projects in coal, iron, and bauxite mining, as well as uranium extraction in Queensland and the Northern Territory. In 1966–1967, Japan displaced Britain as Australia's biggest customer, taking a large proportion of the country's meat production and, even more significantly, its metal ores. See Dyster, *Australia in the International Economy in the Twentieth Century*, 248. In Canada, the government began to open up northern lands for large-scale projects to transport oil and gas from the Arctic to the south, as well as for hydroelectric development projects. By 1960, 80 percent of foreign capital invested in Canada was American and three quarters of oil and gas was foreign-controlled. See Norrie, *A History of the Canadian Economy*, 418 and 424. For other arguments connecting the emergence of indigenous rights claims with the mining boom, see Peterson, "Common Law, Statutory Law, and the Political Economy of the Recognition of Indigenous Australian Rights in Land"; and Sanders, *Native People in Areas of Internal National Expansion*.

6. The concept of "citizens plus" is defined by the Canadian political scientist Alan Cairns as stressing "the virtues of a common citizenship as well as the reinforcement of difference." He critiques a nation-to-nation argument that emerged in Canada in the 1990s that he claims downplays the importance of shared ideals of citizenship. As he explains, the idea that indigenous peoples in Canada bear distinct rights does denote collective identities and national ambitions. Cairns makes the point that the concept also describes "goals of Aboriginal peoples in Australia . . . [who] will have a national loyalty to their Aboriginal first nation and a civic loyalty to the Australia state." Cairns, *Citizens Plus*, 8–10. See also the discussion of the emergence and use of the term in Indian activism later in the chapter.

7. Quoted in Berndt, "The Gove Dispute," 260 and 262.

8. 1 April 1969, Signed by Village Council of Yirrkala. AEWP, box 3.

9. "Assimilation of Aborigines," *Canberra Times*, 19 October 1951, 4.

10. Parliament of the Commonwealth of Australia, *Report from the Select Committee on Grievances of Yirrkala Aborigines*, 9.

11. On the science of racial absorption, see Anderson, *The Cultivation of Whiteness*, 244–247.

12. The term "assimilation" is used broadly by many scholars to refer to a wide range of policies and practices over different periods of time. Some scholars use assimilation to refer to policies in the nineteenth century concerned with the civilization of native tribes and land alienation. See, for instance, Armitage, *Comparing the Policy of Aboriginal Assimilation*, and Miller, *Skyscrapers Hide the Heavens*. Others use assimilation to refer to practices in the twentieth century including child removal and the education of indigenous children in residential schools. See, for instance, Jacobs, *White Mother to a Dark Race*. No settler state had a long-term and crystal-clear policy of assimilation, and some scholars have pointed out that such ideas were in fact a product of certain culturalist ideas that began to circulate more widely in the post–World War II era. Australian historians in particular have differentiated between early twentieth-century policies that were "protectionist" and that treated Aborigines as subjects of colonial rule and post–World War II governmental ideas that proposed the assimilation of Aborigines as a program of modernization that would enable them to claim full citizenship in Australia. See Rowse, *White Flour, White Power*, chapter 7; and McGregor, "Wards, Words, and Citizens."

13. Therefore Tim Rowse argues that assimilation policy "signifies a doctrine of nation-hood better than it defines a distinct and internally coherent practice of government." Rowse, *White Flour, White Power*, 107.

14. In both countries, indigenous men who were considered "civilized" because they had given up their Indian treaty status in Canada or did not live in an Aboriginal settlement in Australia had the right to vote in provincial and federal elections prior to the 1960s, but these rights were not always exercised. See Stretton and Finnimore, "Black Fellow Citizens." See also Attwood and Markus, *The 1967 Referendum, or When Aborigines Didn't Get the Vote*. For a comparison of voting practices after the unconditional enfranchisement of indigenous peoples in the northern regions of both countries, see Loveday and Jaensch, "Indigenes and Electoral Administration, Australia and Canada."

15. Until changes in 1985, status Indian women who married non-status (Indian or non-Indian) men lost their own status and became Canadian citizens, whereas white women who married status Indian men gained Indian status without losing Canadian citizenship. The selective gender bias of the legislation tended to diminish the numbers of those who claimed status, since more status Indian women married non-status men than the other way around. Critics of the act therefore termed Indian women "citizens minus," playing on the widely used term in the 1970s and 1980s that status Indians were "citizens plus." See Jamieson, *Indian Women and the Law in Canada*. For a critical discussion of the 1985 reform of these requirements, see Green, "Canaries in the Mine of Citizenship." For a comparison of Canadian and Australian policies toward indigenous women, see McGrath and Stevenson, "Gender, Race, and Policy."

16. Miller, *Skyscrapers Hide the Heavens*, 326.

17. Perkins, *A Bastard Like Me*, 8.

18. See Clark, *Aborigines and Activism*, 150–179. One of the Australian freedom riders, Ann Curthoys, went on to become an eminent Australian historian and she published a collective memoir of the protest. Curthoys, *Freedom Ride*.
19. Attwood and Markus, *The 1967 Referendum*.
20. See Attwood and Markus, *The 1967 Referendum*, xi.
21. McHugh, *Aboriginal Title*, 112 and 151.
22. Taffe, *Black and White Together*, 94–95; 171; 187–188.
23. Attwood, *Rights for Aborigines*, chapter 1.
24. For example, "Petition to King George V," in Attwood and Markus, *Thinking Black*, 35–36.
25. Maynard, *Fight for Liberty and Freedom*.
26. Attwood, *Rights for Aborigines*, chapter 12.
27. However, for a critique of the policy of self-determination on the ground, see Cowlishaw, "Erasing Culture and Race."
28. See Rowley, *The Destruction of Aboriginal Society*. Later in the decade historians and activists began to use the Roman term *terra nullius* in critiquing the colonization of Australia. Notable was Henry Reynolds's use in his path-breaking book *The Law of the Land*. He did so to emphasize the racism inherent in colonial endeavor, and to put pressure on the law to begin to recognize Aboriginal land rights. On the reception of Reynolds's work, especially by the courts, see Attwood and Griffiths, "Introduction," *Frontier, Race, Nation*, 23–34. Historian Andrew Fitzmaurice has shown that the moral force of natural law has frequently been used to critique unjust conquest in European legal traditions. Indeed, he points out that the idea of *terra nullius* is itself an idea that was developed to expose rather than justify the excesses of colonization. According to Fitzmaurice, the resurfacing of the idea in historical writing of the 1970s and 1980s in Australia, and which influenced the court in the *Mabo* decision, is another moment in this counter-tradition: "Mabo is not good history and it may not be very good common law, but it is clearly continuous with a Western judicial tradition that attempted to rescue liberty (or in this case, liberal democracy) from the threat posed by the dispossession of indigenous people." See Fitzmaurice, "The Genealogy of *Terra Nullius*," 16. As other legal historians have argued, dispossession did not occur simply through the imposition of legal doctrines but rather through practice, in which the criminalization of Aboriginal subjects was key. See Ford, *Settler Sovereignty*; and Ward, "Constructing British Authority in Australasia." For a useful review of the scholarship, see Laidlaw, "Breaking Britannia's Bounds?"
29. See, for example, "Vesteys Sell Most of Australian Ranches," *Independent*, 5 July 1992, www.independent.co.uk.
30. Dyster, *Australia in the International Economy*, 243.
31. For a discussion of land rights as emerging from the protests of Aboriginal people whose lands were becoming increasingly urbanized, see Goodall, *Invasion to Embassy*, chapter 22.

32. Attwood, *Rights for Aborigines*, 262.
33. Attwood, *Rights for Aborigines*, 267.
34. H. C. Coombs, information note for Minister re Wattie Creek, 30 September 1971, Aboriginal Land Rights Policy, A1209/93 1971/6008 Part 2, NAA.
35. Coombs, information note for Minister re Wattie Creek.
36. Rowse, *Rethinking Social Justice*, 62–79.
37. The Minister for Aboriginal Affairs in South Australia, Don Dunstan, referred to ILO Convention 107 explicitly in defending the need for a moral recognition that Aboriginal people had been wronged. See Rowse, *Rethinking Social Justice*, 69.
38. Professor A. A. Abbie, quoted in Rowse, *Rethinking Social Justice*, 73.
39. Acting Director of Aboriginal Affairs D. L. Busbridge, quoted in Rowse, *Rethinking Social Justice*, 77.
40. "Aboriginal land rights campaign" [nd] Council for Aboriginal Rights, MS 12913, Box 5/17, State Library of Victoria.
41. On identity politics as primarily concerned with the right to self-definition, see Farred, "Endgame Identity?" See also Yuval-Davis, *Gender and Nation*.
42. See, for example, Carter, "'Your Great Mother across the Salt Sea'"; De Costa, "Identity, Authority, and the Moral Worlds of Indigenous Petitions"; and Niezen, *The Origins of Indigenism*, chapter 2.
43. The scholarship is extensive. General accounts of the emergence of treaty-making as settler colonial practice are given by Banner, *How the Indians Lost Their Land*, chapter three, and *Possessing the Pacific*, chapter two. For a nationally framed Canadian account, see Miller, *Compact, Contract, Covenant*. For a treaty made and forgotten, and the reasons for its forgetting, in Australia, see Attwood, *Possession*.
44. Harring, *White Man's Law*, 18–29. On arguments within the Colonial Office about indigenous rights, see also Hickford, *Lords of the Land*, especially 124 ff.
45. See Harring, *White Man's Law*, chapter six. Legal historian Kent McNeil argues that the case must be understood within a broader Social Darwinist context of civilizing Indians. See McNeil, "Social Darwinism and Judicial Conceptions of Indian Title in Canada in the 1880s."
46. On Indian interpretations of treaties, see Borrows, "Wampum at Niagara"; Fumoleau, *As Long As This Land Shall Last*; Treaty 7 Elders, *The True Spirit and Original Intent of Treaty 7*; Venne, "Understanding Treaty 6."
47. See Carter, *Aboriginal People and Colonizers of Western Canada to 1900*, especially chapter 8; and Miller, *Skyscrapers Hide the Heavens*, especially chapter 11.
48. On the history of reserves in Canada, see Harris, *Making Native Space*.
49. Daniel, *A History of Native Claims Processes in Canada 1867–1979*.
50. Foster, "We Are Not O'Meara's Children."
51. Kelly, quoted in Foster, "We Are Not O'Meara's Children," 84.
52. For a discussion, see Leslie, "Assimilation, Termination or Integration? The Development of Canadian Indian Policy, 1943–1963."

53. Member of Parliament Thomas Barnett, *House of Commons Debates*, 26th Parliament, 3rd Session, 21 June 1965, 2691.

54. Department of Indian Affairs and Northern Development, *Statement of the Government of Canada on Indian Policy*. The most thorough account of the making of this policy and its aftermath is given in Weaver, *Making Canadian Indian Policy*.

55. Trudeau, "Approaches to Politics [1970]," in Graham, *The Essential Trudeau*, 64.

56. Trudeau, "Official Statement by the Prime Minister: The Just Society [1968]," in Graham, *The Essential Trudeau*, 19.

57. Weaver argues that the Canadian Centennial celebrations in 1968 increased national curiosity about the past and provided a framework for a historical reassessment of Indian-settler relations. At the same time, the Canadian public was becoming more aware of civil rights in the United States and other minority rights issues. See Weaver, *Making Canadian Indian Policy*, 13.

58. The conservative critique of a special rights discourse—that it entitles some people to benefits not available to all—would not gain much traction until the legal efforts of indigenous people and negotiations with settler states began to bear fruit in the form of title awards and monetary compensation in the 1980s and 1990s.

59. Cardinal, *The Unjust Society*, 30. However, according to legal scholar Douglas Sanders, the Nisga'a leader Frank Calder, who would soon become renowned for leading the first aboriginal title case in court in Canada, supported the emphasis on equality in the White Paper, although he also wanted land claims recognized. See Sanders, "The Nishga Case," 13.

60. The idea that Indians bore an "additional status" with political implications for their standing had been discussed in earlier Canadian scholarship. J. G. McGilp, for instance, had described Indians as "possess[ing] a special status as an addition to their Canadian citizenship." J. G. McGilp, "The Relations of Canadian Indians and Canadian Governments."

61. Hawthorn, *A Survey of the Contemporary Indians of Canada*, 13.

62. Hawthorn, *A Survey of the Contemporary Indians of Canada*, 6.

63. Indian Chiefs of Alberta, *Citizens Plus*, 5. According to historian Laurie Drees, the Indian Association of Alberta used funds they had won from the Department of Indian Affairs to pay a research firm to compile this response. Laurie Maijer Drees, *The Indian Association of Alberta*, 169.

64. On the other hand, other emergent leaders were more circumspect about what treaties really meant. George Manuel critiqued a meeting of analysts from the Prime Minister's Office and Indian leaders in 1968 during a Human Rights Conference as simply a "replay" of treaty signings. "At the luncheon meeting the Prime Minister was trying to persuade us to surrender to them what little we had left of our heritage." Manuel, quoted in Weaver, *Making Canadian Indian Policy*, 95.

65. See Chapter 4.

66. Foster, Raven, and Webber, *Let Right Be Done*, introduction.

67. See Chapter 4.
68. *Calder v. Attorney-General of B.C.*, S.C.R. 313, (1973), para. 346.
69. Foster, Raven, and Webber, *Let Right Be Done*, 4–6.
70. National Indian Brotherhood statement on Calder case, 31 January 1973, Indian Claims Commission Files, vol. 5, 1970–1976, RG 33–115, LAC.
71. "Indians Have More Land Rights than He [Trudeau] Thought," announced the headline in the national newspaper the *Globe and Mail* in the aftermath of the decision, 8 February 1973, 8. See also Miller, *Compact, Contract, Covenant*, chapter 9.
72. Indigenous activists began to make explicit these transnational connections as they came to recognize "the widespread, almost global nature of the crises they faced." Niezen, *The Origins of Indigenism*, 30.

CHAPTER 2

1. The Gove land rights case was the subject of a monograph by the anthropologist Nancy Williams, who worked for Yolngu leaders. Motivated by the failure of the judge in the case to understand that Yolngu people did indeed maintain property rights, she considered the almost incommensurable differences between Yolngu and English ways of thinking about land, belonging, and property. Published in 1986, before the creation of a nationwide statute that enabled Aboriginal groups to mount native title claims in 1993, Williams made a case for how indigenous land tenure might be recognizable in settler common law. See Williams, *The Yolngu and Their Land*.
2. Stanner, *After the Dreaming*, 25.
3. Alan Dearn, "Gove: A Dream in Dreamtime but for Whom?" *The Australian*, 7 January 1969.
4. The peninsula was of strategic importance during World War II because of its proximity to Southeast Asia. The Royal Australian Air Force established a base on the peninsula and built roads and several landing strips. The Gove peninsula was named after an airman who died there. He is commemorated in a small plaque in the center of Nhulunbuy.
5. See Berndt and Berndt, *Arnhem Land*.
6. Parliament of the Commonwealth of Australia, *Report from the Select Committee on Grievances of Yirrkala Aborigines*, 9.
7. McKenzie, *Mission to Arnhem Land*, 68–85; Morphy, "Mutual Conversion?" 43.
8. McKenzie, *Mission to Arnhem Land*, 80.
9. Morphy, "Mutual Conversion?"
10. For a discussion of Wells's actions and motivations, see Attwood, *Rights for Aborigines*, chapter 9.
11. For the argument that many Aborigines on large reserves saw these lands as "Aboriginal country," see Berndt, "A Long View," 8.
12. See Attwood, *Rights for Aborigines*, chapter 12, for a more extensive discussion of this history.

13. See "Royal Commission into Aboriginal Land Rights in the Northern Territory, 1973–1974: A discussion between Sir Edward Woodward, Dr. Nicholas Peterson and Professor Max Charlesworth [ca. 1985]," AEWP, box 2.

14. Woodward, *One Brief Interval*, 98.

15. Correspondence between Purcell and Little, October 1969, "Gove Land Rights Case," AEWP, box 3. See also McHugh, *Aboriginal Title*, 74–75.

16. Little to Dadynga (Roy) Marika, 23 January 1972, "Gove Land Rights Case," AEWP, box 3.

17. See references to *Amodu Tijani v. Secretary, Southern Nigeria* [1921] and *Tee-Hit-Ton Indians v. United States* [1955] in AEWP, box 3

18. Barwick, "How Prof. Bill Stanner Recruited a Canadian," 11.

19. *Geita Sebea v. Territory of Papua* [1941], 67 CLR 544. For a discussion of the influence of the Papua and New Guinea experience on Australia in the field of law, see Douglas and Finnane, *Indigenous Crime and Settler Law*, 109, 112.

20. Woodward recalled that the problem of translating Aboriginal notions of ownership into common law categories only "came later as we began to talk to our Aboriginal clients and to anthropologists and started to get some feel for the Aboriginal approach to land holding. . . . [T]here was no concept of boundaries in Aboriginal thinking, since they didn't need to have precise definition between one group's land and another group's land in the same way that European citizens find it necessary to draw precise borders." See "A discussion between Sir Edward Woodward, Dr. Nicholas Peterson and Professor Max Charlesworth," AEWP, box 2.

21. Memorandum of advice in the matter of the land rights of the Aboriginal clans of East Arnhem Land. A.E. Woodward and J. D. Little, Owen Dixon chambers, 28 June 1968. AEWP, box 3.

22. Originally, the first named plaintiff was Mathaman, the elder brother of Milirrpum. He died in January 1970 and Milirrpum, who then became head of the Rirratjingu claim, also took over as first named plaintiff in the legal case.

23. Affidavit of Dadynga Marika, AEWP, box 3.

24. Affidavit of Dadynga Marika.

25. See, for example, letter from Yirrkala Aborigines to General Secretary of FCAATSI, quoted in Berndt, "The Gove Dispute."

26. Affidavit of Dadynga Marika.

27. Williams, *The Yolngu and Their Land*, 29.

28. *Canberra Times*, 17 November 1970, 8.

29. See "Judge on History of White Shame," in *The Age*, 28 April 1971.

30. Submission of plaintiffs' counsel: final address for the plaintiffs, [nd], Purcell Collection, MS 1146, box 19.

31. Defence of defendant Commonwealth of Australia, 2 April 1970, Purcell Collection, MS 1146, box 19.

32. *Milirrpum v. Nabalco*, 149.

33. Indeed, very similar wording to Blackburn's was used by the Earl of Birkenhead in discussing the Southern Rhodesia Land case, decided by the Privy Council in 1914. The case set a precedent for many "native land" disputes in British settler colonies later in the century including this one. Notably, Birkenhead argued that in colonial situations, native custom had to be accommodated to the "developed system of jurisprudence, the very elements of which are strange and may even be repellant to the native mind." Birkenhead, *Famous Trials of History*, 212.

34. See Richard Refshauge, "Blackburn, Sir Richard Arthur (Dick) (1918–1987)," Australian Dictionary of Biography, National Centre of Biography, Australian National University, adb.anu.edu.au/biography.

35. *Milirrpum v. Nabalco Pty Ltd*, 153.

36. *Milirrpum v. Nabalco Pty Ltd*, 153.

37. Some missionaries, notably the Reverend Lawrence Threlkeld, had given evidence on Aboriginal laws and custom in murder cases. See Castles, *An Australian Legal History*, 530; and Ford, *Settler Sovereignty*, 179.

38. *Regina v. Discon and Baker* (1968), 67 DLR (2d) 619. While the judge in this case admitted the evidence of the anthropologist, Wilson Duff, he treated it as being a matter of conjecture and did not give it much weight. The decision went against the Squamish defendants who were found guilty of hunting without a license.

39. "Folklore as Evidence of Land Ownership," *Canberra Times*, 17 June 1970, 17.

40. "Submission of plaintiffs' counsel—Aboriginal evidence," Purcell collection, MS 1146, box 19.

41. W. E. H. Stanner, "Notes on opening statement, Milirrpum & ors v. Nabalco and The Commonwealth," AEWP, box 3.

42. "Submission of plaintiffs' counsel—Aboriginal evidence," Purcell collection, MS 1146, box 19.

43. *Milirrpum v. Nabalco*, 154.

44. *Milirrpum v. Nabalco*, 157.

45. For a longer discussion of the reputation principle and Blackburn's use of it, see, Johnson, "The Gove Land Rights Case and the Problem of History in a Decolonising Australia."

46. *Milirrpum v Nabalco*, 266.

47. *Milirrpum v Nabalco*, 157. See Wigmore, *A Treatise on the Anglo-American System of Evidence in Trials at Common Law*, sections 1563 and 1592.

48. Anthropologist Ian McIntosh argues that in the mid-twentieth century, Yolgnu leaders had developed a practice of "non-disclosure" about some of their sacred and foundational beliefs to outsiders, as they sought to retain control over their lives and lands. See McIntosh, "Missing the Revolution!"

49. 1 April 1969, Signed by Village Council of Yirrkala. AEWP, box 3.

50. Evidence of Aboriginal Witnesses, Dadynga Marika, Purcell collection, MS 1146, Box 5 Item B.

51. *Canberra Times*, 17 June 1970.

52. Report of day's proceedings to Attorney-General, Canberra, 26 May 1970, A432/145 1968/649 part 9, NAA.
53. "A discussion between Sir Edward Woodward, Dr. Nicholas Peterson and Professor Max Charlesworth [ca. 1985/6?]," AEWP.
54. Evidence of Aboriginal Witnesses, Milirrpum Marika, Purcell collection, MS 1146, Box 5 Item B.
55. Williams, *The Yolngu and Their Land*, 158.
56. Williams, *The Yolngu and Their Land*, 23 and 158. In his film *Where the Green Ants Dream* (1984), which draws loosely on the *Milirrpum* case, Werner Herzog casts the problem of translation in absolute terms. The film depicts the untranslatability of a Yolngu worldview into a capitalist order. In the central moment of the film, a so-called "mute," the "last of his tribe," gives a testimony before the court that no one, not even other Aboriginal witnesses, can understand.
57. "Evidence of Anthropologists," Purcell collection, MS 1146 Box 5 Item B#3, AIATSIS.
58. W. E. H. Stanner (1969), "The Yirrkala Case: Some General Principles of Aboriginal Land-holding," unpublished paper, AEWP, box 3.
59. Stanner, *After the Dreaming*, 41.
60. See the Berndt Museum of Anthropology, University of Western Australia, www.berndt.uwa.edu.au.
61. See Minoru, "Reading Oral Histories from the Pastoral Frontier." A revised version of the Berndt's paper was published in 1987. According to Minoru, A. P. Elkin, who had sent the Berndts to the Northern Territory, did not want the report they wrote published because he thought it would have more impact on the government and industry if it were kept confidential.
62. Berndt to Purcell, 25 February 1970, AEWP, box 3.
63. Berndt, "The Gove Dispute."
64. Berndt, "The Gove Dispute," 265.
65. *Milirrpum v Nabalco*, 270–271.
66. *The Australian*, 2 July 1971, and *Canberra Times*, 7 May 1971, 3.
67. Memo: Ministerial Committee on Aboriginal Affairs, 1 December 1971, from Department of Education and Science, M 442/11 part 2, NAA.
68. For a reassessment of the Liberal-Country government's response to *Milirrpum v. Nabalco*, see Viney, *Aborigines, Law and the Settler State*.
69. Australian Council of Churches, "A Submission to the Ministerial Committee on Aboriginal Affairs by the Australian Council of Churches on Aboriginal Land Rights, November 1971," Council for Aboriginal Rights, MS 12913, Box 10/9.
70. *The Age*, 31 January 1970.
71. [Petition] Signed by R. Marika, Daymbalipu Munugurr; and W. Wunungmurra. Presented to PM 6 May 1971 at Canberra. Also in Yolngu. AEWP.
72. *The Age*, 7 May 1971.
73. Roy Marika to Purcell, 24 September 1970, AEWP.

74. Galarrwuy Yunupingu, quoted in Barrie Pittock, "Aborigines and Land Rights" [ca. 1971], Council for Aboriginal Rights, MS 12913, Box 26/1.
75. Yunupingu, "Address by Galarrwuy Yunupingu, Chairman of the Northern Land Council, to National Press Club Luncheon, Canberra, November 10, 1977," FCAATSI, MS 3759, box 35, series 25, 17.
76. Yunupingu, "Address by Galarrwuy Yunupingu."

CHAPTER 3

1. Morrow, *Northern Justice*, 80.
2. Helm, "Indian Dependency and Indian Self-Determination: Problems and Paradoxes in Canada's Northwest Territories."
3. "Indian Brotherhood Explains Freeze," *Tapwe*, 11 April 1973.
4. Blake, quoted in Helm, *The People of Denedeh*, 263.
5. The northern arctic area of the NWT was inhabited by a majority of Inuit people. In 1999 much of this region was separated from the NWT and became the province of Nunavut.
6. Ray, *The Canadian Fur Trade in the Industrial Age*, chapter 8.
7. In 1955, only about 15 percent of residents of the NWT had been educated at government schools, and most of those were the children of the few white residents in the region. By 1967, 90 percent of school-aged children were in school, the majority of whom were indigenous. Some young men and women, including those who would become prominent in the land rights campaign, were heading south for tertiary study. See Helm, *The People of Denedeh*, 133-134. As Kenneth Coates points out, parents with school-aged children were forced to choose between receiving government subsidies if they stayed in the settlements and sent their children to school, or "continue nomadic patterns and forfeit the subsidy." Coates, *Canada's Colonies*, 193.
8. Zaslow, *The Northward Expansion of Canada*, 289.
9. Helm, *The People of Denedeh*, 133–134. See also Zaslow, *The Northward Expansion of Canada*, chapter 10, for a discussion of the increasing native population and its relative economic and social opportunities.
10. Helm, *The People of Denedeh*, 134.
11. Canada, *The Canada Year Book 1975*, 147.
12. Diefenbaker, "A New Vision," opening campaign speech, 12 February 1958, Winnipeg, www.usask.ca/diefenbaker. In the speech, Diefenbaker explicitly recalled his own childhood in the "early days" of the western prairies (in 1903 his family moved from Ontario to what would become the province of Saskatchewan when his father took up a new teaching position there). On the idea of the North as a "discursive formation," see Grace, *Canada and the Idea of the North*. Janice Cavell argues that Diefenbaker did not see himself so much as an "heir to a great tradition that began at Confederation" but rather highlighted the efforts of explorers more

marginal to the national story who had emphasized the value of Canada's north. See Cavell, "The Second Frontier," 365.

13. See Zaslow, *The Northward Expansion of Canada*, chapter 12.

14. Berger, "The True North Strong and Free," 4–5.

15. On the building of railways across Canada and the political costs of these, see Friesen, *The Canadian Prairies*, 171–81.

16. Diefenbaker, "A New Vision."

17. Lajeunesse, "Lock, Stock and Icebreakers." The Canadian government's gradualist approach was manifested in bureaucratic changes. In 1953, for instance, parliament changed the name of the Department of Resources and Development to that of Northern Affairs and National Resources (DNANR). The name change was meant to indicate a "belief that the area was on the threshold of a period of accelerated development." The new department co-ordinated federal activities in the north and commissioned a series of reports on conditions of Indian life in the 1950s and 1960s. See Canada, "Department of Northern Affairs and National Resources, Canada."

18. See Carrothers, *Report of the Advisory Commission on the Development of Government in the Northwest Territories.*

19. For a critical discussion, see Bean, "Colonial Political Institutions in the Northwest Territories."

20. Department of Northern Affairs and Natural Resources, *Peoples of the Northwest Territories*, 39.

21. Quoted in Helm, *The People of Denedeh*, 257–258.

22. Drybone quoted in Helm, *The People of Denedeh*, 261–262.

23. Abel, *Drum Songs*, 246. See also Braden, *The Emergence of Native Interest Groups.*

24. Dene Nation, *Denedeh*, 24–25; 17.

25. Berger, "Mackenzie Valley Pipeline Inquiry: Preliminary Materials" [nd], Mackenzie Valley Pipeline Inquiry records, RG126, Vol 75.

26. Aboriginal Affairs and Northern Development Canada, "Order in Council Setting up Commission for Treaty 8, P.C. no 2749." Available at www.aadnc-aandc.gc.ca.

27. See Chapter 1.

28. The major published account of the making of Treaties 8 and 11 was written by René Fumoleau, a French priest of the Oblates of Mary Immaculate who had lived in the NWT since 1953. *As Long as This Land Shall Last* is still regarded as the seminal account of the two treaties. Fumoleau's documentary evidence was critical in the caveat case. See also Coates and Morrison, *Treaty Research Report No. 11 (1921).*

29. For instance, the Oblate Bishop Gabriel Breynat, who was invited by the government to be a member of the treaty party in 1921, believed that "my signature will be seen forever, together with those of our great chiefs ... to bear witness, for future generations, to the good faith of the contracting parties." He was sorely disappointed on discovering that the treaty terms "were prepared in advance to be imposed upon them rather than freely discussed in a spirit of reconciliation and

mutual concessions." Quoted in Fumoleau, *As Long as This Land Shall Last*, 208 and 163.

30. Aboriginal Affairs and Northern Development Canada, "Report of the Commissioner for Treaty 11, 12 October 1921." www.aadnc-aandc.gc.ca. On the boycotts, see Fumoleau, *As Long as This Land Shall Last*, 192.

31. See, for example, *R. v. Sikyea* (1962) 40 WWR 494. The case concerned the unlawful shooting of a duck out of season by an Indian man, Michael Sikyea, who appealed the fine he was served because he argued the treaty he had helped negotiate in 1921 guaranteed him his rights to shoot whenever he liked.

32. "Indian Brotherhood Explains Freeze," *Tapwe*, 11 April 1973.

33. Pearson, "Native Rights in the Northwest Territories," 285 and 278.

34. See Chapter 1.

35. For a brief discussion, see McHugh, *Aboriginal Title*, 70–71.

36. Sissons, *Judge of the Far North*, 157.

37. For example, a cartoon in a northern newspaper showed someone in traditional native dress holding a gun and pointing it at three government officials, with the speech bubble, "Buzz off or I'll give you a couple of wounded knees." Between the figures a hastily erected sign, held up with stones, read "Land Freeze." *News of the North*, 18 April 1973.

38. Steve Hume, *Edmonton Journal*, 16 May 1973.

39. Hume, *Edmonton Journal*, 16 May 1973.

40. Pearson, "Native Rights in the Northwest Territories," 283.

41. Indian Brotherhood of the NWT, "Budget Submission Regarding Research Leading to a Settlement of Indian Land Claims in the N.W.T.," 1 August 1973, Indian Claims Commission Files, RG 33–115, 9-2-5, LAC.

42. [Legal submissions] Morrow fonds, MS 261, Box 50/166.

43. *Re Paulette and Registrar of Land Titles,* para. 320.

44. *Re Paulette and Registrar of Land Titles,* para. 320.

45. Transcript of *Re Paulette*, 9 July 1973, Morrow fonds, MS 261, Box 50/166.

46. Transcript of *Re Paulette*, 9 July 1973.

47. Eber, *Images of Justice*. Sissons was invoking the eighteenth-century English jurist William Blackstone's exhortation to "bring justice to everyman's door." See Blackstone, *Commentaries on the Laws of England,* book three, chapter four, 30.

48. Morrow, *Northern Justice*, 207.

49. Quoted in Eber, *Images of Justice,* 19. See also Rowe, *Assimilation through Accommodation*, 63.

50. *News of the North,* 25 July 1973.

51. *News of the North,* 25 July 1973.

52. *The Globe and Mail*, 28 July 1973.

53. Morrow, *Northern Justice*, 153.

54. *Edmonton Journal,* 17 May 1973.

55. Transcript of *Re Paulette*, 10 July 1973, 63.

56. Transcript of *Re Paulette*, 17 July 1973, 347–348.

57. *Re Paulette and Registrar of Land Titles,* para. 314.

58. Transcript of *Re Paulette*, 12 July 1973, 156.

59. Transcript of *Re Paulette*, 30 July 1973, 505–506.

60. Transcript of *Re Paulette*, 30 July 1973, 492–498.

61. Transcript of *Re Paulette*, 20 August 1973, 569–570. See also Helm, *The People of Denedeh*, 250; and Asch, "From *Terra Nullius* to Affirmation," 31–32.

62. Nelson et al., *Report of the Commission Appointed to Investigate the Unfulfilled Provisions of Treaties 8 and 11,* 3–4.

63. The commission recommended against establishing reserves. Depicting Indians in the north as being in a "transitional stage," the commissioners argued that the idea of reserves now smacked of paternalism. The government's job was to encourage Indians to enter the mainstream economy so that they would "eventually become integrated into the Canadian way of life." Therefore, the commissioners recommended individual Indians should be provided fee simple (or individual) title to the plots of land they resided on and that bands should be given cash settlements for the lands they had ceded and annuity payments from mineral gas and oil resources. Payments to bands should be held in trust by the government. None of the commission's recommendations were put into effect.

64. Transcript of *Re Paulette*, 10 July 1973, 94.

65. See Ford, *Settler Sovereignty,* and Introduction to this volume.

66. Slattery, "Understanding Aboriginal Rights." See Introduction to this volume.

67. *Re Paulette and Registrar of Land Titles (No. 2),* p. 313. Morrow reiterated the idea of reliving the past in his memoirs: "As we moved from settlement to settlement, I felt as though I was back in the time of treaty signings." Morrow, *Northern Justice,* 172.

68. He took these citations from documents prepared by Fumoleau.

69. Napoleon, "Delgamuukw."

70. Steve Hume, *Oilweek,* 30 July 1973

71. *Native Press,* 15 September 1973.

CHAPTER 4

1. Examining the work of commissions of inquiry in early twentieth-century South Africa, Adam Ashforth argues that these institutions were primarily concerned with the "legitimation of States by helping to create a framework of knowledge which allows those who act in the name of the State to distinguish their roles and goals from those of Society." Ashforth, "Reckoning Schemes of Legitimation," 4–5. See also Ashforth, *The Politics of Official Discourse in Twentieth-Century South Africa.* Using a similar Foucauldian framework, Adam Sitze argues that commissions of inquiry under colonial rule were a "device for the sovereign to pose for itself the question of why and how its bio-political strategies had failed or were failing, in a recurrent attempt to calibrate

and fine-tune those strategies, to adjust the relation between government and population in an endless effort to achieve a fit between the two." Sitze, *The Impossible Machine*, 138.

2. Laidlaw, "Investigating Empire," 749.

3. Carole Pateman has argued that the "settler contract" is a version of the social contract in which settler societies that benefited from the dispossession of indigenous peoples concealed injustices so that the moral justification of settlement as a beneficial project would hold. Pateman argues that the settler contract cannot—in any historical moment—be delegitimated while the settler state remains intact, particularly in the courts to which indigenous peoples take their claims since those institutions have a vested interest in maintaining the sovereign status quo. This theoretical critique misses the ways commissioners and indigenous activists and leaders themselves debated the concept of the social contract in the space of the commission, proposing a reconsideration of national history and state authority. See Pateman, "The Settler Contract." See also Nichols, "Indigeneity and the Settler Contract Today." The argument made in this chapter resonates with that of Christopher Bayly, who demonstrates that Indian intellectuals "believed that they could rewrite the liberal discourse so as to strip it of its coercive colonial features and re-empower it as an indigenous ideology, but one still pointing towards universal progress." Bayly, *Recovering Liberties*, 3–4. Likewise, as Dipesh Chakrabarty has argued, notions such as the social contract, which are derived from a European political heritage, may be inadequate for describing the complexities of life under colonialism but they are nonetheless indispensable for pushing forward political claims. See Chakrabarty, *Provincializing Europe*, introduction.

4. Minute of a Meeting of the Committee of the Privy Council, P.C. 1969-2405, 19 December 1969, *Indian Claims Commission Files*, "ICC Terms of Reference," RG33-115, LAC. On the longer history of discussions about the creation of a claims commission, beginning immediately after World War II, see Milroy, "Aboriginal Policy-Making and Dispute Resolution Processes."

5. Manuel to Trudeau, 1 June 1972, RG 33-115, Volume 3, LAC.

6. See, for example, "Union of New Brunswick Indians: Rights and Treaty Research Proposal," 30 November 1971, in RG 33–115, Volume 1, I/C 9-2-8, LAC; and, "Indian Association of Alberta research program," [n.d.], RG 33–115, Volume 1, I/C 9-2-9, LAC.

7. Minute of a Meeting of the Committee of the Privy Council, 19 December 1969.

8. Chrétien to Moses, 4 June 1970, RG 33–115 Volume 3, LAC.

9. Manuel to Trudeau, 1 June 1972.

10. For example, Barber explained to a parliamentary committee that he was trying to "foster native research, not to attempt to do it on their behalf." See "Parliamentary questions," 22 March 1973, RG 33–115, Volume 1, I/C 9-1-1, LAC. See a similar claim made in a paper by Barber, "Indian Claims Processes," 6 December 1974, in RG 2-C-4, Volume 2707, LAC.

11. Barber to Robertson, July 1970, RG 33–115, Volume 5, LAC. The ad hoc nature and limited extent of Privy Council funding, however, sent some organizations into financial crisis. In 1972, the National Indian Brotherhood complained that funding "has been a token in terms of total requirements. . . . Not only must budgeting for this research be increased substantially, but funds must also be forthcoming regularly, on a dependable basis, so that needless deficits with their concomitant cancellations, postponements, waste and needless frustrations can be avoided." Manuel to Robertson, 21 April 1972, RG 33–115, Volume 4, LAC.

12. Canada, *The Canada Year Book*, 1975, 91.

13. Special Inquiry for Elder Indians' Testimony, 27–28 August 1977, RG 33–108, Volume 1, LAC.

14. Role of the Commissioner as Accepted by the Federation of Saskatchewan Indians, May 28 1973, RG 33 115, Volume 3, LAC.

15. F.S.I. Interim Report, 1973, RG 33–115, Volume 7, 10-1-11, LAC.

16. Department of Indian Affairs and Northern Development, "Communiqué," 9 March 1971, RG 33 115, Volume 3, LAC.

17. Manuel, *The Fourth World*, 237; and Rudolph C. Rÿser, "The Legacy of Grand Chief George Manuel," www.cwis.org/GML/manuel.

18. Lloyd Barber interviewed on CBC television, 10 April 1972, transcript, RG 33 115, Volume 3, LAC.

19. *Montreal Star*, 3 April 1972.

20. Barber to Woodward, 5 September 1973, RG 33 115, Volume 3, LAC.

21. Peterson, "Aboriginal Land Rights: Northern Territory Australia," 446.

22. John Newfong, "The Aboriginal Embassy: Its Purpose and Aims," *Identity*, July 1972, 5. See also Goodall, *Invasion to Embassy*, 339–351.

23. Whitlam quoted in Curran, *The Power of Speech*, 92.

24. Whitlam, "It's Time for Leadership," election speech delivered at Blacktown Civic Centre, New South Wales, 13 November 1972. Online at Whitlam Institute, University of Western Sydney, cem.uws.eud.au.

25. Letters patent, no. 8, issued 8 February 1973, A2880, 28/5/2, 1974-1975, NAA.

26. "A discussion between Sir Edward Woodward, Dr. Nicholas Peterson and Professor Max Charlesworth," [ca. 1985/6?], AEWP, box 2 "Aboriginal Land Rights Commission."

27. "Remove Judge, Plea by Blacks," *Australian*, 5 May 1973.

28. [Petition to HM The Queen from the Larakia/Larrakia people regarding land rights for presentation during HRH The Princess Margaret's visit to Darwin], A2354, 1973/86 attachment 1, NAA.

29. See Buchanan, *We Have Bugger All* [n.p.].

30. Woodward, *Aboriginal Land Rights Commission: Second Report*, 53

31. Woodward, *Aboriginal Land Rights Commission: Second Report*, 50–51.

32. See Peterson, "Common Law, Statutory Law, and the Political Economy of the Recognition of Indigenous Australian Rights in Land."

33. Charles Perkins claimed, "The view held at that time [the mid-1970s] was that land rights were being neglected and they wanted to put their views to government. . . . With this general feeling in the air we decided to establish a land council." Perkins, "When We Started Marching," in Wright, *Take Power Like This Old Man Here,* 18–19.

34. Marika to Council of Aboriginal Affairs, 4 April 1975, Council of Aboriginal Affairs Report, Box 2, AEWP.

35. For example, see Woodward, *Aboriginal Land Rights Commission: Second Report,* 3.

36. Anthropologists began critiquing this emphasis in the early 1980s. See Hiatt, *Aboriginal Landowners: Contemporary Issues in the Determination of Traditional Aboriginal Land Ownership,* especially the chapters by Keen, "A Question of Interpretation," and Hiatt, "Traditional Land Tenure and Contemporary Land Claims."

37. Woodward, "United Voice," [n.d.], Box 2, AEWP.

38. Woodward, "United Voice," [n.d.], AEWP.

39. See *Milirrpum v. Nabalco,* especially 266–267.

40. Woodward, *Aboriginal Land Rights Commission: Second Report,* 2.

41. Woodward, *Aboriginal Land Rights Commission: Second Report,* 162.

42. Quoted in Wright, *Take Power Like This Old Man Here,* 25.

43. This is the Kenbi land claim. For a Larrakia perspective on the claim, see Larrakia Nation website, www.larrakia.com. See also, Parsons, "Kenbi Land Claim—25 Years On."

44. "A discussion between Sir Edward Woodward, Dr. Nicholas Peterson and Professor Max Charlesworth."

45. Hiatt pointed out the paradox that land rights focused attention on traditional land tenure as never before—where tradition was often understood by judges as representing an unchanging past—but at the same time, legal proceedings highlighted the dynamism and adaptive nature of these relationships. See Hiatt, "Traditional Land Tenure and Contemporary Land Claims." See also Povinelli, "Indigenous Politics in Late Liberalism."

46. It is not clear why Woodward preferred the term "inalienable freehold title" to "native title." Nicolas Peterson, who worked with Woodward on the commission as a consulting anthropologist, surmised that Woodward thought the former term was a more "regular form" and easier to use than having to define a new kind of title. Personal communication with Peterson, 3 July 2014. It may have also been the case that he thought "inalienable freehold title" was more politically palatable.

47. "A discussion between Sir Edward Woodward, Dr. Nicholas Peterson, and Professor Max Charlesworth."

48. Woodward, *Aboriginal Land Rights Commission: Second Report,* 7.

49. Woodward, *Aboriginal Land Rights Commission: Second Report,* 6.

50. Woodward, *One Brief Interval,* 139. Jesuit activist and legal scholar Frank Brennan, a long-time defender of Aboriginal land rights in Australia, echoed this sentiment.

"Australia is distinctive," he explained, "because our history of land rights is so brief, our approach so pragmatic and belated, and our commitment to land rights so re-freshingly new, fragile, and wavering." Brennan, *Standing in Deep Time*.

51. Woodward, *Aboriginal Land Rights Commission: First Report*, 1–3.

52. Aboriginal Land Commissioner. *First Report, 7 April 1977–30 June 1977*, 2.

53. Aboriginal Land Commissioner. *Report for year ended 30 June 1981*, 6.

54. Rose, "Women and Land Claims."

55. Aboriginal Land Commissioner, *First Report*, 8.

56. Aboriginal Land Commissioner, *Report for Year Ended 30 June 1981*, 7.

57. Rubuntja quoted in Central Land Council, *The Land Is Always Alive*, 12.

58. Bauman, "Shifting Sands," 211.

59. Peter Sutton has argued for the importance of the transcript in land claims hearings "particularly to the objectors, and in terms of equity and of doing things in a fair and just way. It is important that those who are not supporting the claim have access to an accurate transcript of what was said, usually because they have much less competence than the other parties in knowing what anyone said at any time and what it meant. You also get a chance to correct errors that otherwise end up becoming quoted in the final address." See Sutton, *The Relative Strengths of Oral and Written Evidence*, 23.

60. Rose, "Women and Land Claims," 2.

61. See Central Land Council, *The Land Is Always Alive*, 10.

62. Woodward to Whitlam, 26 March 1973, in box 2, AEWP.

63. Frances Abele argues that Andrew Cowan, director of the CBC at the time, was sympathetic to the civil rights movement in the United States and to a "national native movement" in Canada. He hoped that broadcasting the community hear-ings would create a national consciousness among indigenous peoples, by bringing together scattered communities at the same time to listen to political news. He also promoted the hiring of Indian broadcasters, in order to create publicly known figures within and across these communities. Phoebe Nahanni, quoted below, was one of those broadcasters. See Abele, "The Berger Inquiry and the Politics of Transformation in the Mackenzie Valley," 102 ff.

64. Frank T'sleie in Watkins, *Dene Nation*, 16; see also CBC digital archive, "The Berger Inquiry," 5 August 1975, www.cbc.ca/archives.

65. The Declaration was passed on July 19, 1975. Copies of the Dene declaration were published in *News of the North* and *The Drum* (Inuvik) in August 1975. See also a copy republished in Watkins, *The Dene Nation*, 3–4.

66. See also Coulthard, *Red Skin, White Masks*, chapter 2.

67. A. J. Macdonald, unpublished paper presented at "Conditions of Settler Colonialism symposium."

68. See also Dyck, "Aboriginal Peoples and Nation-States"; Deloria and Lytle, *The Nations Within*. Kymlicka refers to "national minorities" in a similar way—those whose "historical homelands" have been taken over by later colonizers. See Kymlicka, *Multicultural Citizenship*, chapter 5.

69. Manuel, *The Fourth World*, 236. The argument came full circle in the 1990s, as tribal peoples from a number of African countries including Tanzania sought entry into the United Nations Working Group on Indigenous Peoples, claiming justice and self-determination alongside indigenous delegations from the Pacific and across the Americas. See Muehlebach, " 'Making Place' at the United Nations," 436.

70. Manuel, *The Fourth World*, 260.

71. Canada, *House of Commons Debates*, 30th Parliament, 1st Session, Volume 8, 23 July 1975, 7859–7860.

72. Senator Grosart, *Debates of the Senate*, 30th Parliament, 1st Session, Volume 1, 11 March 1975, 623.

73. Leroy Little Bear, "A Concept of Native Title," submission to the Berger Commission, RG 126, Vol 75, LAC.

74. Little Bear, "A Concept of Native Title."

75. Berger, *Northern Frontier, Northern Homeland*, xxii.

76. Phoebe Nahanni, 22 April 1974, Preliminary Hearings Transcript: 46, RG 126, Volume 75, LAC.

77. "A voice," 24 April 1974, Preliminary Hearings Transcript: 64, RG 126, Volume 75, LAC.

78. Lowe, *A Strategic Analysis of the Union of British Columbia Indian Chiefs*, 41–43.

79. Slattery, "The Constitutional Guarantee of Aboriginal and Treaty Rights," 232. See also McNeil, "The Constitutional Rights of the Aboriginal Peoples of Canada."

80. Audra Simpson argues that the Oka "crisis" was so significant because it "pronounced the structure of settler colonialism" that is, as inherently eliminatory. Simpson, *Mohawk Interruptus*, 147.

81. See Report of the Royal Commission on Aboriginal Peoples, available at www.aadnc-aandc.gc.ca.

82. For a critique of the evidentiary strictures of the *Native Title Act* see, for example, Ketley and Ozich, " 'Snapshots of Adventitious Content.' "

83. This was the case for Yorta Yorta native title claimants, who claimed lands straddling the border of the states of Victoria and New South Wales in densely settled southeastern Australia. Their claim failed because the presiding judge, Justice Olney, argued that the "tide of history" had washed away their native title rights. According to Olney, "Notwithstanding the genuine efforts of members of the claimant group to revive the lost culture of their ancestry, native title rights and interests once lost are not capable of revival." *The Members of the Yorta Yorta Aboriginal Community v. the State of Victoria & Ors* (1998), para. 121. Yorta Yorta were deeply disappointed with the decision. See for example, "Yorta Yorta People Declare Native Title Dead," ABC television, 18 December 2002, available at www.abc.net.au.

84. For example, the National Aboriginal Conference (NAC) proposed in 1980 that Aboriginal and non-Aboriginal Australians make a "compact" that they called a "makarrata," adopting a Yolngu word that, the NAC explained, "means things are alright again after a conflict." See National Aboriginal Conference Secretariat, "Memo to all

Aboriginal Organizations, 25 August 1980," AIATSIS library, available at: www.aiatsis. gov.au. The term was later dropped from official discussions once it was learned that "makarrata" in fact referred to the retributive practice of spearing offenders in the thigh. See Rowse, "A Spear in the Thigh for Senator Evans." The idea of a treaty is still on the agenda of some Aboriginal leaders and intellectuals, although now rendered in the terms of national reconciliation. Legal scholar Larissa Behrendt has argued, "The idea of recognition and respect through a formal process of a treaty is often referred to as nation-building—as a way of making a stronger, more united and more tolerant society." See Behrendt, "Foreword," in Read, Meyers, and Reece, *What Good Condition?*, xi.

CHAPTER 5

1. Māori Television, *Nga Tamatoa: Forty Years On* (2012); Harris, *Hikoi*, 27. See also, "Nga Tamatoa," in *Karanga Voices*.
2. Fleras and Spoonley, *Recalling Aotearoa*, 237.
3. For detailed accounts of new Maori activism, see Walker, *Ka Whawhai Tonu Matou*: 210–215; and Ward, *An Unsettled History*, chapter 1.
4. See Ward, *A Show of Justice*. On race-mixing and amalgamation, see Salesa, *Racial Crossings*.
5. On demographic changes in the immediate postwar decades, see Pool, *Te Iwi Maori*, 141–153. The counting of the Maori population over this period was subject to a significant change in policy, as Pool explains: from 1975 Maori could self-identify for electoral purposes; and from 1986 they could self-identify on the national census. The increase in people claiming Maori descent was due to cultural factors rather than a rise in fertility and drop in mortality. Indeed, in the 1970s, Pool claims that there was a marked "fertility decline" in the Maori population. Moreover, there was a significant out-migration of Maori people, mainly to Australia. In 1966, 862 Maori were recorded as living in Australia; by 1986, there were more than 25,900 people of Maori descent in that country. See Pool, *Te Iwi Maori*, especially chapter 8. See also Lashley, "Economic and Social Issues Affecting New Zealand's Maori Population."
6. See Williams, *Panguru and the City*.
7. See Ausubel, *The Fern and the Tiki*. Some New Zealand critics also examined racial conflict. See, for example, Thompson, "Community Conflict in New Zealand."
8. Hunn, *Report on Department of Maori Affairs*, 15.
9. Hunn, *Report on Department of Maori Affairs*, 15. In a critical response to the Hunn Report, the Maori Synod of the Presbyterian Church complained that the Maori population was being "forced into taking steps towards its own elimination." Maori Synod, *A Maori View of the Hunn Report*, 8.
10. *New Zealand Parliamentary Debates*, 353 (1967), 3657. Maori freehold land was held by multiple owners with fractionated interests who might not agree on how to use it, as the authors of a government-commissioned report into Maori land-holding

observed. This was Prichard and Waetford, *Report of Committee of Inquiry into Laws Affecting Maori Land and Powers of the Maori Land Court.* Another critic of government proposals noted, however, that the problem for Maori landholders was not simply fragmentation but also that individualized landholding had not been accompanied by programs for economic development. Few landholders had ready access to enough capital to make their land productive. See Kawharu, "Pacific Commentary: The Prichard-Waetford Inquiry into Maori Land."

11. Walker, *Ka Whawhai Tonu Matou,* 207. See also Harris, *Hikoi,* 24. The name of the wars has been the subject of ongoing discussion among historians but they are now generally referred to as the New Zealand Wars, the title of James Belich's revisionist study. This name reinvigorates the early twentieth-century historian James Cowan's usage, and emphasizes that the wars were about sovereignty rather than simply land. See Belich, *The New Zealand Wars and the Victorian Interpretation of Racial Conflict.*

12. The Native Land Court turned customary land into "freehold title" for Maori land owners. This made land held by customary tenure (in Maori language, the term is "papatupu," which refers to "hard ground" or that which is firmly fixed) available for private sale. The court has been dubbed by some historians an "engine of destruction." See Williams, *"Te Kooti Tango Whenua."* See also O'Malley, *Agents of Autonomy,* 241; King, "Between Two Worlds."

13. Submission of the Tairawhiti District Maori Council and certain Wairoa-Gisborne-East Coast incorporations to the Maori Affairs Committee of Parliament, September 1967, reprinted in Kawharu, *Maori Land Tenure,* 344.

14. Dewes, "Waitangi Day 1968: Some Food for Thought," *Comment,* June 1968, 13.

15. See the "Treaty is a FRAUD" poster from the late 1970s, *Te Ara, Encyclopedia of New Zealand,* available at www.teara.govt.nz.

16. Orange, *The Treaty of Waitangi,* 241–242.

17. In 1971, one of the preeminent New Zealand historians of the postwar period Keith Sinclair, for instance, compared race relations in the country with other settler states and argued that a "humanitarian imperial ideology" was deeply embedded in the New Zealand psyche, one which reinforced a belief on the part of the majority that Maori were superior "natives" and could be incorporated into the settler state. Sinclair, "Why Are Race Relations in New Zealand Better than in South Africa, South Australia, or South Dakota?"127.

18. Walker, *Ka Whawhai Tonu Matou.*

19. See Harris, *Hikoi,* 48.

20. Māori Television, *Nga Tamatoa.*

21. For example, Harris argues that Nga Tamatoa challenged the "old guard" to "face new choices and strategies for articulating Māori grievances and engaging with the State." Harris, *Hikoi,* 25. See also Walker, *Ka Whawhai Tonu Matou,* 186–219.

22. Harris, *Hikoi,* 38.

23. Harris, *Hikoi,* 70.

24. "Te Roopu o te Matakite march on Parliament 1975," available at www.nzhistory. net.nz.

25. See Fox, "Globalising Indigeneity?" 423–424.

26. Harris, *Hikoi*, 75.

27. Historian Ranginui Walker argues that the seats were not meant to provide Maori with real power. Walker, "The Māori People: Their Political Development," 382. However, historian Claudia Orange argues that the enabling legislation, among a raft of other measures, expressed a "thread of idealism" that upheld some of the promises of the treaty. Orange, *The Treaty of Waitangi*, 184.

28. The number of seats in the Maori electorate was not made proportionate to the Maori population until 1993. Between 1950 and 1975, for instance, Maori children were included in the definition of "general European population" in order to calcuate the number of general or "European" electorate seats. Significantly, in the same year as the Maori Affairs Amendment Act was passed (1967), an Electoral Amendment Act made it possible for non-Maori to stand for Maori seats, and for Maori to stand for non-Maori seats. Non-Maori have subsequently stood for Maori seats, but none have yet been elected. Several Maori contenders have won general electorate seats. See Parliamentary Library Research Paper, "The Origins of the Maori Seats."

29. Manuel, *The Fourth World*, 237. For a more recent discussion of the Maori seats in regard to possibilities in Canada, see Fleras, "Aboriginal Electoral Districts for Canda: Lessons from New Zealand."

30. According to Kai Tahu leader Sir Tipene O'Regan, who was at the time a Labour Party member, the Labour deputy leader Bill Rowling was strongly opposed to these aspects of the bill and was ultimately successful in "muzzling Rata's intent." See O'Regan, "Impact on Māori—a Ngāi Tahu Perspective," 42.

31. Minister of Forests to Minister of Maori Affairs [n.d.], ABWN 6095 W5021 382 13/201 part 1, ANZ.

32. Minister of Maori Affairs, Matiu Rata, Memorandum for Cabinet, 16 July 1975, AAFD 811 W4198/91 244/1/1 part 5, ANZ.

33. The Waitangi Tribunal was subsequently awarded the power to issue a binding recommendation where it finds that a claim is well founded and concerns Crown-owned lands. In its thirty-three-year history, however, it has used this power only once. See also Melvin, "The Jurisdiction of the Waitangi Tribunal," 24-25.

34. Oliver, *Claims to the Waitangi Tribunal*, 10.

35. David Williams to Duncan McIntyre, Minister of Maori Affairs, 7 June 1977, AAMK 869 1592a 19/14/1 part 1, ANZ.

36. Interview with Eddie Durie, by Rigby and Young.

37. Interview with Eddie Durie, by Rigby and Young.

38. Interview with Eddie Durie, by Rigby and Young.

39. Interview with Eddie Durie, by Rigby and Young.

40. In court, the defendants argued for mitigation due to cultural reasons, which the judge did not accept although most of the charges were dropped. Maori activists have continued to challenge charges laid against them in the course of protest action. Often they have argued for the customary and cultural priorities of their own people in so doing.

41. On the "No Maoris, No Tour" protests, see Harris, *Hikoi*, 32.

42. See Richards, *Dancing on Our Bones*; and Maclean, "Football as Social Critique." As Charlotte MacDonald argues, protests of South African rugby tours were where many of the "generational and identity struggles" of the 1960s and 1970s played out in New Zealand. See MacDonald, "Ways of Belonging: Sporting Spaces in New Zealand History," 269–296.

43. Whetu Tirakatene-Sullivan to Minister of Maori Affairs, 5 June 1980, AAMK 869 W709A 19/14 part 5, ANZ.

44. Chief Judge Durie to Minister of Maori Affairs, 27 November 1981, AAMK 869 709b 19/14/1 part 2, ANZ.

45. "Treaty of Waitangi Hui, 4–6 February 1985, Report of Proceedings." ABGX W3706 Box 13, 1, Treaty of Waitangi Amendment Bill, ANZ.

46. ABGX W3706 Box 13, 1, Treaty of Waitangi Amendment Bill, ANZ.

47. Interview with Maarire Goodall, 20 March 2006.

48. Dewes, "Waitangi Day 1968," 13.

49. Interview with Maarire Goodall. My emphasis.

50. *Law Commission Act* (1985), s. 5 (2) (a). For brief but useful discussions of biculturalism see, Lashley, "Economic and Social Issues Affecting New Zealand's Maori Population" 14; and Callister, "Attitudes to Biculturalism in New Zealand." For an earlier expression of what it means to become "bicultural" at a personal level, see Ritchie, *Becoming Bicultural*.

51. Fleras and Spoonley, *Recalling Aotearoa*, 232, 237.

52. Ross, "Te Tiriti O Waitangi," 154.

53. Michael Belgrave emphasizes the importance that Maori leaders who signed the treaty placed on being "promised inclusion in the British Empire." Belgrave, *Historical Frictions*, 62.

54. As historian M. P. K. Sorrenson later examined, the British colonial office used a template derived from some African treaties of cession in giving instruction for the drawing up of the treaty. See Sorrenson, "Treaties in British Colonial Policy: Precedents for Waitangi." Stuart Banner identifies "pre-emption" clauses in treaties made with Native Americans after 1789. He points out that preemption is in fact a "misleading name; it was not a right to buy land from the Indians *before* other purchasers, but instead a denial of the ability of other purchasers to purchase at all." Banner, *How the Indians Lost Their Land*, 135.

55. For a discussion of the impact of Ross's article, see Belgrave, *Historical Frictions*, 49–51. See also Sorrenson, "Towards a Radical Reinterpretation of New Zealand History."

56. See, for example, Awatere, *Maori Sovereignty*.
57. *Treaty of Waitangi Act*, 1975, preamble.
58. For a discussion of treaty principles emerging from early tribunal reports and sem-inal court cases, see Hayward, " 'Flowing From the Treaty's Words.' "
59. McNair, *The Law of Treaties*, 365.
60. See also Waitangi Tribunal, *Report of the Waitangi Tribunal on the Manukau Claim*.
61. Waitangi Tribunal, *Report of the Waitangi Tribunal on the Orakei Claim*, para. 11.3.2
62. See Ward, *An Unsettled History*, 37–38.
63. Hawke, "Economic Trends and Economic Policy, 1938–1992," 438. See also Kelsey, *Reclaiming the Future*, introduction.
64. Waitangi Tribunal, "Interim Report to Minister of Maori Affairs on State-Owned Enterprises Bill 8.12.86."
65. Nicholls, "A Comment from the NZ Maori Council," 38.
66. See, for example, McHugh, *Aboriginal Title*, 3, 8.
67. *New Zealand Maori Council v. Attorney-General*, 651.
68. *New Zealand Maori Council v. Attorney-General*, 642.
69. On this point, see the discussion in Sharp, *Justice and the Maori*, 273–274.
70. *New Zealand Maori Council v. Attorney-General*, 664.
71. *New Zealand Maori Council v. Attorney-General*, 664. My emphasis.
72. *New Zealand Maori Council v. Attorney-General*, 662.
73. Baragwanath, "Arguing the Case for the Appellants," 29.
74. *New Zealand Maori Council v. Attorney-General*, 657.
75. Cited in *New Zealand Maori Council v. Attorney-General*, 674. See also, New Zealand Maori Council, *Kaupapa—Te Wahanga Tuatahi*, 10.
76. *New Zealand Maori Council v. Attorney-General*, 17.
77. New Zealand Maori Council, *Kaupapa—Te Wahanga Tuatahi*, 5.
78. O'Regan, "Impact on Māori—a Ngāi Tahu Perspective," 48.

CHAPTER 6

1. Sharp, *Justice and the Maori*, 266.
2. For instance, Kelsey has argued that the advent of biculturalism as official policy was a "passive revolution" in which the state tried to reassert Pakeha hegemony through "the inclusion of new social groups . . . by making sufficient concessions to secure their allegiance without any expansion of their real economic and polit-ical power." See Kelsey, "Treaty Justice in the 1980s," 109. See also Augie and Fleras, *Recalling Aotearoa*, 236–240.
3. Some of this history is also told in the Waitangi Tribunal report on the claim, and Young, *Woven by Water*.
4. Statement of claim, reprinted in Waitangi Tribunal, *The Whanganui River Report*, appendix 1, 350.

5. The tribunal heard the claim to the river under urgency. The claim to land in the broader Whanganui region was slated for hearing after the river hearings, and the land claims were not brought into the district inquiry process until 2007.

6. "Opening Submissions of Counsel for Claimants," document A77, para 1.1, Whanganui River Inquiry Hearings, Waitangi Tribunal archive.

7. Young, *Woven by Water*, 17.

8. See, for example, Brett Printing and Publishing, *The "Rhine of Maoriland": Panorama of New Zealand's Greatest River, the Wanganui.*

9. See Young, *Woven by Water*

10. Whanganui River, Investigation of Title to Its Bed, 3 November 1938.

11. Whanganui River, Investigation of Title to Its Bed, 3 November 1938.

12. Whanganui River, Investigation of Title to Its Bed, 3 November 1938.

13. Court minutes often referred to Māori witnesses giving customary evidence by their first names.

14. Whanganui River, Investigation of Title to Its Bed, 10–11.

15. See also Waitangi Tribunal, *The Whanganui River Report*, 200–201.

16. For a discussion of the case history, see Waitangi Tribunal, *The Whanganui River Report*. See also Young, *Woven by Water*, especially chapters 11 and 12.

17. *In Re the Bed of the Wanganui River*, 446–447.

18. Record of addresses, submissions, and evidence: in the Māori Appellate Court, in the matter of an Order of the Court of Appeal of New Zealand, 7 December 1956, findings sent to Court of Appeal, 6 June 1958, 2.

19. Te Atihaunui could have taken the case to the Privy Council in Britain, but the cost was prohibitive and they decided against it. See Waitangi Tribunal, *The Whanganui River Report*, 233.

20. Petition presented to Matiu Rata, Minister of Māori Affairs, by Titi Tihu and H. Amohia, 20 December 1975. The petitioners presented another petition to National's Minister of Māori Affairs Duncan McIntyre in 1977, and in 1978 wrote to the Queen. Whanganui River Inquiry Hearings, Tribunal archive, B8 (a).

21. Mt. Egmont Vesting Act (1978), preamble, available at www.nzlii.org.

22. Ben Couch, minister of Māori Affairs to Morgan, Cooney Lees & Morgan, 28 January 1982, Whanganui River Inquiry Hearings, Tribunal archive, B8 (a).

23. ANF Harris for secretary, to minister of Māori Affairs, 21 January 1982. Whanganui River Inquiry Hearings, Tribunal archive, B8 (a).

24. I. J. Hyslop, District Solicitor, to Director-General of Lands, 4 March 1982. Whanganui River Inquiry Hearings, Tribunal archive, B8 (a).

25. National Parks Act, S. 30 (2) (1980), available at www.nzlii.org.

26. Statement of Claim, Te Iwi o Whanganui, Whanganui River Inquiry Hearings, Tribunal archive, document 1.1.

27. Quoted in Waitangi Tribunal, *The Whanganui River Report*, 56.

28. Quoted in Waitangi Tribunal, *The Whanganui River Report*, 56.

29. Brief of evidence of Archie Te Atawhai Taiaroa, Whanganui River Inquiry Hearings, Tribunal archive, document B8. Emphasis in original.
30. The Working Group was established in 1982. The efforts of the World Council of Indigenous Peoples, led by George Manuel (see Chapter 4) were crucial to its creation. For a discussion of the Working Group, see Niezen, *The Origins of Indigenism*, 161.
31. Whanganui River Māori Trust Board, "The Whanganui River Charter on Tino Rangatiratanga and Iwi Water Rights," 1993, available at www.wrmtb.co.nz.
32. See Anaya, *Indigenous Peoples in International Law*.
33. Muehlebach, "'Making Place' at the United Nations," 416.
34. Waitangi Tribunal, *The Whanganui River Report*, 79.
35. The chiasmus (inverted parallelism) in the proverb, where "au" and "awa" switch positions in each of the parallel clauses, performs syntactically the ontological meaning that the personal subject and the river are mutually constituting although distinct parts of a whole. Chiasmus, and other kinds of parallelism, is common to many ritual languages; it is frequently used in biblical scripture in particular. See for example, Fox, "'Our Ancestors Spoke in Pairs.'"
36. Matiu Mareikura submission, Whanganui River Inquiry Hearings, Tribunal archive, document B11.
37. Matiu Mareikura submission, Whanganui River Inquiry Hearings.
38. See Sinclair, *Prophetic Histories*.
39. Whanganui River Māori Trust Board, www.wrmtb.co.nz.
40. "Synopsis of Closing Submissions of Counsel for the Crown," Whanganui River Inquiry Hearings, Tribunal archive, document D19 (c), paras 118–119.
41. "Synopsis of Closing Submissions of Counsel for the Crown," para 8.
42. "Synopsis of Closing Submissions of Counsel for the Crown," para 118.
43. "Synopsis of Closing Submissions of Counsel for the Crown," paras. 5–9.
44. On the "clash of cultures" between law and history in the tribunal as observed by one chairperson, see Williams, "Truth, Reconciliation and the Clash of Cultures in the Waitangi Tribunal."
45. Waitangi Tribunal, *The Whanganui River Report*, 79.
46. Transcript of Cross-Examination of Fergus Sinclair, Whanganui River hearing, Waitangi Tribunal, 22 June 1994, 4, Whanganui River Inquiry Hearings, Tribunal archive, document C24.
47. Transcript of cross-examination of Fergus Sinclair, 5.
48. Sharp, "Recent Juridical and Constitutional Histories of Maori," 31. Canadian historian Arthur Ray, who appeared as an expert witness in numerous treaty and native title cases, cautions that in court, "the litigating parties cannot await the possibility of a stable academic consensus," which means that historians "must bear in mind that their primary responsibility is to the court rather than to their clients." Ray, "Native History on Trial," 272. See also, Ward, "History and Historians before the Waitangi Tribunal;" and Sorrenson, "Towards a Radical Reinterpretation of New Zealand History."

49. Oliver, "The Future behind Us," 9. On this issue, see also Curthoys, Genovese, and Reilly, *Rights and Redemption*, chapter 5.

50. Some tribes have gone into direct negotiation with the government rather than engaging in the tribunal hearing and report-writing process.

51. There has been extensive argument about the spelling of the town. Colonists spelled both the name of the river and the town without the "h" which is softly aspirated in the Whanganui dialect. In 1991, the name of the river was officially changed to "Whanganui." In referenda in 2006 and 2009, local voters said they preferred to keep the township's name without the "h." Both spellings are now officially correct.

52. For a discussion of the plaque and the statue of John Ballance, a minister of Māori Affairs and Premier, who was beheaded during the occupation, see Morris, "Men Alone, in Bronze and Stone: A Tale of Two Statues," 65–67.

53. *New Zealand Herald*, 16 March 1995, 7. See also Moon, "The History of Moutoa Gardens and Claims of Ownership," 347.

54. *New Zealand Herald*, 16 March 1995, 7

55. See, for instance, *Evening Post*, 18 March 1995, 11; *New Zealand Herald*, 31 March 1995, 18.

56. *Evening Post*, 18 March 1995, 11.

57. *Dominion*, 4 March 1995, 6.

58. *New Zealand Herald*, 16 March 1997, 7.

59. *Dominion*, 1 February 1997, 17.

60. *Dominion*, 4 October 1997, 25.

61. Waitangi Tribunal, *The Whanganui River Report*, 91.

62. Hamish Ensor quoted in Dominy, "White Settler Assertions of Native Status," 363. Anthropologist Michèle Dominy, who worked with high country farmers, points out how their expressions draw on an "emerging rhetoric of primordial affinities grounded in attachment to place." "White Settler Assertions of Native Status," 371. See also Dominy, *Place and Identity in New Zealand's High Country*.

63. Dominy, "White Settler Assertions of Native Status," 365.

64. Waitangi Tribunal, *The Whanganui River Report*, 99.

65. Personal communication with Paul Hamer, 22 September 2014.

66. Waitangi Tribunal, *The Whanganui River Report*, 35.

67. Waitangi Tribunal, *The Whanganui River Report*, 343.

68. Ken Shirley in *New Zealand Herald*, 5 July 1999, A13.

69. Waitangi Tribunal, *The Whanganui River Report*, xix.

70. Ratu Sir Kamisese Mara, *The Pacific Way*.

71. A process that Chief Judge Durie advocated in other writing at the time. See for example, Durie, "Will the Settlers Settle?"

72. See "Whanganui River Settlement: Ratification Booklet for Whanganui Iwi," available at www.wrmtb.co.nz.

EPILOGUE

1. On the treaty claims process pejoratively termed an "industry" in New Zealand, see Scott, *The Travesty of Waitangi*. Some critics have argued that there is a "brown-washing" of New Zealand's history going on as a consequence of this "industry." See, for example, the blog www.treatygate.wordpress.com.

2. In Australia, "History Wars" raged at the end of the 1990s and into the 2000s. Influenced by historians critical of work in the new field of Aboriginal history, Liberal (conservative) Prime Minister John Howard, in power from 1996 to 2007, refused to issue an apology to Aboriginal people removed from their families, known as the "Stolen Generations." He argued that Australians should be proud of their past, not apologetic for it. The term "black armband history" was coined by the historian Geoffrey Blainey. See Blainey, "A Balance Sheet on Our History." For a general account, see Clark and Macintyre, *The History Wars*. In Canada, Thomas Flanagan, an academic and later special advisor to Conservative Prime Minister Stephen Harper, provoked similar acrimony concerning the status of indigenous peoples and the value of their oral histories. See Flanagan, *First Nations? Second Thoughts*.

3. In New Zealand, a furor erupted in 2004 when Maori leaders took to court their protests about the Labour government's Foreshore and Seabed Act (2003), which removed the possibility of claiming such areas as subject to native title. Their claim was successful, triggering anger and resentment among the Pakeha public who wanted unrestricted access to the beach. See Ruru, "A Politically Fuelled Tsunami."

4. See "The Vision," Idle No More, available at www.idlenomore.ca.

5. See Coulthard, *Red Skin, White Masks*; Simpson, *Mohawk Interruptus*; and Simpson and Smith, *Theorizing Native Studies*, introduction.

6. Paul Daley, "The Man Who Renounced Australia," *The Guardian*, 26 August 2014, www.theguardian.com.

7. O'Regan in Melbourne, ed., *Maori Sovereignty*, 158–159.

8. The declaration was at first rejected by the governments of Canada, Australia, New Zealand, and the United States because they claimed that they were already dealing with indigenous peoples' claims on their own terms. Some indigenous leaders and academics interpreted this refusal as exhibiting a fear of secession, driven by conservative politics against indigenous rights. See, for example, Davis, "The United Nations Declaration on the Rights of Indigenous Peoples." However, Kirsty Gover has recently reinterpreted the refusal of the settler states as evidence of a "distinctive 'western settler-state' view of the relationship between liberal principles of equality and historical indigenous rights to self-governance and property that is shaped by the ways in which indigenous claims have been settled in those countries." As she points out, the "multilateralism" that settler states have engaged in with indigenous polities in the last three decades is, remarkably, unique to them. Gover,

"Settler-State Political Theory, 'CANZUS' and the UN Declaration on the Rights of Indigenous Peoples." The four settler states did eventually sign the declaration.

9. In an extremely important decision on aboriginal title in Canada in 2014, the Supreme Court found that the Tsilhqot'in nation did have title to 440, 000 hectares of land in interior British Columbia. The decision overturned a previous ruling by the British Columbia Court of Appeal that this "semi-nomadic tribe" could not establish aboriginal title because it did not use the land in question all the time. *Tsilhqot'in Nation v. British Columbia* (2014) SCC 44 [2014] 2 S.C.R. 256.

10. Johnson, "Reconciliation, Indigeneity and Postcolonial Nationhood in Settler States."

Bibliography

UNPUBLISHED MATERIAL
Australia

Australia. Legal Action—Land on Gove Peninsular. A5882/1, CO 566, 1968-1971. NAA.

Australia. Mathaman, Mungurrawuy, Daymbalipu and others versus Nabalco Pty Ltd and the Commonwealth. A432, 1968/649, parts 1-26. NAA.

Australia. [Personal Papers of Prime Minister Fraser] Aborigines [Cabinet submissions relating to Aboriginal reserves, Australian Council of Churches submission relating to Aboriginal land rights]. M442/1 1 Part 2. NAA.

Australia. Royal commissions. A2880, 28/5/2, 1974-1975. NAA.

Council for Aboriginal Rights. Papers. MS 12913, Box 5/17, State Library of Victoria.

Federal Council for the Advancement of Aborigines and Torres Strait Islanders Collection. MS 3759. AIATSIS.

Purcell, Francis Xavier collection. MS 1146. AIATSIS.

Woodward, Sir Albert Edward. Papers. 102/26, 1968-2002. University of Melbourne Archives, Melbourne, Australia.

Canada

Canada. Indian Claims Commission fonds. RG33-115, Volume 1, I/C 9-1-1—10-1-11, "Research (In-House)," 1966-1977, LAC.

Canada. Indian Claims Commission fonds. RG33-115, Volume 3, "ICC Terms of Reference," 1966-1977, LAC.

Canada. Indian Claims Commission fonds. RG33-115, Volume 4, "Funding Indian Research," 1966-1977, LAC.

Canada. Indian Claims Commission fonds. RG33-115, Volume 5, "National Indian Brotherhood," 1966-1977, LAC.

Canada. Indian Claims Commission fonds. RG33-115, Volume 7, 1966-1977, LAC.
Canada. Indian Claims Commission fonds. RG33-115, Volume 10, "National Indian Brotherhood," 1966-1977, LAC.
Canada. Canadian Indian Rights Commission fonds. RG2-C-4, Volume 2707, 1975-1978, LAC.
Canada. Mackenzie Valley Pipeline Inquiry records, RG126, Vol 75, LAC.
Canada. Special Inquiry for Elder Indians' Testimony. RG33-108, Volume 1, 1977, LAC.
Morrow, William George. Fonds. University of Calgary Special Collections, MS 261.

New Zealand

Interview with Eddie Durie, interviewed by David Young and Barry Rigby, 7 March 2001, OHInt-0797-03, *Waitangi Tribunal Oral History Project*, ATL.
Interview with Maarire Goodall, interviewed by Miranda Johnson, Oriental Bay, Wellington, 20 March 2006.
New Zealand. Cabinet Office: Maori Affairs, 1973–1978. AAFD 811 W4198/91 244/1/1 part 5, ANZ.
New Zealand. Lands and Survey. Treaty of Waitangi Act and Decisions of the Tribunal, ABWN 6095 W5021 382 13/201 part 1, ANZ.
New Zealand. Maori Affairs Committee, Treaty of Waitangi Bill no 172/1-2, Hon. M. Rata ABGX, W3706, box 13, 3, ANZ.
New Zealand. Notes of evidence given before Whanganui River Reserves Commission 1916-1917. ABWN 8926 W 5278 81/228.2, ANZ.
New Zealand. Treaty of Waitangi Policy and General. AAMK 869 W709A 19/14 part 5, ANZ.
New Zealand. Waitangi Tribunal general 1975. AAMK 869 1592a 19/14/1 part 1, ANZ.
New Zealand. Waitangi Tribunal—General. AAMK 869 709b 19/14/1 part 2, ANZ.
Waitangi Tribunal archive. Whanganui River Inquiry Hearings, Wai 167, Waitangi Tribunal, Wellington.
Macdonald, A. J. Unpublished paper presented at "Conditions of Settler Colonialism." Symposium held at the University of Chicago, 25–26 April 2008.

LEGAL CASES

Calder et al. v. Attorney-General of British Columbia (1973) SCR 313.
Delgamuukw v. British Columbia (1997) 3 SCR 1010.
In Re the Bed of the Wanganui River (1955) 419 NZLR.
Mabo v. Queensland (no. 2) (1992) HCA 23.
Milirrpum v. Nabalco Pty Ltd and the Commonwealth of Australia (1971), 17 FLR.
New Zealand Maori Council v. Attorney-General [1987] 1 NZLR 641.
Re Paulette and Registrar of Land Titles (No. 2) (1973) 42 DLR (3d) 8.
Regina v. Discon and Baker (1968) 67 DLR (2d) 619.

The Members of the Yorta Yorta Aboriginal Community v. the State of Victoria & Ors. (1998), FCA 1606.

Whanganui River, Investigation of Title to its Bed, Proceedings in Maori Land Court, 3 November 1938.

PUBLISHED MATERIAL

Abel, Kerry. *Drum Songs: Glimpses of Dene History.* Montreal: McGill-Queen's University Press, 1993.

Abele, Frances. *The Berger Inquiry and the Politics of Transformation in the Mackenzie Valley.* Ph.D. thesis, York University, 1983.

Aboriginal Land Commissioner. *First Report, 7 April 1977–30 June 1977.* Canberra: Commonwealth Government Printer, 1978.

Aboriginal Land Commissioner. *Report for Year Ended 30 June 1981.* Canberra: Australian Government Publishing Service, 1982.

Anaya, S. James. *Indigenous Peoples in International Law,* 2nd ed. New York: Oxford University Press, 2004.

Anderson, Benedict. *Imagined Communities: Reflections on the Origin and Spread of Nationalism.* London: Verso, 1983.

Anderson, Warwick. *The Cultivation of Whiteness: Science, Health and Racial Destiny in Australia.* Melbourne: Melbourne University Press, 2002.

Anghie, Anthony. "Finding the Peripheries: Sovereignty and Colonialism in Nineteenth-Century International Law." *Harvard International Law Journal,* 40, 1 (1999): 1–80.

Armitage, Andrew. *Comparing the Policy of Aboriginal Assimilation: Australia, Canada and New Zealand.* Vancouver: University of British Columbia Press, 1995.

Arvin, Maile. "Analytics of Indigeneity." In Stephanie Nohelani Teves, Andrea Smith, Michelle H. Rahetja. *Native Studies Keywords.* Tuscon: University of Arizona Press, 2015: 119-129.

Asch, Michael. "From *Terra Nullius* to Affirmation: Reconciling Aboriginal Rights with the Canadian Constitution." *Canadian Journal of Law and Society,* 17 (2002): 23–40.

Asch, Michael and Norman Zlotkin. "Affirming Aboriginal Title: A New Basis for Comprehensive Claims Negotiations." In Michael Asch, ed., *Aboriginal and Treaty Rights in Canada: Essays on Law, Equality, and Respect for Difference.* Vancouver: University of British Columbia Press, 1997: 208–229.

Ashforth, Adam. *The Politics of Official Discourse in Twentieth-Century South Africa.* Oxford: Clarendon Press and Oxford University Press, 1990.

Ashforth, Adam. "Reckoning Schemes of Legitimation: On Commissions of Inquiry as Power/Knowledge Forms." *Journal of Historical Sociology,* 3, 1 (March 1990): 1–22.

Attwood, Bain. *Possession: Batman's Treaty and the Matter of History.* Carlton, Vic: Miegunyah Press, 2009.

Attwood, Bain, *Rights for Aborigines*. Crows Nest, NSW: Allen & Unwin, 2003.

Attwood, Bain and Tom Griffiths, "Introduction." In *Frontier, Race, Nation: Henry Reynolds and Australian History*. Melbourne: Australian Scholarly Publishing, 2009: 3–52.

Attwood, Bain and Andrew Markus. *The 1967 Referendum, or When Aborigines Didn't Get the Vote*. Canberra: Australian Institute of Aboriginal and Torres Strait Islander Studies, 1997.

Attwood, Bain and Andrew Markus. *Thinking Black: William Cooper and the Australian Aborigines' League*. Canberra: Aboriginal Studies Press, 2004.

Ausubel, David. *The Fern and the Tiki: An American view of New Zealand: National Character, Social Attitudes, and Race Relations*. Sydney: Angus and Robertson, 1960.

Awatere, Donna. *Maori Sovereignty*. Auckland: Broadsheet, 1984.

Banner, Stuart. *How the Indians Lost Their Land: Law and Power on the Frontier*. Cambridge, MA: Harvard University Press, 2005.

Banner, Stuart. *Possessing the Pacific: Land, Settlers and Indigenous People from Australia to Alaska*. Cambridge, MA: Harvard University Press, 2007.

Baragwanath, Hon. Justice David. "Arguing the Case for the Appellants." In Jacinta Ruru, ed., *"In Good Faith": Symposium Proceedings Marking the 20th Anniversary of the* Lands *Case*. Wellington: New Zealand Law Foundation, 2008: 23–36.

Barwick, Diane. "How Prof. Bill Stanner Recruited a Canadian." *Aboriginal Treaty News*, 9 (1983): 11.

Basso, Keith H. *Wisdom Sits in Places: Landscape and Language among the Western Apache*. Albuquerque: University of New Mexico Press, 1996.

Bauman, Toni. "Shifting Sands: Towards an Anthropological Praxis." *Oceania*, 71, 3 (2001): 202–225.

Bayly, Christopher. *Recovering Liberties: Indian Thought in the Age of Liberalism and Empire*. Cambridge: Cambridge University Press, 2012.

Bean, Wilf. "Colonial Political Institutions in the Northwest Territories," *Dene Rights*, 4, 7 [ca. 1977]: 46–47.

Belich, James. *Replenishing the Earth: The Settler Revolution and the Rise of the Angloworld, 1783–1939*. Oxford: Oxford University Press, 2009.

Belich, James. *The New Zealand Wars and the Victorian Interpretation of Racial Conflict*. Auckland: Auckland University Press, 1986.

Belgrave, Michael. *Historical Frictions: Maori Claims and Reinvented Histories*. Auckland: Auckland University Press, 2005.

Belmessous, Saliha, ed. *Native Claims: Indigenous Law against Empire, 1500–1920*. Oxford: Oxford University Press, 2011.

Berger, Carl. "The True North Strong and Free." In Peter Russell, ed., *Nationalism in Canada*. Toronto: McGraw-Hill of Canada, 1966.

Berger, Thomas. *Northern Frontier, Northern Homeland: The Report of the Mackenzie Valley Pipeline Inquiry*. Ottawa: Minister of Supply and Services Canada, 1977.

Berndt, R. M. "The Gove Dispute: The Question of Australian Aboriginal Land and the Preservation of Sacred Sites." *Anthropological Forum*, 1, 2 (1964): 258–295.

Berndt, R. M. "A Long View: Some Personal Comments on Land Rights." *Australian Institute of Aboriginal Studies Newsletter*, 16 (1981): 5–20.

Berndt, R. M. and Catherine H. Berndt. *Arnhem Land: Its History and Its People.* Melbourne: F. W. Cheshire, 1954.

Biolsi, Thomas. "Imagined Geographies: Sovereignty, Indigenous Space, and American Indian Struggle." *American Ethnologist* 32, 2 (2005): 239–259.

Birkenhead, Earl of. *Famous Trials of History.* New York: George H. Dorian, 1926.

Blackstone, William. *Commentaries on the Laws of England: In Four Books.* Philadelphia: Rees Welsh, 1902–1915.

Blackton, Charles S. "Australian Nationality and Nativism: The Australian Natives' Association, 1885–1901." *Journal of Modern History* 30, 1 (1958): 37–46.

Blainey, Geoffrey. "A Balance Sheet on Our History." *Quadrant* (July/August 1993): 10–15.

Borrows, John. "Wampum at Niagara: The Royal Proclamation, Canadian Legal History, and Self-Government." In Michael Asch, ed., *Aboriginal and Treaty Rights in Canada: Essays on Law, Equality, and Respect for Difference.* Vancouver: University of British Columbia Press, 1997: 155–172.

Braden, George. *The Emergence of Native Interest Groups and Their Impact on the Political and Economic Development of the Northwest Territories, 1969 to 1975.* MA thesis, Dalhousie University, 1976.

Brennan, Frank. *Standing in Deep Time; Standing in the Law: A Non-Indigenous Australian Perspective on Land Rights, Land Wrongs and Self-Determination.* 2005. www.uniya.org.

Brett Printing and Publishing. *The "Rhine of Maoriland": Panorama of New Zealand's Greatest River, the Wanganui.* Auckland, ca. 1910.

Buchanan, Cheryl. *We Have Bugger All: The Kulaluk Story.* Carlton, Vic.: Race Relations Department, Australian Union of Students, 1974.

Byrnes, Giselle. *The Waitangi Tribunal and New Zealand History.* Melbourne: Oxford University Press, 2004.

Cairns, Alan. *Citizens Plus: Aboriginal Peoples and the Canadian States.* Vancouver: University of British Columbia Press, 2000.

Callister, Paul. "Attitudes to Biculturalism in New Zealand: Asking the Wrong Questions, Getting the Wrong Answers?" Callister and Associates, working paper, 2011.

Canada. *The Canada Year Book 1972.* Ottawa: Census and Statistics Office, 1972.

Canada. *The Canada Year Book 1975.* Ottawa: Census and Statistics Office, 1975.

Canada. "Department of Northern Affairs and National Resources, Canada." *Polar Record*, 7, 50 (1955): 421–422.

Canadian Broadcasting Corporation digital archive, "The Berger Inquiry," 5 August 1975, www.cbc.ca/archives.

Cardinal, Harold. *The Unjust Society: The Tragedy of Canada's Indians*. Edmonton: M. G. Hurtig, 1969.

Carrothers, A. W. R. *Report of the Advisory Commission on the Development of Government in the Northwest Territories*. Ottawa, 1966.

Carter, Sarah. *Aboriginal People and Colonizers of Western Canada to 1900*. Toronto: University of Toronto Press, 1999.

Carter, Sarah. "'Your Great Mother across the Salt Sea': Prairie First Nations, the British Monarchy, and the Vice-Regal Connection to 1900." *Manitoba History*, 48 (Autumn–Winter 2004–2005): 34–48.

Castles, Alex. *An Australian Legal History*. Sydney: Law Book Company, 1982.

Cavell, Janice. "The Second Frontier: The North in English-Canadian Historical Writing." *Canadian Historical Review*, 83, 3 (2002): 364–389.

Central Land Council. *The Land Is Always Alive: The Story of the Central Land Council*. Alice Springs: Central Land Council, 1994.

Chakrabarty, Dipesh. *Provincializing Europe: Postcolonial Thought and Historical Difference*. Princeton: Princeton University Press, 2000.

Chatterjee, Partha. *The Nation and Its Fragments: Colonial and Postcolonial Histories*. Princeton, NJ: Princeton University Press, 1993.

Chesterman, John and Brian Galligan. *Citizens without Rights: Aborigines and Australian Citizenship*. Cambridge: Cambridge University Press, 1997.

Clark, Anna and Stuart Macintyre. *The History Wars*. Melbourne: Melbourne University Press, 2003.

Clark, Jennifer. *Aborigines and Activism: Race, Aborigines and the Coming of the Sixties to Australia*. Crawley, WA: University of Western Australia Press, 2008.

Clifford, James. "Identity in Mashpee." In *The Predicament of Culture: Twentieth-Century Ethnography, Literature, and Art*. Cambridge, MA: Harvard University Press, 1988: 277–348.

Coates, Kenneth S. and William R. Morrison, *Treaty Research Report No. 11 (1921)*. Ottawa: Treaties and Historical Research Centre, Indian and Northern Affairs Canada, 1986.

Coates, Kenneth S. *Canada's Colonies: A History of the Yukon and Northwest Territories*. Toronto: James Lorimer, 1985.

Comaroff, John L. "Colonialism, Culture and the Law: A Foreword." *Law and Social Inquiry*, 26, 2 (2001): 305–314.

Coulthard, Glen. *Red Skin, White Masks: Rejecting the Colonial Politics of Recognition*. Minneapolis: University of Minnesota Press, 2014.

Cover, Robert. "Violence and the Word." In Martha Minow, Michael Ryan, and Austin Sarat, eds., *Narrative, Violence and the Law: The Essays of Robert Cover*. Ann Arbor: University of Michigan Press, 1986.

Cowlishaw, Gillian. "Erasing Culture and Race: Practicing 'Self-Determination.'" *Oceania*, 68, 3 (1998): 145–169.

Crosby, Alfred. *Ecological Imperialism: The Biological Expansion of Europe, 900–1900.* Cambridge: Cambridge University Press, 1986.

Curran, James. *The Power of Speech: Australian Prime Ministers Defining the National Image.* Carlton, Vic.: Melbourne University Press, 2004.

Curran, James and Stuart Ward. *The Unknown Nation: Australia after Empire.* Melbourne: Melbourne University Press, 2010.

Curthoys, Ann. *Freedom Ride: A Freedom Rider Remembers.* Crows Nest, NSW: Allen & Unwin, 2002.

Curthoys, Ann, Ann Genovese, and Alexander Reilly. *Rights and Redemption: History, Law and Indigenous Peoples.* Sydney: University of New South Wales Press, 2008.

De Costa, Ravi. "Identity, Authority, and the Moral Worlds of Indigenous Petitions." *Comparative Studies in Society and History*, 48, 3 (2006): 669–698.

Daniel, Richard C. *A History of Native Claims Processes in Canada 1867–1979.* Ottawa: Research Branch, Department of Indian & Northern Affairs, 1980.

Davis, Megan. "The United Nations Declaration on the Rights of Indigenous Peoples." *Indigenous Law Bulletin*, 6, 30 (2007): 6–8.

Deloria, Vine. *Behind the Trail of Broken Treaties: An Indian Declaration of Independence.* New York: Dell, 1974.

Deloria, Vine Jr. and Clifford M. Lytle. *The Nations Within: The Past and Future of American Sovereignty.* New York: Pantheon Books, 1984.

Denoon, Donald. *Settler Capitalism: The Dynamics of Dependent Development in the Southern Hemisphere.* Oxford: Oxford University Press, 1983.

Dene Nation. *Denedeh: A Dene Celebration.* Toronto: McClelland & Stewart, 1984.

Department of Indian Affairs and Northern Development. *Statement of the Government of Canada on Indian Policy.* Ottawa: Queen's Printer, 1969.

Department of Northern Affairs and Natural Resources. *Peoples of the Northwest Territories.* Ottawa: DNANR, 1958.

Dominy Michèle D. "White Settler Assertions of Native Status." *American Ethnologist*, 22, 2 (1995): 358–374.

Dominy Michèle D. *Place and Identity in New Zealand's High Country.* Lanham, MD: Rowman & Littlefield, 2001.

Douglas, Heather and Mark Finnane. *Indigenous Crime and Settler Law: White Sovereignty after Empire.* Basingstoke: Palgrave Macmillan, 2012.

Drees, Laurie Maijer. *The Indian Association of Alberta: A History of Political Action.* Vancouver: University of British Columbia Press, 2002.

Durie, E. J. T. "Will the Settlers Settle? Cultural Conciliation and the Law." *Otago Law Review*, 8, 4 (1996): 449–465.

Duthu, Bruce. *American Indians and the Law.* New York: Penguin, 2008.

Dyck, Noel, "Aboriginal Peoples and Nation-States: An Introduction to Analytical Issues." In Noel Dyck, ed., *Indigenous Peoples and the Nation-State: Fourth World Politics in Canada, Australia and Norway*. St John's: University of Newfoundland, 1985:1–26.

Dyster, B., et al. *Australia in the International Economy in the Twentieth Century*. Cambridge: Cambridge University Press, 1990.

Eber, Dorothy Harley. *Images of Justice: A Legal History of the Northwest Territories as Traced through the Yellowknife Courthouse Collection of Inuit Sculpture*. Montreal: McGill-Queen's University Press, 1997.

Elkins, Caroline and Susan Pederson, eds. "Introduction: Settler Colonialism: A Concept and Its Uses." In *Settler Colonialism in the Twentieth Century: Projects, Practices, Legacies*. London: Routledge, 2005: 1–20.

Evans, Julie, Patricia Grimshaw, David Phillips, and Shurlee Swain. *Equal Subjects, Unequal Rights: Indigenous People in British Settler Colonies, 1830–1910*. Manchester: Manchester University Press, 2003.

Fabian, Johannes. *Time and the Other: How Anthropology Makes Its Object*. New York: Columbia University Press, 1983.

Farred, Grant. "Endgame Identity? Mapping the New Left Roots of Identity Politics." *New Literary History*, 31, 4 (2000): 627–648.

Fitzmaurice, Andrew. "The Genealogy of *Terra Nullius*." *Australian Historical Studies*, 129, 1 (2007): 1–16.

Flanagan, Thomas. *First Nations? Second Thoughts*. Montreal: McGill-Queen's University Press, 2000.

Fleras, Augie and Paul Spoonley. *Recalling Aotearoa: Indigenous Politics and Ethnic Relations in New Zealand*. Auckland: Oxford University Press, 1999.

Fleras, Augie. "Aboriginal Electoral Districts for Canada: Lessons from New Zealand." In Robert A. Milen, ed., *Aboriginal Peoples and Electoral Reform in Canada*. Toronto: Dundurn Press, 1991.

Ford, Lisa. *Settler Sovereignty: Jurisdiction and Indigenous People in America and Australia, 1788–1836*. Cambridge, MA: Harvard University Press, 2010.

Ford, Lisa. "Locating Indigenous Self-Determination in the Margins of Settler Sovereignty." In Ford and Tim Rowse, eds. *Between Indigenous and Settler Governance*. Abingdon, Oxon: Routledge, 2013, 1–11.

Foster, Hamar, Heather Raven, and Jeremy Webber, eds. *Let Right Be Done: Aboriginal Title, the Calder Case, and the Future of Indigenous Rights*. Vancouver: University of British Columbia Press, 2007.

Foster, Hamar. "We Are Not O'Meara's Children: Law, Lawyers, and the First Campaign for Aboriginal Title in British Columbia, 1908–28." In Hamer Foster, Heather Raven and Jeremy Webber, eds., *Let Right Be Done: Aboriginal Title, the Calder Case, and the Future of Indigenous Rights*. Vancouver: University of British Columbia Press, 2007: 61–84.

Fox, James J. "'Our Ancestors Spoke in Pairs:' Rotinese Views of Language, Dialect and Code." In Richard Bauman and Joel Sherzer, eds., *Explorations in the Ethnography of Speaking.* London: Cambridge University Press, 1974: 65–85.

Fox, Karen. "Globalising Indigeneity? Writing Indigenous Histories in a Transnational World." *History Compass*, 10, 6 (2012): 423–439.

Friesen, Gerald, *The Canadian Prairies: A History.* Toronto: University of Toronto Press, 1984.

Frow, John and Meaghan Morris. "Two Laws: Response to Elizabeth Povinelli." *Critical Inquiry*, 25, 3 (1999): 626–630.

Fumoleau, René. *As Long as This Land Shall Last: A History of Treaty 8 and Treaty 11, 1870-1939.* Calgary: University of Calgary Press, 2004.

Gelder, Ken and Jane Jacobs. *Uncanny Australia: Sacredness and Identity in a Postcolonial Nation.* Carlton, Vic.: Melbourne University Press, 1998.

Good, Reginald. "Admissibility of Testimony from Non-Christian Indians in the Colonial Municipal Courts of Upper Canada/Canada West." *Windsor Yearbook of Access to Justice*, 23, 1 (2005): 55–94.

Goodall, Heather. *Invasion to Embassy: Land in Aboriginal Politics in New South Wales, 1770–1972.* St Leonards, NSW: Allen & Unwin, 1996.

Gover, Kirsty. *Tribal Constitutionalism: States, Tribes and the Governance of Membership.* Oxford: Oxford University Press, 2010.

Gover, Kirsty. "Settler-State Political Theory, 'CANZUS' and the UN Declaration on the Rights of Indigenous Peoples." *European Journal of International Law*, 26, 2 (2015): 345–373.

Gover, Kirsty. "When Tribalism Meets Liberalism: Human Rights and Indigenous Boundary Problems in Canada." *University of Toronto Law Journal* 64, 2 (2014): 206–242.

Grace, Sherrill E. *Canada and the Idea of the North.* Montreal: McGill-Queen's University Press, 2001.

Graham, Ron, ed. *The Essential Trudeau.* Toronto: McClelland & Stewart, 1998.

Green, Joyce. "Canaries in the Mine of Citizenship: Indian Women in Canada." *Canadian Journal of Political Science*, 34, 4 (2001): 715–738.

Haebich, Anna. *Spinning the Dream: Assimilation in Australia 1950–1970.* Fremantle: Fremantle Press, 2008.

Harring, Sidney L. *White Man's Law: Native People in Nineteenth-Century Canadian Jurisprudence.* Toronto: Osgoode Society for Canadian Legal History, 1998.

Harris, Aroha. *Hikoi: Forty Years of Māori Protest.* Wellington: Huia, 2004.

Harris, Cole. *Making Native Space: Colonialism, Resistance, and Reserves in British Columbia.* Vancouver: University of British Columbia Press, 2002.

Harrison, Noel. *Graham Latimer: A Biography.* Wellington: Huia, 2002.

Havemann, Paul, ed. *Indigenous Peoples' Rights in Australia, Canada & New Zealand.* Auckland: Oxford University Press, 1999.

Hawke, Gary. "Economic Trends and Economic Policy, 1938–1992." In Geoffrey W. Rice, ed., *The Oxford History of New Zealand*, 2nd ed. Auckland: Oxford University Press, 1992.

Hawthorn, H. B. *A Survey of the Contemporary Indians of Canada: A Report on Economic, Political and Educational Needs and Policies in Two Volumes*, vol. 1. Ottawa: Indian Affairs Branch, 1966.

Hayward, Janine. " 'Flowing From the Treaty's Words': The Principles of the Treaty of Waitangi." In Hayward and Nicola R. Wheen, eds. *The Waitangi Tribunal: Te Roopu i te Tiriti o Waitangi*. Wellington: Bridget Williams Books, 2004: 29-40.

Helm, June. *The People of Denedeh: Ethnohistory of the Indians of Canada's Northwest Territories*. Montreal: McGill-Queen's University Press, 2001.

Helm, June. "Indian Dependency and Indian Self-Determination: Problems and Paradoxes in Canada's Northwest Territories." In Ernest L. Schusky, ed. *Political Organization of Native North Americans*. Washington: Smithsonian Institute, 1980: 215-242.

Hiatt, L. R. "Traditional Land Tenure and Contemporary Land Claims." In L. R. Hiatt, ed., *Aboriginal Landowners: Contemporary Issues in the Determination of Traditional Aboriginal Land Ownership*. Sydney: University of Sydney Press, 1984.

Hickford, Mark. *Lords of the Land: Indigenous Property Rights and the Jurisprudence of Empire*. Oxford: Oxford University Press, 2011.

Hobsbawm, Eric and Terence Ranger, eds. *The Invention of Tradition*. Cambridge: Cambridge University Press, 1983.

Hopkins, A. G. "Rethinking Decolonization." *Past & Present*, 200 (2008): 211-247.

Hoxie, Frederick E. "Retrieving the Red Continent: Settler Colonialism and the History of American Indians in the US." *Ethnic and Racial Studies*, 31, 6 (2008): 1153-1167.

Hunn, J. K. *Report on Department of Maori Affairs with Statistical Supplement*. Wellington: Government Printer, 1961.

Hunn, J. K. *Integration of Maori and Pakeha*. Wellington: Department of Maori Affairs, 1962.

Indian Chiefs of Alberta. *Citizens Plus: A Presentation by the Indian Chiefs of Alberta to the Right Honourable P. E. Trudeau, Prime Minister and the Government of Canada*. Edmonton, 1970.

Ivison, Duncan. "Decolonizing the Rule of Law: Mabo's Case and Postcolonial Constitutionalism." *Oxford Journal of Legal Studies*, 17, 2 (1997): 253–279.

Ivison, Duncan. *Postcolonial Liberalism*. Cambridge: Cambridge University Press, 2002.

Ivison, Duncan, Paul Patton, and Will Sanders, eds. *Political Theory and the Rights of Indigenous Peoples*. Cambridge: Cambridge University Press, 2000.

Jacobs, Margaret. *White Mother to a Dark Race: Settler Colonialism, Maternalism, and the Removal of Indigenous Children in the American West and Australia, 1880–1940*. Lincoln: University of Nebraska Press, 2009.

Jamieson, Kathleen. *Indian Women and the Law in Canada: Citizens Minus*. Ottawa: Advisory Council on the Status of Women, 1978.

Johnson, Miranda. "The Gove Land Rights Case and the Problem of History in a Decolonising Australia." In Bain Attwood and Tom Griffiths, eds., *Frontier, Race, Nation: Henry Reynolds and Australian History*. Melbourne: Australian Scholarly Publishing, 2009: 305–329.

Johnson, Miranda. "Reconciliation, Indigeneity and Postcolonial Nationhood in Settler States." *Postcolonial Studies*, 14, 2 (2011): 187–201.

Johnston, Harold. *Report of Proceedings of Royal Commission Appointed to Inquire into Maori Claims in Relation to the Bed of the Whanganui River, 26 April 1950*. Wellington, 1950.

Kauanui, J. Kēhaulani. "Indigenous." In Bruce Burgett and Glenn Hendler, eds. *Keywords for American Cultural Studies Second Edition*. New York: New York University Press, 2014: 133-137.

Kawharu, I. H. "Pacific Commentary: The Pichard-Waetford Inquiry into Maori Land," *Journal of the Polynesian Society*, 76, 2 (1967): 205–214.

Kawharu, I. H. *Maori Land Tenure: Studies of a Changing Institution*. Oxford: Clarendon Press, 1977.

Keating, Paul. "Redfern Speech." www.antar.org.au.

Keen, Ian. "A Question of Interpretation: The Definition of 'Traditional Aboriginal Owners' in the Aboriginal Land Rights (N.T.) Act." In L. R. Hiatt, ed., *Aboriginal Landowners: Contemporary Issues in the Determination of Traditional Aboriginal Land Ownership*. Sydney: University of Sydney, 1984: 24–45.

Kelsey, Jane. *Reclaiming the Future: New Zealand and the Global Economy*. Wellington: Bridget Williams Books, 2000.

Kelsey, Jane. "Treaty Justice in the 1980s." In Paul Spoonley, David Pearson, and Cluny Macpherson, eds., *Nga Take: Ethnic Relations in Aotearoa/New Zealand*. Palmerston North: Massey University Press, 1992.

Ketley, Harriet and Clare Ozich. "'Snapshots of Adventitious Content': The Assessment of Oral and Historical Evidence in Native Title Claims." In Christine Choo and Shawn Hollbach, eds., *History and Native Title: Studies in Western Australian History*. Perth: University of Western Australia, 2003: 83–94.

King, Michael. "Between Two Worlds." In Geoffrey W. Rice, ed., *The Oxford History of New Zealand*, 2nd ed. Auckland: Oxford University Press, 1992.

Knafla, Louis A. and Haijo Westra. *Aboriginal Title and Indigenous Peoples: Canada, Australia, and New Zealand*. Vancouver: University of British Columbia Press, 2010.

Kymlicka, Will. *Multicultural Citizenship: A Liberal Theory of Minority Rights*. Oxford: Oxford University Press, 1995.

Laidlaw, Zoe. "Breaking Britannia's Bounds? Law, Settlers, and Space in Britain's Imperial Historiography." *Historical Journal*, 55, 3 (2012): 807–830.

Laidlaw, Zoe. "Investigating Empire: Humanitarians, Reform and the Commission of Eastern Inquiry." *Journal of Imperial and Commonwealth History*, 40, 5 (2012): 749–768.

Laidlaw, Zoe and Alan Lester, eds. *Indigenous Communities and Settler Colonialism: Land Holding, Loss and Survival in an Interconnected World*. Basingstoke: Palgrave Macmillan, 2015.

Lajeunesse, Adam. "Lock, Stock and Icebreakers: Defining Canadian Sovereignty from Mackenzie King to Stephen Harper." *Calgary Papers in Military and Strategic Studies, Occasional Paper*, no.1, 2008.

Lake, Marilyn and Henry Reynolds. *Drawing the Global Colour Line: White Men's Countries and the Question of Racial Equality*. Melbourne: Melbourne University Press, 2008.

Langton, Marcia. "The Hindmarsh Island Bridge Affair: How Aboriginal Women's Religion Became an Administerable Affair." *Australian Feminist Studies*, 11, 24 (1996): 211–217.

Lashley, Marilyn. "Economic and Social Issues Affecting New Zealand's Maori Population." In Srikanta Chatterjee and Stuart Birks, eds., *The New Zealand Economy: Issues and Policies*, 4th ed. Palmerston North: Dunmore Press, 2001.

Leslie, John F. *Assimilation, Termination or Integration? The Development of Canadian Indian Policy, 1943–1963*. Ph.D. thesis, Carleton University, 1999.

Lowe, Lana C. *A Strategic Analysis of the Union of British Columbia Indian Chiefs*. MA thesis, University of Victoria, 2004.

Loveday, Peter and Dean Jaensch. "Indigenes and Electoral Administration, Australia and Canada." *Electoral Studies*, 6, 1 (1987): 31–40.

Lurie, N. O. "The Indian Claims Commission." *Annals of the American Academy of Political and Social Science*, 436 (1978): 97–110.

Lyotard, Jean-Francois. *The Differend: Phrases in Dispute*, tr. Georges Van Den Abbeele. Minnesota: University of Minnesota Press, 1988.

Macdonald, Charlotte. "Ways of Belonging: Sporting Spaces in New Zealand History." In Giselle Byrnes, ed., *The New Oxford History of New Zealand*. Melbourne: Oxford University Press, 2009: 269–296.

Maclean, Malcolm. "Football as Social Critique: Protest Movements, Rugby and History in Aotearoa, New Zealnd." *International Journal of the History of Sport*, 17, 2–3 (2000): 255–277.

Manuel, George and Michael Posluns. *The Fourth World: An Indian Reality*. New York: Free Press, 1974.

Maori Synod of the Presbyterian Church of New Zealand. *A Maori View of the Hunn Report*. Christchurch, 1961.

Mara, Ratu Sir Kamisese. *The Pacific Way: A Memoir*. Honolulu: University of Hawai'i Press, 1997.

Maynard, John. *Fight for Liberty and Freedom: The Origins of Australian Aboriginal Activism*. Canberra: Aboriginal Studies Press, 2007.

McGilp, J. G. "The Relations of Canadian Indians and Canadian Governments." *Canadian Public Administration*, 6, 3 (1963): 299–308.

McGrath, Ann and Winona Stevenson. "Gender, Race, and Policy: Aboriginal Women and the State in Canada and Australia." Joint issue of *Labour/Le Travail*, 38, and *Labour History*, 71 (1996): 37–53.

McGregor, Russell. "Wards, Words and Citizens: A. P. Elkin and Paul Hasluck on Assimilation." *Oceania*, 69, 4 (1999): 243–259.

McHugh, Paul. *Aboriginal Societies and the Common Law: A History of Sovereignty, Status, and Self-determination.* Oxford: Oxford University Press, 2004.

McHugh, Paul. *Aboriginal Title: The Modern Jurisprudence of Tribal Land Rights.* Oxford: Oxford University Press, 2011.

McIntosh, Ian S. "Missing the Revolution! Negotiating Disclosure on the pre-Macassans (Bayini) in North-East Arnhem Land." In Martin Thomas and Margo Neale, eds., *Exploring the Legacy of the 1948 Arnhem Land Expedition.* Canberra: ANU E-Press, 2011: 337–354.

McKenzie, Maisie. *Mission to Arnhem Land.* Adelaide: Rigby Limited, 1976.

McMillen, Christian. *Making Indian Law: The Hualapai Land Case and the Birth of Ethnohistory.* New Haven, CT: Yale University Press, 2007.

McNeill, Kent. "Social Darwinism and Judicial Conceptions of Indian Title in Canada in the 1880s." *Journal of the West* 38, 1 (1999): 68–76.

McNeil, Kent. "The Constitutional Rights of the Aboriginal Peoples of Canada." *Supreme Court Law Review*, 4 (1982): 255–265.

Melbourne, Hineani. *Maori Sovereignty: The Maori Perspective.* Auckland: Hodder Moa Beckett, 1995.

Melvin, Geoff. "The Jurisdiction of the Waitangi Tribunal." In Janine Hayward and Nicola R. Wheen, eds. *The Waitangi Tribunal: Te Roopu i te Tiriti o Waitangi.* Wellington: Bridget Williams Books, 2004: 15-28.

Merlan, Francesca. "Indigeneity: Global and Local." *Current Anthropology*, 50, 3 (2009): 303–334.

Merry, Sally Engle. "Law and Colonialism." *Law and Society Review*, 25, 4 (1991): 889–922.

McNair, Arnold Duncan. *The Law of Treaties.* Oxford: Clarendon Press, 1961.

Miller, J. R. *Compact, Contract, Covenant: Aboriginal Treaty-Making in Canada.* Toronto: University of Toronto Press, 2009.

Miller, J. R. *Skyscrapers Hide the Heavens: A History of Indian-White Relations in Canada*, 3rd ed. Toronto: University of Toronto Press, 2000.

Milroy, Leigh Ogston. *Aboriginal Policy-Making and Dispute Resolution Processes: A History of the Concept of a Tribunal for the Adjudication of Specific Land Claims in Canada.* MA thesis, University of Victoria, 2002.

Minoru, Hokari. "Reading Oral Histories from the Pastoral Frontier: A Critical Revision." *Journal of Australian Studies*, 72 (2002): 21–28.

Moon, Paul. "The History of Moutoa Gardens and Claims of Ownership." *Journal of the Polynesian Society*, 105, 3 (1996): 347–365.

Moran, Anthony. "The Psychodynamics of Australian Settler-Nationalism: Assimilating or Reconciling with the Aborigines?" *Political Psychology* 23, 4 (2002): 667–701.

Morphy, Howard. "Art and Politics: The Bark Petition and the Barugna Statement." Sylvia Kleinert and Margo Neale, eds., *The Oxford Companion to Aboriginal Art and Culture*. Melbourne: Oxford University Press, 2000: 100–102.

Morphy, Howard. "Mutual Conversion? The Methodist Church and the Yolngu, with Particular Reference to Yirrkala." *Humanities Research*, 11, 1 (2005): 41–53.

Morris, Ewan. "Men Alone, in Bronze and Stone: A Tale of Two Statues." *Journal of New Zealand Studies*, 13 (2012): 62–76.

Morrow, William G. and W. H. Morrow. *Northern Justice: The Memoirs of Mr. Justice William G. Morrow*. Toronto: University of Toronto Press, 1995.

Muehlebach, Andrea. "'Making Place' at the United Nations: Indigenous Cultural Politics at the U.N. Working Group on Indigenous Populations." *Cultural Anthropology*, 16, 3 (2001): 415–448.

Nadasdy, Paul. *Hunters and Bureaucrats: Power, Knowledge, and Aboriginal-state Relations in the Southwest Yukon*. Vancouver: University of British Columbia Press, 2003.

Napoleon, Val. "Delgamuukw: A Legal Straitjacket for Oral Histories?" *Canadian Journal of Law and Society*, 20, 2 (2005): 123–155.

Nelson, Walter H. et al. *Report of the Commission Appointed to Investigate the Unfulfilled Provisions of Treaties 8 and 11 as They Apply to the Indians of the Mackenzie District*. Prince Albert, Saskatchewan: The Commission, 1959.

Nettheim, Garth. "'Peoples' and 'Populations': Indigenous Peoples and the Rights of Peoples." In James Crawford, ed., *The Rights of Peoples*. Oxford: Clarendon Press, 1988.

Nettheim, Garth. "The Mabo Response in Australia: Reconciliation or Continuing Conquest?" *Anthropology Today*, 10, 1 (1994): 8–11.

New Zealand Maori Council, *Kaupapa—Te Wahanga Tuatahi*. February 1983.

Nicholls, Jim. "A Comment from the NZ Maori Council," In Jacinta Ruru, ed., *"In Good Faith": Symposium Proceedings Marking the 20th Anniversary of the Lands Case*. Wellington: New Zealand Law Foundation, 2008: 37–38.

Nichols, Robert. "Indigeneity and the Settler Contract Today." *Philosophy and Social Criticism*, 39, 2 (2013): 165–186.

Niezen, Ronald. *The Origins of Indigenism: Human Rights and the Politics of Identity*. Berkeley: University of California Press, 2003.

Norrie, Kenneth et al. *A History of the Canadian Economy*. Toronto: Harcourt Brace Canada, 1996.

Norman, Heidi. *What Do We Want? A Political History of Aboriginal Land Rights in New South Wales*. Canberra: Aboriginal Studies Press, 2015.

Oliver, W.H. *Claims to the Waitangi Tribunal*, Wellington: Waitangi Tribunal Division, Department of Justice, 1991.

Oliver, W. H. "The Future Behind Us: The Waitangi Tribunal's Retrospective Utopia." In *Histories, Power and Loss: Uses of the Past: A New Zealand Commentary*. Andrew Sharp and Paul G. McHugh, eds. Wellington: Bridget Williams Books, 2001: 9–29.

O'Malley, Vincent. *Agents of Autonomy: Maori Committees in the Nineteenth Century*. Wellington: Huia, 1998.

Orange, Claudia. *The Treaty of Waitangi*. Wellington: Allen & Unwin, 1987.

O'Regan, Sir Tipene. "Impact on Māori—a Ngāi Tahu Perspective." In Jacinta Ruru, ed., *"In Good Faith": Symposium Proceedings Marking the 20th Anniversary of the Lands Case*. Wellington: New Zealand Law Foundation, 2008: 41–50.

Pagden, Anthony. "Fellow Citizens and Imperial Subjects: Conquest and Sovereignty in Europe's Overseas Empires." *History and Theory*, 44, 4 (2005): 28–46.

Parliament of the Commonwealth of Australia, House of Representatives, *Report from the Select Committee on Grievances of Yirrkala Aborigines, Arnhem Land Reserve*, Canberra: Commonwealth Government Printer, 1963.

Parliamentary Library Research Paper. "The Origins of the Maori Seats." Parliamentary Library, Wellington, 2003/2009, www.parliament.nz.

Parsons, David. "Kenbi Land Claim—25 Years On." *Indigenous Law Bulletin*, 4, 8 (1998): 15–16.

Pateman, Carole. "The Settler Contract." In Carole Pateman and Charles Mills, *Contract and Domination*. Cambridge: Polity Press, 2007: 35–78.

Pearson, Ronald H. "Native Rights in the Northwest Territories—The Caveat Case." *Alberta Law Review* 12 (1974): 278–290.

Perkins, Charles. *A Bastard Like Me*. Dee Why West, NSW: Ure Smith, 1975.

Peterson, Nicolas. "Common Law, Statutory Law, and the Political Economy of the Recognition of Indigenous Australian Rights in Land." In L. Knafla and H. Westra, eds., *Aboriginal Title and Indigenous Peoples*. Vancouver: University of British Columbia Press, 2010: 171–184.

Pocock, J. G. A. *The Ancient Constitution and the Feudal Law: A Study of English Historical Thought in the Seventeenth Century*. Cambridge: Cambridge University Press, 1957.

Pool, Ian. *Te Iwi Maori: Population Past, Present, and Projected*. Auckland: Auckland University Press, 2013.

Povinelli, Elizabeth A. "The State of Shame: Australian Multiculturalism and the Crisis of Indigenous Citizenship." *Critical Inquiry*, 24, 2 (1998): 575–610.

Povinelli, Elizabeth A. "Critical Response: The Cunning of Recognition: A Reply to John Frow and Meaghan Morris." *Critical Inquiry*, 25, 3 (1999): 631–637.

Povinelli, Elizabeth A. *The Cunning of Recognition: Indigenous Alterities and the Making of Australian Multiculturalism*. Durham, NC: Duke University Press, 2002.

Povinelli, Elizabeth A. "Indigenous Politics in Late Liberalism." In Jon Altman and Melinda Hinkson, eds., *Culture Crisis: Anthropology and Politics in Aboriginal Australia*. Sydney: University of New South Wales Press, 2010: 17–31.

Prichard, I. and H. T. Waetford. *Report of Committee of Inquiry into Laws Affecting Maori Land and Powers of the Maori Land Court.* Wellington, Department of Maori Affairs, 1965.

Raibmon, Paige. *Authentic Indians: Episodes of Encounter from the Late-Nineteenth-Century Northwest Coast.* Durham, NC: Duke University Press, 2005.

Ramos, Alcida Rita. *Indigenism: Ethnic Politics in Brazil.* Madison: University of Wisconsin Press, 1998.

Ray, Arthur J. *The Canadian Fur Trade in the Industrial Age.* Toronto: University of Toronto Press, 1990.

Ray, Arthur. "Native History on Trial: Confessions of an Expert Witness." *Canadian Historical Review* 84, 2 (2003): 253–273.

Read, Peter, Gary Meyers, and Bob Reece, eds. *What Good Condition?Reflections on an Australian Aboriginal Treaty 1986–2006.* Canberra: Aboriginal History Inc. and ANU E-Press, 2006.

Refshauge, Richard. "Blackburn, Sir Richard Arthur (Dick) (1918–1987)." Australian Dictionary of Biography, National Centre of Biography, Australian National University, adb.anu.edu.au/biography.

Reynolds, Henry. *The Law of the Land.* Melbourne: Penguin, 1987.

Richards, Trevor. *Dancing on Our Bones: New Zealand, South Africa, Rugby and Racism.* Wellington: Bridget Williams Books, 1999.

Ritchie, James. *Becoming Bicultural.* Wellington: Huia, 1992.

Ritter, David. "The 'Rejection of *terra nullius*' in *Mabo*: A Critical Analysis." *Sydney Law Review*, 18, 1 (1996): 5–33.

Rose, Deborah Bird. "Women and Land Claims." In Mary Edmunds, ed., *Land, Rights, Laws: Issues of Native Title.* Canberra: Australian Institute of Aboriginal and Torres Strait Islander Studies, 1995.

Rosenthal, Harvey D. *Their Day in Court: A History of the Indian Claims Commission.* New York: Garland, 1990.

Ross, Ruth. "Te Tiriti O Waitangi: Texts and Translations." *New Zealand Journal of History*, 6, 2 (1972): 129–157.

Rowe, Andrea W. *Assimilation through Accommodation: Practice, Rhetoric and Decisions in the Territorial Court of the Northwest Territories 1955–1972*, Master of Laws thesis, University of Toronto, 1990.

Rowley, Charles Dunford. *The Destruction of Aboriginal Society.* Sydney: Penguin, 1972.

Rowse, Tim. "A Spear in the Thigh for Senator Evans." In Klaus Neumann, Nicholas Thomas, and Hilary Ericksen, eds., *Quicksands: Foundational Histories in Australia and Aotearoa New Zealand.* Sydney: University of New South Wales Press, 1999.

Rowse, Tim. "Global Indigenism: A Genealogy of a Non-Racial Category." In A. Holland and B. Brookes, eds., *Rethinking the Racial Moment: Essays on the Colonial Encounter.* Newcastle: Cambridge Scholars Publishing, 2011: 229–253.

Rowse, Tim. "Indigenous Heterogeneity." *Australian Historical Studies* 45, 3 (2014): 297–310.

Rowse, Tim. *Rethinking Social Justice: From "Peoples" to "Populations."* Canberra: Aboriginal Studies Press, 2012.

Rowse, Tim. *White Flour, White Power: From Rations to Citizenship in Central Australia.* Cambridge: Cambridge University Press, 1998.

Ruru, Jacinta. "A Politically Fuelled Tsunami: The Foreshore/Seabed Controversy in Aoteaora Me Te Wai Pounamu/New Zealand." *Journal of the Polynesian Society*, 113, 1 (2004): 57–72.

Russell, Peter. *Recognising Aboriginal Title: The Mabo Case and Indigenous Resistance to English-Settler Colonialism.* Sydney: University of New South Wales Press, 2005.

Salesa, Damon. *Racial Crossings: Race, Intermarriage and the Victorian British Empire.* Oxford: Oxford University Press, 2011.

Sanders, D. E. *Native People in Areas of Internal National Expansion: Indians and Inuit in Canada.* Copenhagen: International Working Group for Indians Affairs, 1973.

Sanders, D. E. "The Nishga Case." *BC Studies*, 19 (1973): 3–20.

Scholtz, Christa. *Negotiating Claims: The Emergence of Indigenous Land Claim Policies in Australia, Canada, New Zealand and the United States.* New York: Routledge, 2006.

Scott, Stuart C. *The Travesty of Waitangi: Towards Anarchy.* Dunedin: Campbell Press, 1995.

Sharp, Andrew. *Justice and the Māori: Māori Claims in New Zealand Political Arguments in the 1980s.* Auckland: Oxford University Press, 1990.

Sharp, Andrew "Recent Juridical and Constitutional Histories of Maori." In Andrew Sharp and Paul McHugh, eds., *Histories, Power and Loss: Uses of the Past: A New Zealand Commentary.* Wellington: Bridget Williams Books, 2001: 31–60.

Simpson, Audra. *Mohawk Interruptus: Political Life Across the Borders of Settler States.* Durham: Duke University Press, 2014.

Simpson, Audra and Andrea Smith, eds. *Theorizing Native Studies.* Durham, NC: Duke University Press, 2014.

Sinclair, Karen. *Prophetic Histories: The People of the Maramatanga.* Wellington: Bridget Williams Books, 2002.

Sinclair, Keith. "Why Are Race Relations in New Zealand Better than in South Africa, South Australia, or South Dakota?" *New Zealand Journal of History*, 5, 2 (1971): 121–127.

Sissons, Jeffrey. *First Peoples: Indigenous Cultures and Their Futures.* London: Reaktion Books, 2005.

Sissons, John Howard. *Judge of the Far North: The Memoirs of Jack Sissons.* Toronto: McClelland and Stewart, 1968.

Sitze, Adam. *The Impossible Machine: A Genealogy of South Africa's Truth and Reconciliation Commission.* Ann Arbor: University of Michigan Press, 2013.

Slattery, Brian. "The Constitutional Guarantee of Aboriginal and Treaty Rights." *Queen's Law Journal*, 8 (1982–1983): 232–273.

Slattery, Brian. "Understanding Aboriginal Rights." *Canadian Bar Review*, 66, 4 (1987): 727–783.

Smith, L. R. *The Aboriginal Population of Australia*. Canberra: Australian National University, 1980.

Sorrenson, Keith. "Towards a Radical Reinterpretation of New Zealand History: The Role of the Waitangi Tribunal." In I. H. Kawharu, ed. *Waitangi: Maori and Pakeha Perspectives of the Treaty of Waitangi*. Auckland: Oxford University Press, 1989: 158-178.

Sorrenson, Keith. "Treaties in British Colonial Policy: Precedents for Waitangi." In William Renwick, ed., *Sovereignty and Indigenous Rights: The Treaty of Waitangi in International Contexts*. Wellington: Victoria University Press, 1991.

Stanner, W. E. H. *After the Dreaming: The 1968 Boyer Lectures*. Sydney: Australian Broadcasting Commission, 1969.

Stanner, W. E. H. "The Yirrkala Land Case: Dress-Rehearsal (1970)." In *White Man Got No Dreaming: Essays 1938–1973*. Canberra: Australian National University Press, 1979.

Stretton, Pat and Christine Finnimore. "Black Fellow Citizens: Aborigines and the Commonwealth Franchise." *Australian Historical Studies*, 25, 101 (1993): 521–535.

Sutton, Peter. *The Relative Strengths of Oral and Written Evidence*. Proof and Management of Native Title: Summary of Proceedings of a Workshop, University House. Canberra: Australian Institute of Aboriginal and Torres Strait Islander Studies, 1994.

Taffe, Sue. *Black and White Together, FCAATSI: The Federal Council for the Advancement of Aborigines and Torres Strait Islanders, 1958–1973*. St. Lucia, Qld: University of Queensland Press, 2005.

Tanner, Helen Hornbeck. "In the Arena: An Expert Witness View of the Indian Claims Commission." In Daniel Cobb, ed., *Beyond Red Power: American Indian Politics and Activism since 1900*. Santa Fe, NM: School for Advanced Research, 2007.

Teves, Stephanie Nohelani, Andrea Smith, and Michelle H. Rahetja. "Indigeneity." *Native Studies Keywords*. Tuscon: University of Arizona Press, 2015: 109-118.

Thomas, Allan, ed. *Karanga Voices—Volume 1: Calls and Chants*. Wellington: Asia Pacific Archive, School of Music, Victoria University of Wellington, 2001.

Thompson, Richard. "Community Conflict in New Zealand: A Case Study," *Race*, 3, 1 (1961): 28–38.

Treaty 7 Elders and Tribal Council, Walter Hildebrandt, Dorothy First Rider, and Sarah Carter. *The True Spirit and Original Intent of Treaty 7*. Montreal: McGill-Queen's University Press, 1996.

Tsing, Anna Lowenthaupt. "*Adat*/Indigenous: Indigeneity in Motion." In Carol Gluck and Tsing, eds., *Words in Motion: Toward a Global Lexicon*. Durham, NC: Duke University Press, 2009: 40–66.

Turner, Frederick Jackson. "The Significance of the Frontier in American History." (1893). In Turner, *The Frontier in American History*. New York: Henry Holt, 1920.

Venne, Sharon. "Understanding Treaty 6: An Indigenous Perspective." In Michael Asch, ed., *Aboriginal and Treaty Rights in Canada: Essays on Law, Equality, and Respect for Difference*. Vancouver: University of British Columbia Press, 1997: 173–207.

Viney, Fiona. *Aborigines, Law and the Settler State: The Gove Land Rights Case and Political Change, 1968–1972*. MA thesis, Monash University, 2013.

Viswanthan, Gauri. "Ireland, India, and the Poetics of Internationalism." *Journal of World History*, 15, 1 (2004): 7–30.

Waitangi Tribunal. "Interim report to Minister of Maori Affairs on State-Owned Enterprises Bill 8.12.86," *Report of the Waitangi Tribunal on the Muriwhenua Fishing Claim—Wai 22*. Waitangi Tribunal: Wellington, 1988, A3.4.1.

Waitangi Tribunal. *Report of the Waitangi Tribunal on the Manukau Claim*. Wellington: The Tribunal, 1989.

Waitangi Tribunal. *Report of the Waitangi Tribunal on the Orakei Claim*. Wellington: The Tribunal, 1987.

Waitangi Tribunal. *The Whanganui River Report*. Wellington: GP Publications, 1999.

Waldron, Jeremy. "Indigeneity? First Peoples and Last Occupancy," *New Zealand Journal of Public and International Law*, 1, 55 (2003): 55–82.

Walker, Ranginui. *Ka Whawhai Tonu Matou: Struggle without End*. Auckland: Penguin Books, 1990.

Walker, Ranginui. "The Māori People: Their Political Development." In Hyam Gold, ed., *New Zealand Politics in Perspective*. Auckland: Longman Paul, 1992.

Ward, Alan. *A Show of Justice: Racial 'Amalgamation' in Nineteenth Century New Zealand*. Auckland: Auckland University Press, 1973.

Ward, Alan. *An Unsettled History: Treaty Claims in New Zealand Today*. Wellington: Bridget Williams Books, 1999.

Ward, Alan. "History and Historians before the Waitangi Tribunal." *New Zealand Journal of History* 24, 2 (1990): 150–167.

Ward, Damen. "Constructing British Authority in Australasia: Charles Cooper and the Legal Status of Aborigines in the South Australian Supreme Court, c. 1840–60." *Journal of Imperial and Commonwealth History*, 34, 4 (2006): 483–504.

Ward, Stuart. "The 'New Nationalism' in Australia, Canada and New Zealand: Civic Culture in the Wake of the British World." In Kate Darian-Smith, Patricia Grimshaw and Stuart Macintyre, eds., *Britishness Abroad: Transnational Movements and Imperial Cultures*. Melbourne: Melbourne University Press, 2007: 231–266.

Watkins, Mel, ed. *Dene Nation: The Colony Within*. Toronto: University of Toronto Press, 1977.

Weaver, John C. *The Great Land Rush and the Making of the Modern World, 1650–1900*. Montreal: McGill-Queen's University Press, 2003.

Weaver, Sally M. *Making Canadian Indian Policy: The Hidden Agenda, 1968–70*. Toronto: University of Toronto Press, 1981.

Webber, Jeremy. "Beyond Regret: Mabo's Implications for Australian Constitutionalism." In Duncan Ivison, Paul Patton, and Will Sanders, eds., *Political Theory and the Rights of Indigenous Peoples*. Cambridge: Cambridge University Press, 2000: 60–88.

Whanganui River Māori Trust Board. "The Whanganui River Chart on Tino Rangatiratanga and Iwi Water Rights." 1993.

Whanganui River Māori Trust Board. "Whanganui River Settlement: ratification booklet for Whanganui Iwi," www.wrmtb.co.nz.

Whitlam, "It's Time for Leadership," election speech delivered at Blacktown Civic Centre, New South Wales, 13 November 1972. Online at Whitlam Institute, University of Western Sydney, cem.uws.eud.au.

Wigmore, John. *A Treatise on the Anglo-American System of Evidence in Trials at Common Law: Including the Statutes and Judicial Decisions of All Jurisdictions*, 5 vols. Boston: Little, Brown, 1904.

Wilkinson, Charles F. *Blood Struggle: The Rise of Modern Nations*. New York: W. W. Norton, 2005.

Williams, David. *"Te Kooti Tango Whenua": The Native Land Court, 1864–1909*. Wellington: Huia, 1999.

Williams, Joe. "Truth, Reconciliation and the Clash of Cultures in the Waitangi Tribunal." *Australia & New Zealand Law & History E-Journal, Keynote Speech* (2005): 234-238.

Williams, Melissa Matutina. *Panguru and the City: Kāinga Tahi, Kāinga Rua: An Urban Migration History*. Wellington: Bridget Williams Books, 2015.

Williams, Nancy M. *The Yolngu and Their Land: A System of Land Tenure and the Fight for Its Recognition*. Stanford: Stanford University Press, 1986.

Williams, Robert A. Jr. *The American Indian in Western Legal Thought: The Discourse of Conquest*. New York: Oxford University Press, 1990.

Wolfe, Patrick. "Land, Labor and Difference: Elementary Structures of Race." *American Historical Review*, 106, 3 (2001): 866–905.

Wolfe, Patrick. "Settler Colonialism and the Elimination of the Native." *Journal of Genocide Research*, 8, 4 (2006): 123–144.

Woodward, A. E. *Aboriginal Land Rights Commission: First Report*. Canberra: Australian Government Publishing Service, 1973.

Woodward, A. E. *Aboriginal Land Rights Commission: Second Report*. Canberra: Government Printer of Australia, 1974.

Woodward, A. E. *One Brief Interval: A Memoir*. Melbourne: Miegunyah Press, 2005.

Wright, Alexis, ed. *Take Power Like This Old Man Here: An Anthology of Writings Celebrating Twenty Years of Land Rights in Central Australia, 1977–1997*. Alice Springs: IAD Press, 1998.

Young, David. *Woven by Water: Histories from the Whanganui River*. Wellington: Huia, 1998.

Yuval-Davis, Nira. *Gender and Nation*. London: Sage, 1997.

Zaslow, Morris. *The Northward Expansion of Canada 1914–1967*. Toronto: McClelland and Stewart, 1988.

Index

Note: Photographs are indicated by italic page numbers.